WISDOM

The Principal Thing

WISDOM

The Principal Thing

Don Manley

WINEPRESS WP PUBLISHING

Printed in the United States of America.

Packaged by WinePress Publishing, PO Box 428, Enumclaw, WA 98022. The views expressed or implied in this work do not necessarily reflect those of WinePress Publishing. Ultimate design, content, and editorial accuracy of this work are the responsibility of the author.

Unless otherwise indicated, Scripture references are from the New Scofield® Study Bible, King James Version, © 1967 by Oxford University Press, Inc.

Scripture quotations identified NAS are from the New American Standard Bible, © 1960, 1962, 1963, 1968, 1971, 1973, 1975, 1977 by The Lockman Foundation.

Scripture quotations identified RSV are from the Revised Standard Version of the Bible, © 1946, 1952, 1971, 1973 by the Division of Christian Education of the National Council of the Churches of Christ in the United States of America.

Scripture quotations identified TLB are taken from The Living Bible © 1971. Used by permission of Tyndale@ House Publishers, Inc., Wheaton, IL 60189.

The images used herein on pages 52, 57, 58, 60, 61, 86, 88, 90, 91, 119, 120, 127, 150, 161-164, 167, 168, 177, 179-182, 187, 189, 197, 284 and 301 were obtained from IMSI's MasterClips Collection, 1895 Francisco Blvd. East, San Rafael, CA 94901-5506, USA.

ISBN 1-57921-372-3
Library of Congress Catalog Card Number: 2001087750

Don Manley has given us the fruit of much work, investigation, and thought. *Wisdom — The Principal Thing* is a practical and pastoral commentary that focuses on primary truths and personal directives found in this amazing Old Testament wisdom book. This commentary is not a detailed verse-by-verse explanation of Hebrew idioms and cultural/historical backgrounds; rather it is an expository presentation of key truths and teachings in Proverbs written from a New Testament perspective with consistent life-applications for today. For those wanting insights into the wisdom of Proverbs and its challenge for us today, this commentary will give understanding and "what to do" application. Written with numerous helpful outlines, lists, and visual aids, the study can be used by a wide variety of readers and could be a teacher's "manual" for group study. Don Manley's commentary makes Wisdom the principal thing, and helps us to learn wisdom and live wisely.

David L. Olford, Ph.D.
President,
The Stephen Olford Center for Biblical Preaching,
Memphis Tennessee

There are infinite ways to know error. There is only one way to know truth. This is to rely wholly on the inerrant Word of God. Don Manley has taken this wonderful book of wisdom and broken it down so it may be used by students and pastors alike. There are deep insights, yet it is so practical. I recommend it without reservation.

Dr. Dale Prince
Resident Minister
Olford Ministries International
Memphis, Tennessee

The Commentary on Proverbs provides the pastor and lay person with a fine interpretation of the book of Proverbs, topical studies of important subjects found throughout the book, and the only description of the ideal woman as seen from God's point of view. The author explains the meaning of each proverb in clear and concise terms and offers insightful contemporary applications of the teachings found in Proverbs.

This commentary is a needed resource which will assist both the individual and family to apply God's wisdom to future planning and day-to-day decisions making.

Edward E. Hogg, Ed.D., Ph.D.
President,
Trinity College and Theological Seminary
Newburgh, Indiana

This is Monumental Work done by Don Manley and provides an excellent and informative way to understand God's Wisdom in Proverbs.

Your life will be greatly enriched by reading it and everyone can be certain to have God's guarantee of Eternal life by just accepting God's gift on page 208, Pillar #7.

Dr. A. Ray Stanford
Founder and President Emeritus of
Florida Bible College

This book makes clear the practical truth so desperately needed for Godly living in the family and in society. It is a gold mine of wisdom spelled out for all to understand. The commentary is filled with jewels of truth that could bring back much needed holy living and a national revival.

I was surprised at the size of the project, amazed at the careful analysis, and blessed by my review of the great truths expounded. I earnestly recommend this splendid volume to all who love the Lord and pray for a revival for our beloved country.

Robert A. Miller, D.D.
Founder & President Emeritus of the
Southwest Institute of Biblical Studies
Miami, Florida

Don Manley's excellent book on Proverbs is obviously the fruit of many years of diligent labour. It has potential to be a great blessing to the entire Christian Church. The exposition of the text is faithful, thoughtful and extremely practical. The unusual format in which the book is laid out, makes it an outstanding tool for studying this sadly neglected part of the Bible, either privately or corporately. I warmly commend it; we have much need of this wisdom today.

Dr. Eric J. Alexander
formerly Senior Minister of St. George's
Tron Church, Glasgow, Scotland

I found it to be quite helpful in its practical orientation, directed toward a lay audience, with a special emphasis on the doctrine of God and the identification of qualities in Christians that are pleasing to the Lord. The book does a good job of drawing out the implications from the short maxims that we find in the text of Proverbs itself. Its easy-to- use, flowing design will be a welcomed Sunday school guide for many youth pastors and adult pastors.

Edward N. Martin, Ph.D.
Vice President for Academic Affairs
Dean of Philosophy and History
Trinity College and Seminary
Newburgh, Indiana

Don Manley set out to provide a work that brings the richness of the Proverbs to bear on our lives. He reminds us of God's great gift of wisdom for our living in a readable, useful, and wonderful way.

Thomas A. Kinchen, President
The Baptist College of Florida

Don Manley's work on Proverbs is excellent. It becomes obvious very early in the study that it is rich in illustrations. Practical applications to life could well be a summary of the book. This material will be helpful to pastors and others as they teach and preach from Proverbs. I recommend this book to you for spiritual development, interesting reading, and excellent research.

John Sullivan
Executive Director-Treasurer
Florida Baptist Convention

This practical commentary on Proverbs will be a welcome and soon to become a well-worn addition to the library of both pastors and Bible students who have discovered the lack of such a definitive work on the bookstore and library shelves.

Without using worn out clichés and out-of-date applications, the author has presented a cogent, concise, and timely commentary which has been needed for several decades.

Thomas R. Rodgers, D.Min.
Chairman, Trinity College and Seminary
Newburgh, Indiana

Dedication

*To my wife,
Anne,
for encouraging me in ministry, for being my
co-laborer, my best friend, my lover, my most
constructive critic, my teacher, and a role model for women.*

Acknowledgments

With gratitude to:

My Lord for guiding, instructing, and helping me in the preparation of this commentary. It was a task beyond my ability, but I sensed His presence throughout the many months of this project.

My secretary Linda Wirshels, for being used of God in suggesting to me one day how nice it would be if I would speak on Proverbs.

My typist Bill Berube, who served me faithfully with his skills throughout this project.

Jean Macfarlane, Ph.D., Professor Emerita of Clearwater Christian College, for her willingness to serve me by proofreading the manuscript.

Christian artist Vester Arnold, for designing the illustrations that I requested for the book.

Anne Manley for her illustration "The Outstretched Hand of God."

Marie Nelson for her unswerving loyalty to me and her enthusiasm for all of my many projects.

Contents

Foreword

My good friend, Don Manley, has asked me to write a brief fore-word to his commentary on Proverbs appropriately titled *Wisdom — The Principal Thing*. I have acceded to his request for three reasons:

First, the Book of Proverbs became especially meaningful to me during a bout with cancer some time ago. As I battled the horrific tortures of chemotherapy, I was strangely drawn to "the wise words" of this fascinating portion of God's revelation. The ethical, moral, and practical counsel that the Holy Spirit gives throughout these chapters resonated in my soul. In fact, during my illness, I wrote thirty-one devotional studies on specific subjects in Proverbs entitled *Windows of Wisdom*.

Second, I want to commend the excellent work of Don Manley in helping us all to understand this book more clearly. In his commentary, he skillfully expounds and applies the essence of God's truth as it relates to godly behavior day by day. His comments, graphics, and insights combine to make the book come alive!

Third, the book is timely. We are living in a day when TRUTH is being fiercely challenged. The postmodernism of accepted relativism and apostate syncretism make it difficult to teach or preach truth, even though we *must never* relent from doing so; but if there is a body of truth for unbelievers and believers alike that cannot be challenged, it is the Book of Proverbs. The sheer sanity, clarity, and testimony of each proverb has an appeal even to "the natural mind." All truth is God's truth, but my experience has shown that truth wrapped up in a proverb is often more palatable to the average person.

So I wish God's richest blessing on this unique presentation of divine truth in the Book of Proverbs. Well did Solomon say: "A word fitly spoken is like apples of gold in settings of silver" (Prov. 25:11).

Dr. Stephen F. Olford
Founder and Senior Lecturer
The Stephen Olford Center
For Biblical Preaching
Memphis, Tennessee

Introduction

The Purpose of This Book

I have, of course, asked God to use this book in any way that pleases Him. I am asking the Lord, however, that He would use it specifically in the following areas:

1. To help the people of God to better understand the important Book of Proverbs.
2. To create a fresh desire within the hearts of God's people to become "students of the Word."
3. To help parents better understand what God expects of them.
4. To serve as a devotional guide and resource book for parents as they teach their children the Book of Proverbs every three years.
5. To aid pastors and teachers as they prepare to speak and teach on Proverbs.

Defining Proverbs

Who Wrote Proverbs?

The book itself testifies that its main author is Solomon. In fact, the opening words of the book are: "The proverbs of Solomon . . ." Chapter 10 also opens with the words "The proverbs of Solomon."

Chapter 25 begins as follows: "These are also proverbs of Solomon. . . ." While Solomon is the main author of Proverbs, Agur is the author of chapter 30, and King Lemuel is the author of chapter 31.

What Is a Proverb?

A proverb is a short, witty saying that conveys a truth in a pointed way. Proverbs were common in the various nations of the ancient Near East. Proverbs are common in our culture as well. Modern day examples would include: "Action speaks louder than words," "Birds of a feather flock together," and "You can't teach an old dog new tricks." Arthur T. Pierson defined the biblical proverb as follows:

> A Proverb is a wise saying in which a few words are chosen instead of many, with a design to condense wisdom into a brief form both to aid memory and stimulate study. Hence proverbs are not only "wise sayings," but "dark sayings"—parables in which wisdom is disguised in a figurative or enigmatic form like a deep well, from which instruction is to be drawn, or a rich mine, from which it is to be dug. Only a profound meditation will reveal what is hidden in these moral and spiritual maxims.[1]

You cannot always claim a proverb for your situation. In the book, *Cracking the Old Testament Codes*, the authors ask us: "What authority does a proverb have? Proverbs 10:4 says, 'Lazy hands make a man poor, but diligent hands bring wealth.' Is this true in every case? Are not some people wealthy even though they are lazy, while others are poor throughout their whole lives even though they are diligent?"[2] The authors proceed to discuss three proposed solutions to this problem question. The first proposed solution is "name and claim." According to this proposal, all a believer has to do is find a promise, claim it by faith, and God will guarantee the desired outcome. The second proposal is the view that "a proverb is not a promise." The third view states more accurately what many of us believe to be true about the Proverbs, and is here repeated:

A third explanation makes an attempt to reinstate the original authority of the proverb as a genre and part of inspired scripture. Their view suggests that a proverb presents a slice of reality. The biblical proverb is always true, since it is simply specifying only one aspect of reality. Diligence does bring wealth, and laziness brings poverty. Though that is a true statement, life is complex with complex acts and complex consequences, and other factors may convolute the consequences. Thus, a lazy person may have a parent who bails him out so he never receives the poverty consequence which should have come upon him. A diligent son may choose friends who squander the wealth acquired by his diligence (see Prov. 1:10 FF). Nevertheless, the proverb is always true in the slice of reality it describes. It does not pretend to describe all of reality, just one segment of it.[3]

The Three Sections of Proverbs

I have divided this book into three sections. The first section covers the first nine chapters of Proverbs. As J. Sidlow Baxter said, these "are a little book in themselves, all devoted to one theme namely, the extolling of wisdom."[4]

The second section covers chapters 10–30. This section deals with many different subjects, and often the subjects change abruptly from verse to verse. These chapters do not lend themselves to analysis by traditional outlining. As Herbert Lockyer said, "All of the proverbs seem to hang as separate pearls on the necklace of truth."[5] The best way to study these chapters is by topic. In preparing to write on these chapters of Proverbs, I first selected what I considered to be the more important topics. I then researched these topics thoroughly and made them the subjects of chapters 10–30 in this book.

The third section of this book deals with Proverbs chapter 31. Unlike chapters 10–30, this chapter has a central theme, all of its subjects are related, and it can, therefore, be analyzed for our profit by outline. The theme of this great chapter is, of course, the virtuous woman. The Holy Spirit places great emphasis upon the concept of the godly woman by giving her an *exclusive* section in Proverbs.

Wisdom –
The Principal Thing

Section One

This section deals with wisdom training in the home.

Hear, ye children, the instruction of the father, and attend to know understanding.

— Proverbs 4:1

1 | Wisdom's Foundation

Reasons for the Proverbs

The proverbs of Solomon, the son of David, king of Israel: To know wisdom and instruction; to perceive the words of understanding; to receive the instruction of wisdom, righteousness, and justice, and equity; to give prudence to the simple, to the young man knowledge and discretion. A wise man will hear, and will increase learning; and a man of understanding shall attain unto wise counsels, to understand a proverb and the interpretation, the words of the wise and their dark sayings. (1:1–6)

The Book of Proverbs opens with a famous trio: Solomon, David, and Israel. These were all chosen by God for His purposes. When God was ready to create the nation Israel, He called a man named Abram out of the pagan city of Ur. From Abram's descendants, God created the nation Israel. Later, David, the shepherd boy, would be chosen of God to be king of Israel. Finally, David's son Solomon would be chosen of God to succeed David as king. The Proverbs are a gift to us from the Creator. These divine sentences come to us from the "lips of the king" (Solomon) (16:10). Although they come from the lips of the king, their origin was God. *Divine sentences never originate in the heart of man.*

This divine collection of sayings was given to us that we might be instructed in "wisdom, righteousness, justice, and equity" (v. 3). The Creator also designed the proverbs to give the "simple" (opposite of the wise) and the young these things: prudence, knowledge, and discretion (v. 4). What an incredible need there is in our society for these divine teachings!

Wisdom's Foundation

The fear of the Lord is the beginning of knowledge, but fools *despise wisdom and instruction.* (1:7)

The *beginning* of knowledge, we are told, is "the fear of the Lord." This is the key verse in Proverbs. It tells us that the *key that unlocks the door* to the vast library of divine knowledge is "the fear of the Lord." God emphasizes in this book that the fear of the Lord and wisdom are related. The phrase "the fear of the Lord" appears fourteen times in Proverbs and is, therefore, a key phrase. Since God uses this phrase repeatedly, it is obviously extremely important that we "fear the Lord." "But what," we ask, "does it mean to fear the Lord?" C.I. Scofield tells us that it means "reverential trust, including the hatred of evil."[1] Merrill Unger explains this "fear" as follows:

> Fear is that affection of the mind that arises with the awareness of approaching danger. The fear of God is of several kinds: superstitious, which is the fruit of ignorance; servile, which leads to abstinence from many sins through apprehension of punishment; and filial, which has its spring in love and prompts to care not to offend God and to endeavor in all things to please Him. It is another term for practiced piety and comprehends the virtue of godly character (Ps. 111:10, Prov. 14:2), whereas its absence is characteristic of a wicked and depraved person (Rom. 3:18). It is produced in the soul by the Holy Spirit, and great blessing is pronounced upon those who possess this trait: His angels protect them (Ps. 34:7); they "abide in the shadow of the Almighty" (91:1). This fear would subsist in a pious soul were there no punishment for sin. It dreads God's displeasure, desires His favor, reveres His

holiness, submits cheerfully to His will, is grateful for His benefits, sincerely worships Him, and conscientiously obeys His commandments. Fear and love must coexist in us in order that either passion may be healthy and that we may please and rightly serve God.[2]

Charles Bridges describes this "fear" as follows:

But what is this *fear of the Lord?* It is that affectionate reverence, by which the child of God bends himself humbly and carefully to his father's law. His wrath is so bitter, and his love so sweet [sic]; that hence springs an earnest desire to please him, and—because of the danger of coming short from his own weakness and temptations—a holy watchfulness and *fear,* "that he might not sin against him" (Heb. 12:28, 29). This enters into every exercise of the mind, every object of life (chapter 23:17).[3]

Ten Benefits of Fearing the Lord

The benefits that we receive for fearing the Lord are many. When we fear the Lord, we honor Him for who He is. When we honor Him, He blesses us. That is not only good theology; it is also "common sense." Here are ten of the benefits that we receive from fearing the Lord:

 The fear of the Lord brings salvation.

*The fear of the Lord is a **fountain of life**, to depart from the snares of death.* (14:27)

Before a person can be saved, he must realize that he is lost because he has sinned against a holy God. Furthermore, he must hear the gospel and accept Christ as his Savior. Until he realizes that the awesome, all-powerful, holy God is holding him accountable for his sins, he will see no need for salvation. The fear of the Lord precedes salvation. The fountain of life mentioned in Proverbs 14:27 is a reference to salvation. Jesus told the woman at the well:

25

But whosoever drinketh of the water of life that I shall give him shall never thirst, but the water that I shall give him shall be in him a well of water springing up into everlasting life. (John 4:14)

Benefit #2   **The fear of the Lord opens the door to the library of divine knowledge.**

*The fear of the Lord is the **beginning of knowledge,** but fools despise wisdom and instruction.* (1:7)

*Then shalt thou understand the **fear of the Lord,** and find the **knowledge of God.*** (2:5)

The subjects of divine wisdom and human wisdom will be discussed in another chapter, but I'd like to point out here that before anyone can attain divine wisdom, he or she must first fear the Lord and come to salvation through His Son Jesus.

Benefit #3   **The fear of the Lord will humble us.**

*The **fear of the Lord** is the instruction of wisdom; and **before honor is humility.*** (15:33)

As we study Scripture and let it get into our hearts, we begin to realize how awesome our God is. As we read about the God who is all powerful, all knowing, and everywhere present, we begin to develop a reverence for Him. We begin to realize how puny we are. We will find ourselves asking as the psalmist did: "What is man that thou art mindful of him?" The fear of the Lord and humility go together.

Benefit #4   **The fear of the Lord will bring us honor.**

The fear of the Lord is the instruction of wisdom; and before honor is humility. (15:33)

Before destruction the heart of man is haughty, and before honor is humility. (18:12)

The formula for destruction is found in Proverbs 18:12. God says that if a man is haughty (proud), he will face destruction. The formula for honor is also found in this verse: **before honor is humility.** We discovered earlier that the fear of the Lord brings humility, and now we discover that humility is followed by honor. Any honor that comes to a man who does not fear the Lord is strictly "man's honor." The Lord will not honor any man or woman who has not first feared Him and experienced biblical humility.

(Benefit #5) **The fear of the Lord will keep us from evil.**

*By mercy and truth iniquity is purged; and by the **fear of the Lord men depart from evil.*** (16:6)

We take sin lightly. We even try to excuse it. We argue: "Well, what's wrong with this? Why is this so wrong? Oh, really, this isn't that bad." As we read Scripture and begin to submit to the God of Scripture, our fear of the Lord increases. As our fear of the Lord increases, our eyes are opened more and more. We begin to see the issues of sin and righteousness a lot clearer, and this causes us to "depart from evil." Parents can protect their children from future evil by *training them from infancy* in Holy Scripture to *fear the Lord.*

(Benefit #6) **The fear of the Lord will cause us to hate evil.**

*The **fear of the Lord** is to **hate evil;** pride and arrogance, and the evil way, and the perverse mouth do I hate.* (8:13)

It is not enough for us to stay away from the wickedness of our culture. We should have a "holy hatred" for the sins of our society that trap and enslave our citizens and destroy their souls. The message that God has for us in the first part of this verse is **if you really fear Me, you will hate evil.** Someone might ask, "But is this a benefit?" It certainly is. There are great blessings from God reserved for those who love the things that He loves and hate the things that He hates.

Benefit #7   **The fear of the Lord will increase our confidence.**

In the **fear of the Lord** there is **strong confidence, and His children shall have a place of refuge.** (14:26)

It is a wonderful thing to go through life with your hand in the hand of the Heavenly Father. As He leads you, cares for you, and protects you, your confidence in Him will increase, and you'll find yourself trusting Him more and more. With confidence you'll be able to say, "I do not know what I will face tomorrow, but *I know who holds tomorrow*, and it's going to be OK."

Benefit #8   **The fear of the Lord will increase our life span.**

By humility and the **fear of the Lord** are riches, and honor, and **life.** (22:4)

The **fear of the Lord prolongeth days,** but the years of the wicked shall be shortened. (10:27)

We realize that there are exceptions to these statements, but as a general rule, fearing the Lord will increase the days of one's life. There are tremendous benefits in health and longevity for those who fear Him. The fear of the Lord is good for physical, emotional, mental, and spiritual health. More will be said about the benefits of righteous living in chapter twenty-two of this book.

Benefit #9 — **The fear of the Lord will increase our material wealth.**

*By humility and the **fear of the Lord** are **riches**, and honor, and life.* (22:4)

The classic example of this great truth is found in the Book of Job, where we read: "There was a man in the land of Uz whose name was Job; and that man was perfect and upright, and one that **feared** God, and eschewed evil." As we know, Job "went through the fire." He lost his children, his health, and his wealth. His friends told him that there must be sin in his life. Job went through some tremendous trials, but he continued to "fear the Lord" (Job 28:28). The outcome of this story is found in Job 42:10, where it says: "And the Lord turned the captivity of Job, when he prayed for his friends; also **the Lord gave Job twice as much as he had before.**" God multiplied Job's wealth because, in spite of his trials and tribulations, he **feared** God.

Benefit #10 — **The fear of the Lord results in a better quality of life.**

Better is little with the fear of the Lord, *than great treasure and trouble therewith.* (15:16)

This scripture clearly teaches that the *better* life is experienced, not necessarily by the rich, but by the one who fears the Lord. There is a wonderful peace and a thrilling joy in the heart of the believer who has a proper fear of the Lord. The peace of God is described in Philippians 4:7 as that "which passeth all understanding. . . ."

Parental Instruction

My son, hear the instruction of thy father, and forsake not the law of thy mother; *for they shall be an ornament of grace unto thy head, and chains about thy neck.* (1:8–9)

We are given the purpose of this book in verses one through six. Verse seven teaches us that there is a foundation called "the fear of the Lord," upon which knowledge is built. "Wisdom training" begins in verse eight with these words: "My son, hear. . . ." This is the first of a series of "wisdom training sessions" in the Book of Proverbs.

The *very first* thing that this son is told in this *first* wisdom session could be paraphrased as follows: "Son, listen to your father and your mother; their instruction heeded will bring you great benefit."

Enticement by Sinners

My son, if sinners entice thee, consent thou not. If they say, Come with us, let us lay wait for blood, let us lurk secretly for the innocent without cause, let us swallow them up alive as sheol, and whole, as those that go down into the pit; we shall find all precious substance, we shall fill our houses with spoil; cast in thy lot among us; let us all have one purse: My son, walk not thou in the way with them; refrain thy foot from their path; for their feet run to evil, and make haste to shed blood. Surely in vain the net is spread in the sight of any bird. And they lay wait for their own blood; they lurk secretly for their own lives. So are the ways of everyone who is greedy of gain, who taketh away the life of the owners thereof. (1:10–19)

Here the son is warned about ungodly men who introduce the young and the naive to their evil way of life. Men of evil, the son is warned, may try to entice him. The Hebrew word translated *entice* in this passage means "to persuade by deception." These ungodly men will almost always use the lure of "quick riches." Notice their enticing words in verse 13: "We shall find all precious substance, we shall fill our houses with spoil." These scriptures have served as a warning for the young throughout history, and with crime and violence escalating in our society, they are needed more now than ever.

After the father warns the son that he might be enticed by ungodly men (v. 10), he gives a vivid example of how these men induce others into a life of sin (vv. 11–13). The father proceeds to

30

tell the son what to do when the allurement comes. "Consent thou not," he tells the son in verse 10. "Walk not thou in the way of them; refrain thy foot from their path," he instructs the son in verse 15.

Finally, the son is told where a life of crime leads. It is a path, he is told, that leads not to fast riches and an easy life, but one that leads to ruin and premature death (vv. 18 and 19). It is a wise father that, with good instruction, insulates his children against the evils that they will face in life.

Observations from This Wisdom Training Session

Fathers should incorporate these points in training their children in the home.

1. Warning concerning enticements (v. 10).
2. Example of enticement (vv. 11–14).

   Here the father gives the son an example of how the process works. He "acts out" the part of the enticer by a technique known as "role playing."

3. Instruction against enticement (vv. 10, 15).
4. Outcome of the enticers, and those that follow them (vv. 16–19).

   How is this father able to accurately predict the outcome? How does he know any better than the son what the future holds for these ungodly people? The father has two advantages over the son:

   A. His knowledge of the Word of God. (He has read what God has said about such individuals.)
   B. His life experiences. (He has known people whose lives have been wrecked by sin.)

Lady Wisdom's Debut

Wisdom crieth outside; *she uttereth her voice* in the streets; *she crieth* in the chief place of concourse, in the openings of the gates; in the city *she uttereth her words*. . . . (1:20–21)

We see Lady Wisdom for the first time in these verses. She comes onto the scene without any introduction. We are not told anything about her background. Who is she? Where did she come from? What is the story of her life? These are the types of questions that come up in our minds as we study the text. The answers to these questions, however, are not found here. We know nothing of her history. She simply appears on the scene proclaiming an important message to the people of the city. Her message has nothing to do with the world of politics or the issues of commerce. Lady Wisdom is seen crying out to the *lost people* of the city delivering a *divine message*. The only thing we are told about her is her name and the fact that she speaks for God.

Lady Wisdom appears again and again in the Proverbs. We will discover that whenever she speaks, she speaks for God. She is described elsewhere in Proverbs as the one who is to be sought after, followed, and not forsaken. She is a fascinating personality, and one that we will discuss in detail in another chapter.

The Offer of Salvation

How long, ye simple ones, will ye love simplicity? And the scoffers delight in their scoffing, and fools hate knowledge? Turn you at my reproof; behold, **I will pour out my spirit unto you, I will make known my words** *unto you.* (1:22–23)

The Lord's message is delivered here by Lady Wisdom. Look at the people He offers salvation to. He is speaking to the "simple," the "scoffers," and "fools." Isn't the love of God amazing? I look at this undesirable bunch and ask myself: "Why would God even bother with these?" Then, I am reminded of my own sin, and all that God has forgiven me. Suddenly, the spotlight that I had focused on the sinners found in verse 22 swings around and focuses on me! I see myself for what I am: a terrible sinner who does not deserve mercy. My question then is no longer focused on the sinners of verse 22, but upon me. The question now becomes, "Why would God even bother with *me*?" Have there not been times when you too have thought about your sins and your failures, and you too have asked: "Why would He even bother with me?" The amazing answer to that disturbing question that sometimes haunts our minds is found in Scripture. The answer is because *God is love* (1 John 4:8). It is a loving God calling out to the lost and the ungodly in verses 22 and 23. He "bothers" with us because He loves us.

There are two things that God always uses to save our souls: His Spirit and His Word. You will find them both in verse 23. He calls out for these sinners to repent. **Turn you at my reproof** . . . (v. 23). Then He promises His Spirit and further enlightenment through His Word to those that do . . . *I will* **pour out my Spirit unto you,** *I will* **make known my words unto you** (v. 23).

Salvation Rejected

Because I have called, and **ye have refused;** *I have stretched out my hand and no man regarded, but* **ye would have** *set at nought all my counsel, and would have* **none of my reproof.** (1:24–25)

What a rebellious race we are! God **called,** but the people **refused** Him (v. 24)! This is pretty much how it has been all through history. God calls. Some are saved. Many refuse His salvation. The "believers" are a minority group today, and always have been. I am extremely grateful that I am a member of this *distinct minority group*, aren't you? Multitudes do just what the people in Proverbs 1:24–25 did—they refuse. They think they are okay without Him. They "feel bad" when convicted with the need to be saved, but they reject Him and continue in their "feel good" religion. They fail to accept the truth, and without divine forgiveness, they can never enter heaven. They do not want to accept the fact that they have evil, wicked hearts and therefore need the salvation that the holy God provides for all who will come to Jesus Christ by faith.

Just how does God **call?** Here are the words of A.R. Fausset, a nineteenth century Church of England clergyman: "God calls externally by His ministers, by His written *Word*, and by His judgements, and inwardly by His awakening appeals, and by the stings of conscience."[4]

The Outstretched Hand of God

The God that called also **stretched out** His hand (v. 24). Here is a picture of a powerful and loving God offering His outstretched hand to those who are spiritually lost. He stretched forth His hand, willing to rescue any who would grasp it. His powerful hand has been extended to the people of earth all through the ages. Many a man has heard God's voice speak to his spirit, and has visualized the divine hand reaching down from heaven to save him from his wretched condition. What exactly does a sinner see when God stretches out His hand to him? He sees a hand that is *powerful*, a hand that is *holy*, a hand that is *loving*, and a hand that *saves*. A picture of the saving hand of God is given to us in the gospel of Matthew. Peter, the apostle, was walking on the water toward Jesus. He began to sink. Fear gripped his heart! He was about to go under! With great urgency, he cried out three little words: "Lord, save me!" Scripture informs us that "*immediately* Jesus stretched forth His hand" (Matt. 14:31) and Peter was saved. Have *you* heard God's call? Have *you* seen His hand reaching down from heaven *to you*? Have *you* cried out to Him, "Lord, save me"?

Here is a summary of the events in Proverbs 1:22–24: The Spirit of God was at work, the Word of God was proclaimed, and the hand of God was extended. The people's response was:

1. They refused his call (v. 24).
2. They regarded not His outstretched hand (v. 24).
3. They rejected His counsel and reproof (v. 25).

God Becomes Angry

I will also laugh at your calamity; I will mock when your fear cometh; when your fear cometh as desolation, and your destruction cometh like a whirlwind; when distress and anguish come upon you. Then shall they call upon me, but I will not answer; they shall seek me early, but they shall not find me; because they hated knowledge, and did not choose the fear of the Lord. They would have none of my counsel; they despised all of my reproof. Therefore shall they eat of the fruit of their own way, and be filled with their own devices. For the turning away of the simple shall slay them, and the prosperity of fools shall destroy them. But whoso hearkeneth unto me shall dwell safely, and shall be quiet from fear of evil. (1:26–32)

All those who reject God's love will eventually receive God's judgment. "It is a fearful thing to fall into the hands of the Living God," we are told in Hebrews 10:31. The above verses (1:26–32) describe a frightening scene. They describe the awful judgment of God upon a people who refused His call, regarded not His outstretched hand, and rejected His counsel and reproof. "Their cry is for deliverance from pain, and not from sin (Jer. 11:11, Ezek. 8:15, Mic. 3:4, Zech. 7:13)," states A.R. Fausset.[5]

"But," say some, "this picture seems so inconsistent with a God of love." We would remind them that these people refused His love. He called to them, but they refused His call. He stretched out His hand to them, but they ignored it. He gave them counsel and reproof, but they rejected it. What is a holy God to do with those who reject His goodness and His offer of salvation? What we see in these verses is the ungodly reaping what they have sown. "Men are free in choosing destruction, so that the blame rests wholly on themselves (Acts 13:46 'Ye judge yourselves unworthy of everlasting life')," noted A.R. Fausset.[6] Charles Bridges said, "The day of grace has its limits (Gen. 6:3, Heb. 4:7). . . . there is a knock which will be the last knock. . . ."[7]

Destruction is seen coming upon this God-rejecting crowd like a hurricane or a tornado. They scoffed and mocked at the things of God (v. 22), so He tells them, *I also will laugh at your calamity; I will mock when your fear cometh* (v. 26). Charles Bridges states: "To be forsaken of God at any time is awful woe (Hos. 9:12); how much more in the time of trouble (1 Sam. 28:15)! But to have His countenance not only turned from us, but turned against us, His eternal frown instead of His smile—this will be hell instead of heaven."[8]

Hope for the Individual

*But **whoso hearkeneth unto me shall dwell safely,** and shall be quiet from fear of evil.* (1:33)

Verses 24–32 speak of the divine judgment upon a society that had rejected the true God. No hope is given for any member of that society in those verses. It is a dismal picture indeed. Hope is restored, however, in verse 33. The first word of that verse ("but") acts as a dividing line. There are unbelievers on one side of the line and believers on the other. Call it "the great divide." Before the great divide, we find God's eternal judgment on unbelievers, and after the great divide we find God's blessing on believers.

The entire subject changes in verse 33. We do not read of any more judgment, destruction, or anguish. The "subjects" are also different, as we have mentioned. They are not unbelievers, but believers. We are reminded in verse 33 that society as a whole may reject God's call, but there is still hope for the individual. The Word of God declares, "Whosoever will, let him take the water of life freely" (Rev. 22:17). So then, after the warning of coming judgment in verses 24–32, God reaches out with love one more time with a message of hope and life: *But **whoso hearkeneth unto me shall dwell safely, and shall be quiet from fear of evil*** (v. 33).

2 | The Importance of Receiving the Word

R eceiving the Word of God is extremely important for us as believers. We cannot grow spiritually without the Word of God. We are told to desire the Word, even as a newborn baby desires milk. First Peter 2:2 says: "As newborn babes, desire the sincere milk of the Word, that ye may grow thereby." This chapter focuses on promises from God that will literally change our lives if we will give His Word *priority*.

> My son, **if thou wilt receive my words,** and **lay up my commandments** with thee, so that thou **incline thine ear unto wisdom,** and **apply thine heart to understanding;** yea, if thou criest after knowledge, and liftest up thy voice for understanding; **if thou seekest her as silver,** and **searchest for her as hidden treasures;** (2:1–4)

What food is to the body, God's Word is to the soul. Christians who do not study God's Word regularly suffer from spiritual malnutrition. Believers do not live defeated, unstable, and unhappy lives when they are spending ample time in the Word of God. God has some wonderful promises in this chapter, but the fulfillment of these promises is not without a price. They are *contingent upon our diligent pursuit of a deeper understanding of God's Word.*

God's Word Must Be:

1. Received into our minds
2. Retained in our hearts
3. Regular in our study

God's Word must be:
1. Received into our minds.

Verse 1 states, "if thou will **receive** my words. . . ." It is not enough to read the Word. It is not enough to hear the Word. The Word must be received. We must **open our minds** and **receive it** if we are to profit. Many people *read* the Word and *hear* the Word and yet their lives never seem to change. They never seem to get the victory over the flesh, and they show very little evidence of growth in Christ. Reason: **The Word must not only be read and heard. It must also be received.**

Matthew Henry said: "We must, accordingly, receive the Word of God with all readiness of mind, and bid it welcome, even the commandments as well as the promises, without murmuring or disputing. *Speak Lord, for thy servant hears.*"[1]

God's Word must be:
2. Retained in our hearts.

Verse 1 also states: "**if thou will . . . lay up** my commandments with thee." To "lay up" His commandments is to hide them in the heart, to store them in the heart, or to treasure them in the heart. "We must not only receive, but retain, the Word of God, and lodge it in our hearts, that it may be always ready to us," warned Matthew Henry.[2] "We must lay hold on all opportunities of hearing the Word of God and listen to it with attention and seriousness, as those that are afraid of letting it slip," said Henry.[3]

God's Word, when retained in our minds, can keep us from falling into sin. The psalmist said: "Thy Word have I hidden in my heart, that I might not sin against thee" (Ps. 119:11). Committing Scripture to memory is very important. The memorization of Scripture should be a regular discipline for every believer. Memorizing Scripture can be a family project. A verse for the week can be selected, and each member of the family can recite the verse during family devotions. The benefits for each member of the family will be immeasurable!

God's Word must be:
3. Regular in our study.

"*[I]ncline thine ear* unto wisdom, and *apply thine heart* unto understanding." The person whose ear is "inclined" unto wisdom is the person who is anxious to hear, to read, and to study the Word of God. "And as you note the emphasis on searching for wisdom as one would search for treasures," states Jay Adams, "you understand something of the urgency, dedication, time, energy and thought that God expects us to devote to the project. Treasure hunters are persistent!"[4] Charles Bridges had this to say on the subject:

> The miner's indefatigable pains; his invincible resolution; his untiring perseverance; *seeking, yea, searching for hid treasures*— such must be our *searching* into the sacred storehouse. To read, instead of "*searching* the scriptures," is only to skim the surface, and gather up a few superficial notions. The rule of success is— Dig up and down the field; and if the search be discouraging, dig again. The patient industry of perusal and re-perusal will open the embosomed treasure. . . . we may read the Scriptures in company—but to *search* them, we must be alone with God. Here we learn to apply ourselves wholly to the Word, and the Word wholly to us. This enriching study gives a purer vein of sound judgment. The mere reader often scarcely knows where to begin, and he performs the routine without any definite object. His knowledge, therefore, must be scanty and ineffective.

Nor is the neglect of this habit less hurtful to the church. All fundamental errors and heresies in the church may be traced to this source—"Ye do err, not knowing the scriptures" (Matt. 22:29). They are mostly based on partial or disjointed statements of truth. Truth separated from truth becomes error.[5]

Life-Changing Promises from God

"My son, **if** thou wilt receive my words . . . **if** thou criest after knowledge . . . **if** thou seekest her as silver . . . **then shalt thou understand**. . . ." (Prov. 2:1–5). The promises of God that we are about to discover are contingent upon our diligent pursuit of a deeper understanding of God's Word. When other activities in our lives have priority over Scripture, we miss much of what God has planned for us. The illustrations that follow will help us to visualize the "priority problem."

Bill's Priority List

Home entertainment
Sports
Hobbies
Friends
Recreation
**Bible study
and
Prayer**

Low Priority

Betty's Priority List

Bible study and prayer
Home entertainment
Sports
Hobbies
Friends
Recreation

High Priority

Notice that Bible study and prayer are not a high priority on Bill's list. This believer is missing out on the exciting, life-changing promises that God offers in Proverbs chapter two.

Betty has put time with the Lord in Bible study and prayer above all of the other activities listed. The Lord will bless this believer by fulfilling the promises of Proverbs chapter two in her life.

If you will fulfill the "if" in verse one, the "if" in verse three, and the "if" in verse four, you will be well on your way to experiencing the promises of God that follow. I've personified each of the promises because they are from the Lord Himself.

Life-Changing Promise #1

"I'll teach you to fear Me."

> ***Then shalt thou understand the fear of the Lord***, *and find the knowledge of God.* (2:5)

Here is the beginning of great things in a person's life. If you will give the Word of God priority in your life, He'll teach you to fear Him. In chapter one, we listed ten benefits that we receive when we fear the Lord. Can you remember any of them? Take a moment and review that list.

Life-Changing Promise #2

"I'll increase your wisdom."

> *Then shalt thou understand the fear of the Lord,* ***and find the knowledge of God.*** *. . . **For the Lord giveth wisdom**. . . . (2:5–6a)*

Solomon knew from experience that "the Lord giveth wisdom" (1 Kings 3:9–12). We are instructed in Proverbs 2:3 to cry out for knowledge and to lift up our voices for understanding. That is exactly what Solomon did. "Wisdom is a *gift*," comments Jay Adams, "graciously imparted to those who seek it for the right reasons, from the right source, in the right way."[6] "Do not, on the other hand, be self-confident, as if you could get it by your own efforts," states A.R. Fausset, "for it is the Lord who gives it, as its Author, even as the Lord is the object to whom all true wisdom tends, and in whom it finds its centre (for 'the fear of the Lord is the beginning of knowledge,' chapter 1 v. 7)."[7]

Looking back over your life, can you not see that since you became a believer and started "receiving" God's words that He has kept His promise to you? Have you grown in wisdom? Has He increased your knowledge? Has not this increased wisdom enabled you to get "both feet on the ground," whereas before salvation you had all you could do to keep one foot down? Has not this increased wisdom and knowledge been a blessing to you?

Now these promises of God are, as we have said, "conditional"— but they are also "continual." As long as we continue to receive His words and honor His commandments, He will continue to increase our wisdom and knowledge. I am excited about this great truth because I, for one, want more wisdom, more knowledge, from Almighty God. As I "look back" and see where I was, I realize God has brought me such a long way! Praise God for what He has done! As I "look at the present," I realize I have such a long way to go. Isn't this true in your life as well? Here is the important thing: As long as you continue to receive His words and honor His commandments, He will continue to increase wisdom and knowledge as you journey through life!

Life-Changing Promise **#3**

"I'll bless you with a wonderful, personal relationship with Me."

For the Lord giveth wisdom: **out of his mouth cometh knowledge** *and* **understanding**. (2:6)

Here we see God speaking, communicating, and teaching. This all speaks of fellowship with Him. He states here that He will teach us wisdom—and out of His mouth He will communicate to us knowledge and understanding. Fellowship with the "Word" is the condition for all these promises. Fellowship with the written Word of God is fellowship with the Living Word, the Lord Himself. God blesses His people with many wonderful blessings, and here is one of the very greatest: the opportunity to have fellowship with Him.

"Truly our fellowship is with the Father, and with His Son Jesus Christ" (1 John 1:3).

Life-Changing Promise #4
"I'll be your shield."

*He layeth up sound wisdom for the righteous: He is a **shield** to them that walk uprightly.* (2:7)

God has a shield of protection for you if you will (verse one) "receive" His "words." I call this the *invisible shield*. With so much wickedness in the world today, we need a shield of protection more than ever. We are involved in a great spiritual battle. The devil and his demons are constantly attacking the things of God and the people of God. They hate the human race, and they especially hate the believers. In fact, their feelings for you are the exact opposite of the Lord's feelings for you. The Lord loves you with an intense love, and they hate you with an intense hatred. The Lord desires to bless the human race with good things. The devil and his demons are out to attack and subdue us with wicked things. I cannot overemphasize the importance of these great truths. **1.** There is a holy God who loves you, wants to bless your life, and wants to make you a godly person. **2.** There is a devil who personally hates you. He wants to wreck your life. He wants you to live an ungodly life. In short, he's out to get you! You need a ***shield of protection from this evil one*** and his vast army of rebellious fallen angels!

Almighty God will be your shield if you will "receive His words" (2:1). If we were fully aware of the ungodly, unseen spiritual forces that are at work all around us, we would certainly live a lot differently. We need to make sure that we are always protected by God's invisible shield. Consider the following verses:

Put on the whole armor of God, that you may be able to stand against the wiles of the devil. For we wrestle not against flesh and blood, but against principalities, against powers, against the rulers of darkness of this world, against spiritual wickedness in high places. Wherefore take unto you the whole armor of God that ye may be able to withstand in the evil day, and having done all, to stand. Stand therefore, having your loins girt about with truth, and having on the breastplate of righteousness; and your feet shod with the preparation of the gospel of peace; above all taking the **shield of faith, wherewith ye shall be able to quench all the fiery darts of the wicked**. *And take the helmet of salvation, and the sword of the spirit which is the* **Word of God.** (Eph. 6:11–17)

My friend, your protection—***the shield of faith,*** the "invisible shield—will stop (v. 16) *all* the fiery darts of the wicked one, if you will just wear it! You wear it by "receiving His words" (Prov. 2:1). We need to be saturated with the Word of God! We should read it, meditate upon it, memorize it, and we should be at the house of the Lord where His holy Word is preached at every opportunity! It's up to us to be sure that the protective shield is in place! Missing church? That scares me! Skipping devotions? Danger! **Without the shield in place, we face powerful enemies unprotected.**

> **For we wrestle** not against flesh and blood, but **against principalities, against powers, against the rulers of the darkness of this world**, against spiritual wickedness in high places. (Eph. 6:12)

Life-Changing Promise **#5**
"I'll preserve your way."

> He keepeth the paths of justice, and **preserveth the way of His saints**. (2:8)

The word translated "preserveth" is the Hebrew word *shâmar* and means "to hedge about, to guard, to protect." The word translated "way" is *derek* and means "a road." The invisible shield mentioned earlier is at work here in a wider measure. In v. 7, the Lord's shield is around the believer to protect him from all of the fiery darts of the wicked. In verse 8, God is seen as guarding the very path or road that the Christian is called to walk. "He *preserveth* (to hedge about, guard, protect) the way of His saints." What a blessing this is. God promises this wonderful shield of protection and then states He'll even guard the road that He puts us on during this journey of life.

Late one very dark night in the Blue Hills of Arizona, our church bus broke down, just after we had dropped off the last teenager following a youth meeting and had started back home. The road was very hilly and full of twists and turns. Home was a few miles away in the valley. My eleven-year-old daughter and I started down that long, dark country road. It was a night as dark as any I have ever seen. We walked side by side but could not see each other. We could not see the road. We were able to follow the road because it was a dirt road with deep ditches on either side. Although we couldn't see, we could *hear*—and what we could hear was not comforting at all! We heard coyotes howling in the distance, and we heard what sounded like vicious dogs barking at us as we walked the road that would lead us to the valley. We finally made it to the valley where there were many homes with outside lights on. We were able to get help from our good friend and church member Earl Dublin. We arrived safely. "Daddy, I'm scared," my daughter had said to me as we started that dark walk. "Don't worry, the Lord will protect us," I told her, but secretly I was more than a little concerned! As we traveled the road that God had placed us on that evening, He watched over us. I believe He had a hedge of protection along the road that night especially for us. We could hear potential dangers, but we stayed on the road where God put us and He brought us safely to the valley.

As you follow the Lord on the path He gives you to follow, there will be times when the way will be unsure, the road will be dark, and your heart will fear the many possible dangers lurking just around the bend. Thank God that not all of the Christian life is like that. The road called *God's Will* is a joyous road to travel, filled with blessings and good things, but there will be times when the road will be dark, and your heart fearful. You may be *almost* able to hear the roar of the lion!

*Be sober, be vigilant; because **your adversary the devil**, as a **roaring lion**, walketh about, seeking whom he may devour.* (1 Pet. 5:8)

If you ever face such a situation, remember this— God has promised:

1. "I will never leave you nor forsake you" (Heb. 13:5).

2. "I will be your shield" Prov. 2:7.

3. "I will guard the road I put you on in life" (Prov. 2:8).

Life-changing Promise **#6**

"I'll give you understanding and discretion."

*Then shalt thou understand righteousness, and justice, and equity; yea, every good path. When wisdom entereth into thine heart, and knowledge is pleasant unto thy soul, **discretion** shall preserve thee, **understanding** shall keep thee.* (2:9–11)

The Book of Proverbs is all about wisdom. The words "wise," "wisdom," "knowledge," "understanding," and "know" appear 226 times in Proverbs. Great things begin to happen when we open our hearts to "receive" His words. "Wisdom" begins to enter our hearts, a bit at a time, and then more and more and more. Wisdom and knowledge are indeed "pleasant unto thy soul" (v. 10).

As we allow the Word of God to enter our hearts, we begin to get "discretion" and "understanding." The Hebrew word translated "discretion" in verse 11 is *mezimmâh,* and it means *a plan.* The Hebrew word that is translated "understanding" in verse 11 is *tâbûwn,* and it means *intelligence.* When a believer begins to grow in wisdom, he soon realizes that he still has his old flesh nature that loves to sin, and he discovers something else. He discovers that he has an enemy named Satan. The growing Christian begins to think thoughts similar to the following: "I am no match for this evil enemy. He is powerful and wicked, and I am weak and so prone to sin. What can I do? How can I stand? What **plan** do I follow? I don't know what to do, but I intend to find out—and fast! I'll ask my pastor what to do to protect myself from this powerful enemy." Pastors and Christian friends should show new believers what they must do to have victory over the world, the flesh, and the devil. We all need a plan to keep us pure for God.

If you diligently pursue Him, He will give you discretion and understanding that will:

DELIVER YOU FROM EVIL MEN
To deliver thee from the way of the evil man, *from men that speak perverse things, who leave the paths of uprightness, to walk in the way of darkness; who rejoice to do evil, and delight in the perverseness of the wicked; whose ways are crooked, and they perverse in their paths. . . . (2:12–15)*

DELIVER YOU FROM EVIL WOMEN
To deliver thee from the strange woman, *even from the foreigner who flattereth with her words; who forsaketh the guide of her youth, who forgetteth the covenant of her God. For her house inclineth unto death, and her paths unto the dead. None that go unto her return again, neither take they hold of the paths of life. . . . (2:16–19)*

HELP KEEP YOU ON THE RIGHT PATH
That thou mayest walk in the way of good men, and keep the paths of the righteous. *For the upright shall dwell in the land, and the perfect shall remain in it. But the wicked shall be cut off from the earth, and the transgressors shall be rooted out of it. (2:20–22)*

We all need a plan from God. Furthermore, God has a plan for each of us. His plan is never deficient. His plan, when followed, will deliver us from evil that might otherwise engulf us! Are you living in God's "plan" for your life? It would be good at this point to go back to the beginning of this chapter and re-read it, and as you do, I believe it will become increasingly clear what one must do to have a plan for spiritual victory. Not just any plan will do. We are dealing with spiritual things. Therefore, we must have a plan that goes above and beyond the human range. Man's plan will not "deliver you from evil." There is only one plan that will accomplish that: God's plan for you.

The Strange Woman

The unclean woman in verse 16 appears time after time in Proverbs. Almighty God warns his "sons" who study this book to beware of her. *She represents all the immoral, wicked women on the planet.* Pay close attention to the things God says about her.

    1. She's a flatterer (v. 16).
    2. Her paths lead to death (v. 18).
    3. She has left the guide of her youth (v. 17).
    4. She has forgotten the covenant of her God (v. 17).

Many Christian authors have stated that the "guide" that she has forsaken is her husband. I ask you to consider that the guide she has forsaken is Conscience. God equips each of us with conscience. It is conscience that accuses us when we do wrong. Proverbs 20:27 states that: "The spirit of man is the **lamp of the Lord,** searching all of the inward parts." That **lamp** is conscience. If it is dark and you have a lamp, you can see. If you forsake the lamp, then you are in total darkness. Notice what the "strange" woman is guilty of in Proverbs 2:17—"She forsaketh the guide of her youth." She threw away the lamp. She did this in her youth. The Hebrew word for youth speaks of childhood or a young person. Most men and women who end up living wicked, evil lives left the guide of their youth in their teenage years. These are the dangerous years. Be especially careful, watchful, and protective of your sons and daughters during those crucial teenage years. Expose them to the right things, and encourage them to have the right kind of friends, and to avoid like the plague anyone or anything that would cause them to *forsake the guide of their youth.*

Forsaking the lamp of the Lord, the guide of our youth, can cause all types of worldly activity and filthiness of the flesh. Every unclean woman, every wicked, perverted man, every homosexual, every lesbian, every atheist at one time had "the lamp" but threw it away! They "forsook the guide of their youth." Romans chapter one tells us of such a people:

> Wherefore, God also gave them up to uncleanness through the lusts of their own hearts, to dishonor their own bodies between themselves, **who exchanged the truth of God for a lie**, and worshipped and served the creature more than the Creator who is blessed forever. Amen. For this cause, God gave them up unto vile affections; for even **the women did exchange the natural use for that which is against nature; and likewise also the men, leaving the natural** use of the woman, burned in their lust one to another, men with men, working that which is unseemly, and receiving in themselves that recompense of their error which was fitting. And even as **they did not like to retain God in their knowledge**, God gave them over to a reprobate mind, to do those things which are not seemly, being filled with all unrighteousness, fornication, wickedness, covetousness, maliciousness, full of envy, murder, strife, deceit, malignity, whisperers, backbiters, haters of God, insolent, proud, boasters, inventors of evil things, disobedient to parents; **without understanding**, covenant breakers, without natural affection, implacable, unmerciful; who, knowing the judgement of God, that they who commit such things are worthy of death, not only do the same, but have pleasure in them that do them. (Rom. 1:24–32)

Every young person will be tempted to disregard the "guide of their youth." In today's world, it is happening at a much younger age. It is our responsibility as parents to see that the conscience is not seared (1 Tim. 4:2) in the lives of our young people.

The Paths of Proverbs Chapter Two

The Pathetic Paths
(avoid these)

- Paths of darkness (vv. 12–13).
- Paths of evil men (v. 15).
- Paths of the wicked woman (v. 18).

The Profitable Paths
(follow these)

- Paths of justice (vv. 8–9).
- Paths of righteousness (v. 9).
- Paths of equity (v. 9).
- Paths of uprightness (v. 13).
- Paths of life (v. 19).
- Paths of the righteous (v. 20).

3 | The God Who Provides Abundantly

From the very beginning of creation, God has been providing for man. Speaking to Adam and Eve in Genesis chapter one, God said: "Behold, I have given you . . . food." All through Scripture we find Him providing all kinds of good things to His people. The apostle Paul reminded the believers in Philippi: "But my God shall supply all your needs according to His riches in glory by Christ Jesus." If you were to make a list from Scripture of all of the things that the Lord provides for you, you would be amazed. The list on your tablet would go on and on, with page after page after page. Our God provides us with many things that we never even think about, or give Him credit for. A careful study of this chapter will reveal that the God of heaven is a God that provides.

God Provides Marvelous Benefits for Keeping His Commandments

*My son, forget not my law, but let thine heart keep my commandments; for **length of days**, and **long life**, and **peace**, shall they add to thee. Let not mercy and truth forsake thee; bind them about thy neck; write them upon the table of thine heart; so shalt thou find **favor** and **good understanding** in the sight of God and man.* (3:1–4)

The Lord declares here that He will provide us with certain benefits if we will keep His commandments in our hearts. These benefits are similar but not identical to the ones promised by the Lord in chapter two. Here are the specific benefits mentioned in verses 1–4:

1. A long life (v. 2).
2. A peaceful life (v. 2).
3. Favor with God (v. 4).
4. Favor with people (v. 4).
5. Wisdom (good understanding) (v. 4).
6. Wisdom recognized by others (v. 4).

The Lord said, "let **thine heart** keep my commandments" (v. 1). It is not enough to keep God's laws and commandments **outwardly**. If we are to please Him, we must keep God's laws and commandments **inwardly.** Jesus condemned the Pharisees because they put on a good outward appearance, but their hearts were far from God.

Where does sin originate? Where are the commandments of God first broken in a believer's life? The commandments of God are not initially broken outwardly, but inwardly, or from the heart.

Isn't it interesting that Solomon failed to do what he instructed his son to do? Isn't it also interesting that the Lord chose Solomon, a man who later failed God so terribly, to give us the Proverbs? Solomon had a great start. He loved the Lord (1 Kings 3:3); he had an audience with the Lord (1 Kings 3:5–14, 9:1–9); and the Lord made him wise, wealthy, and famous (1 Kings 3:11–14, 4:29). He was known in all of the surrounding nations as a great wise man (1 Kings 4:29–33). People came from all over to hear this divinely enlightened man. First Kings 4:34 states:

And there came from all peoples to hear the wisdom of Solomon, from all kings of the earth, who had heard of his wisdom.

Solomon had a great beginning. God blessed him with much wisdom. Solomon walked with God, and blessed the people of his generation with "3,000 proverbs," and over a thousand songs (1 Kings 4:32). God gave the world the Proverbs that we are studying through a godly and a wise Solomon. Later, Solomon, the man of wisdom, did a very unwise thing: he forsook God (1 Kings 11). There came a time when Solomon had God's laws in his head but not in his heart (1 Kings 11:4). Earlier, he had been taught by David, his father, to follow the Lord and was warned of the consequences if he did not (1 Chron. 28:9). His Heavenly Father also instructed and warned him of the consequences if he turned away (1 Kings 9:1–9). God blessed him with wisdom. In spite of the warnings, and the Lord's rich blessings, Scripture records that "Solomon did evil in the sight of the Lord. . . ." (1 Kings 11:6) There is a difference in knowing what to do and doing it. Many men have stood behind pulpits and publicly proclaimed the eternal truths of God but privately had ceased to walk in fellowship with the God whose truths they proclaimed. All of us that know and love the Lord must recognize the dangerous potential that we have of turning away from the Lord. We must be careful not to specialize in criticizing Solomon. Instead, let's look at the mistakes that he made, learn from them, and determine in our hearts that we won't make those same mistakes (Gal. 6:1).

The Solomon Story

- Solomon had a desire to really obey the Lord early in his ministry.
- Solomon followed the Lord early in his ministry.
- Solomon failed to guard his heart carefully.
- Solomon departed from the Lord after he became successful.

Proverbs 4:23 states: "Keep **thy heart** with all diligence; for out of it are the issues of life." The man who gave us those great words failed to do what he instructed us to do. The Word of God informs us: "And the Lord was angry with Solomon, because his **heart** was *turned away* from the Lord God of Israel, who had appeared unto him twice" (1 Kings 11:9). Let the story of Solomon be a warning to all of us. We must give heed to the divine message received by Solomon (Prov. 4:23), repeated by Solomon, and later ignored by Solomon.

We need to remember that this is Solomon the father instructing his son. As we read the "my son" instructional Proverbs, we should keep in mind that God the Father is speaking to all of us through the words of Solomon, the earthly father. Solomon spoke the words, but we can trace the words back to God. Second Timothy 3:16 states that "all scripture is given by inspiration of God. . . ." The word "inspiration" is translated from the Greek word *theopneustos*. In Greek, *theos* is God, and *pneo* means "to breathe." The Greek word "theopneustos" means "God-breathed." That is why the Bible is unique among all of the other books of the world. Men wrote the Bible, just as men (and women) have written all of the other books that have ever come into existence. One of the unique things about the Bible is the fact that men were moved by God to write what they wrote. Second Peter 1:21 reads as follows:

> *For the prophecy came not at any time by the will of man, but holy men of God spoke as they were moved by the Holy Spirit.*

Each of the "my son" instructional Proverbs should be read in the following two ways:

1. The message is for you.

As you read these, keep in mind: *The message is for me.*

God

God is speaking to me.

Here God is speaking to you. He explains to you what He will do for you if you will hear His words and obey Him.

First, read the instruction and let God speak to you through His words. This is one of the primary functions of Scripture. The Holy God speaks to us through His living Word. Hebrews 4:12 states:

> *For the word of God is **living**, and powerful, and sharper than any two-edged sword, piercing even to the dividing asunder of soul and spirit, and of the joints and marrow, and is a discerner of the thoughts and intents of the heart.*

Notice that God tells us His Word is "living." Here is another unique aspect of the Bible: The words are "alive." All books have words, but the words of the Bible speak to us in a unique way because they are God-breathed and have divine life! The words of God are alive, active, and powerful.

As you read through the instruction, remember *the message is for you.* It is for you to read, consider, and do. The Heavenly Father immediately gets your attention with those captivating words: "my son." If you have accepted Jesus Christ as your Savior, you are His son, or His child, and those words are from the Father to you. It makes no difference whether you are male or female, these words are from the Father, and He will speak to you through them. If you are not saved, the loving Lord wants to show you, as you read the instruction, what He has for you if you will receive Him into your life and obey Him.

2. The model is for you.

As you read these, also keep in mind this thought: *The model is for me.*

God

Oh, I get it—God is showing me a model of a godly father.

Here, God is speaking to you using Solomon as the model father. Solomon is seen instructing his son in the ways of godliness and right living. Study carefully the things that God wants you to teach to:

A. Your children.
B. Your grandchildren.
C. Sunday school children.
D. Others.

Second, read the "my son" instructional proverb again with this thought in mind: "God is showing me here what this parent (Solomon) taught his son. Obviously, if I am to be a godly parent, and see my children grow up to live for the Lord, I need to teach these things to my children."

The God Who Provides Abundantly

Have you ever wondered why the Lord didn't say more on the subject of raising children in the New Testament? Search, and you will find only a few brief references in the New Testament that deal specifically with the raising of children. Study the Old Testament and you'll discover that the subject of raising, teaching, and training children is important to God. He could not wait for centuries to reveal His mind on this subject. The men and women of this ancient culture needed God's word on raising families, and He gave it to them. He gave the ten commandments to the children of Israel (Exod. 20:1–17). That's a great start for training children, isn't it? Then, He told His people *what* to teach their children, and *when* to teach their children (Deut. 6:6–9).

Finally, He gave His people the Proverbs. This collection of ancient Near East writings has been a treasure chest of wealth for God-fearing parents through the centuries. Many books, both good and bad, have been written on the subject of raising children. Only one, however, is inspired (God-breathed). That God-given and God-inspired book is the Bible, including Proverbs.

If God's people would dedicate themselves to lives of total obedience to Him, and if they would study and teach the Proverbs to their children, grandchildren, and others (perhaps using the book that you are now reading as a guide), it would soon be a new day in our sin-sick land. Homes would be strengthened. Moms and dads would be blessed of God and have a new sense of destiny. Children would be instructed in the ways of God. Strong biblical homes would be the result. If we had these kinds of homes, God would bless us with strong, great churches. When a nation's homes are godly and strong, and its churches are godly and strong, the entire nation is blessed.

> *Righteousness exalteth a nation, but sin is a reproach to any people.* (14:34)

> *Blessed is the nation whose God is the Lord; and the people whom he hath chosen for His own inheritance.* (Ps. 33:12)

We are in grave danger of forfeiting our Christian heritage to the dark, immoral culture that surrounds us. We must return to the Lord with all of our heart, and take seriously the command to "train up a child in the way he should go" (22:6), or our grandchildren will inherit a spiritual wasteland! God's formula for raising children is not complicated but, on the contrary, is very simple.

God Provided a Formula for Training Children

The father trains his son.

God

The son doesn't forget God.

My son, hear these words.*

I love You, Lord.

Later, a fully grown son

| Train up a child in the way he should go | Proverbs 22:6 | And when he's old he'll not depart from it. |

*Proverbs 1:8, 2:1, 3:1, 4:1, 5:1, 7:1
All training should be Bible-based.

As you share God's Word with your own children and with others, God will certainly speak to them. You should teach God's Word to your children daily.

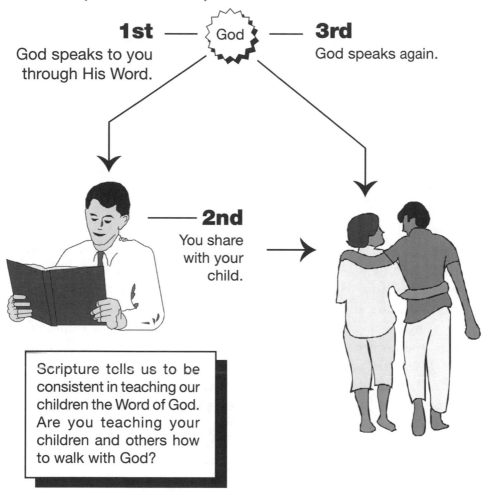

1st — God — **3rd**

God speaks to you through His Word.

God speaks again.

2nd

You share with your child.

Scripture tells us to be consistent in teaching our children the Word of God. Are you teaching your children and others how to walk with God?

"Teach God's Word diligently to thy children. . . ."
- In your house
- When you walk with them
- When you are putting them to bed at night
- When you are getting them up in the morning

— Deut. 6:7 (paraphrase)

God Provides Commandments for Us to Keep

The commandments mentioned in Proverbs 3:1 are from Solomon to his son. They are different from the ten commandments that God gave to Moses (Exod. 20), but there are similarities.

In both Exodus 20 and Proverbs 3:

- The first commandment deals with putting God first in our lives.

- The first four commandments deal with our relationship with God (group A).

- The remaining six deal with our relationship to others (group B).

- There are ten commandments.

Verses one through four, as we mentioned earlier, tell us of certain benefits that people can normally expect if they will "keep my commandments." Before He lists the specific commandments that He has in mind, He emphasizes that we should keep them, and He promises blessings if we do.

This chapter has a very interesting design. The commandments that the Lord gave us are broken up into two groups. Group A deals with the relationship God wants us to have with Him (vv. 5–13). Group B deals with our relationship with others (vv. 25–31). Sandwiched between the two groups of commandments are the "Lady Wisdom" verses (14–20), and another appeal to keep His commandments (vv. 21–24). The justice of the Lord is the subject of verses 32–35, which end the chapter.

There are various subjects covered in this chapter, but the unifying theme is the commandments of the Lord. The emphasis is clearly on the Group A commandments.

The Group A Commandments:
- Are first in position
- Deal with our relationship to the Lord Himself
- Carry wonderful blessings if obeyed.

The Group B commandments:
- Are second in position
- Are separated from the group A commandments
- Deal with our relationships to our fellow man
- No blessing promised for obedience.

Verse Groups of Proverbs 3

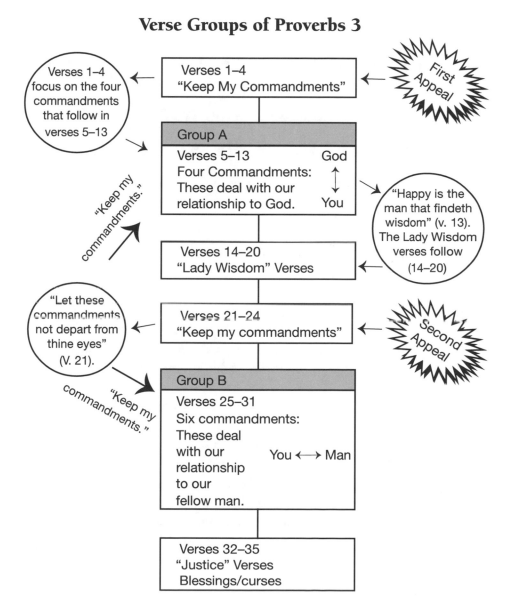

Group A Commandments

This set of four commandments deals with who is going to be in control of our lives: ourselves or the Lord. Trusting Christ as Savior is one thing, but living a life of full submission to the Lord is quite another. The Lord challenges us to give Him the control of our lives. In these first four commandments, He basically says: #1) "Trust Me," #2) "Fear Me," #3) "Hear Me," #4) "Submit to me." Parents need to be sure that they are doing all four of these, and then they need to teach their children by word and by example.

---

1. God provides a commandment for the better life. (vv. 5–6)

> *Trust in the Lord with all thine heart, and lean not unto thine own understanding. In all thy ways acknowledge Him and He shall direct thy paths.* (3:5–6)

"Trust Him," we are told, "with all your heart." There is always the possibility of trusting in other things. Here, the Lord is saying— "Look to Me, only to Me." The first commandment given to Moses was "thou shalt have no other gods before me." There the Lord was saying: "Look to Me, worship Me, only Me." John Wesley, the famous eighteenth century English evangelist, said, "Whatever is loved, feared, delighted in, or depended on more than God, of that we make a god."[1]

Trusting in the Lord "with all your heart" is a daily challenge, for there is always the possibility of trusting Him with less than the whole! Charles Bridges said, "It is the trust of the heart, of all the heart. It is a child-like unwavering confidence in our Father's well-proved wisdom, faithfulness and love."[2]

It is difficult for us to trust because we have all been hurt. Lovers, ministers, politicians, and others whom we thought we could trust have hurt us. There is a great difference here, however. This is the Lord speaking. When *He* says "trust Me," you can trust Him! You can trust His love. He will not betray you, for love is the essence of God. 1 John 4:8 states "God is love." You can trust His wisdom, for He "knoweth all things" (1 John 3:20). You can trust His power to guide you ("is anything too hard for the Lord?" [Gen. 18:14]). If anyone will walk with the Lord, and trust Him to lead, He will do exactly that because "the steps of a good man are ordered by the Lord, and He delighteth in his way" (Ps. 37:23).

Few men and women, in any age, are willing to fully trust Him, and in all their ways acknowledge Him. Will you answer His call to you in Proverbs 3:5–6? Oswald Chambers said, "If you are 'looking unto Jesus,' avoiding the call of the religious age you live in, and setting your heart on what He wants, on thinking on His line— you will be called unpractical and dreamy; but when He appears in the burden and heat of the day, you will be the only one who is ready. Trust no one, not even the finest saint who ever walked the earth, ignore him, if he hinders your sight of Jesus Christ."[3]

What a difficult thing it is to "lean not unto our own understanding." We tend to study the problem, come up with a solution and a "plan," then we ask the Lord (if we *even* remember to do that!) to put His stamp of approval on our plan. That is the *exact* opposite of the first commandment of Proverbs 3. It is certainly not biblical, and at best we could label it "evangelical humanism." We must guard against this evil by making sure each day that our hearts are given over in total to the Lord. How easy is it for us to "lean unto our own understanding?" We think we have to "help God out" sometimes, don't we? We can best help God by keeping out of His way, and letting Him direct our paths. In 1710, Matthew Henry of England said: "In all our conduct we must be diffident of our own judgement, and confident of God's wisdom, power, and goodness, and therefore we must follow providence and not force it. That often proves best which was least our own doing."[4]

"In all thy ways acknowledge Him" is the clarion call of Proverbs 3:6. The Hebrew word for acknowledge means "to know." The word is used in a great variety of senses, such as: perceive and see, find out, discern, to know by experience, to be instructed, be aware of, etc. When we are fully trusting in the Lord, we can expect His direction for all of the affairs of life. We are able to "see" the path He wants us to travel. In Psalm 32:8 He declares: "I will instruct thee and teach thee in the way which thou shall go, I will guide thee with mine eye."

When any believer places himself in the desirable position of being at God's disposal, he doesn't ask questions such as "Is this the Lord? Should I do this?" He will *know* what is of the Lord, and what he is to do, because the Lord who cannot break His word has clearly said: "I will direct thy paths" (3:6). Charles Stanley said, "Whenever you are on the right path, there will always be an incredible sense of peace filling your heart. Everything around you may be in physical upheaval, but deep inside you there is a firm, unshakable peace which has only one source—the Lord Jesus Christ."[5] J. Vernon McGee said: "If you are going down a certain path, doing a certain thing, it is amazing how everything else drops into place." [6]

This is the better life that God has for us if we will keep His commandment found in Proverbs 3:5–6. Oswald Chambers said, "Get into the habit of saying 'speak, Lord,' and life will become a romance."[7]

---

2. God provides a commandment for better health. (vv. 7–8)

Be not wise in thine own eyes; fear the Lord, and depart from evil. It shall be health to thy navel, and marrow to thy bones. (3:7–8)

Being "wise in our own eyes" is in conflict with fearing the Lord. This warning is very similar to the one in verse five. Obviously, trusting in the flesh is a big problem with God's people. It is a problem that, if not dealt with, will prevent us from being all that God wants us to be. We all have a tendency to drift away from the center of God's will. We begin to focus internally instead of on the Lord. Soon, we have lost much of the "fear of the Lord" that He encouraged us to have. What happens when we do not fear the Lord as we should? Evil will rear up its ugly head somewhere in our lives, and what do we often do? We become "wise in our own eyes." Scripture tells us that by the "fear of the Lord men depart from evil" (Prov. 16:6).

When we fear God, we fear sin, for we are keenly aware of the fact that we serve a holy God. He has told us: "Be ye holy; for I am holy" (1 Pet. 1:16). Are you keeping this second commandment in Proverbs 3? Has your fear of the Lord perhaps diminished over a period of time? If so, it's time to take action! Set aside some significant portions of time. Ask the Lord to show you how much time you need. Use this time *strictly* for an opportunity to be alone with God in prayer and the Word. Spend sufficient time with the Lord, confessing your sin, seeking Him, and studying His Word, and soon you'll sense His holy presence. When His powerful presence comes, your fear of Him will certainly return. Isaiah the prophet was so overwhelmed with Almighty God's presence, he cried out: "Woe is me! For I am undone, because I am a man of unclean lips, and I dwell in the midst of a people of unclean lips; for mine eyes have seen the King, the Lord of hosts!" (Isa. 6:5).

The benefit to God's people for keeping this commandment is better health. We all know that a large percentage of our nation's health problems are caused by ungodly living. There is a high price to pay for low living. It causes all kinds of physical problems, diseases, and even death (James 1:14–16). The fear of the Lord, we are told in verse 8, "shall be health to thy navel." The Hebrew word for health here is *riph' ûwth,* and it means "cure." Many people have lost their health through no fault of their own. Others have broken the rules of health for so long, or so badly, that they will never have a good measure of health again. There are, however, millions of others whose health would improve immensely if they would simply take the cure that a loving Lord offers them in verses 7–8. The fear of the Lord results in good health.

> ### 3. God provides a commandment for better wealth. (vv. 9–10)

Honor the Lord with thy substance, and with the first fruits of all thine increase; so shall thy barns be filled with plenty, and thy presses shall burst out with new wine. (3:9–10)

The worldly mind normally does not have any desire to honor the Lord financially. The person who is unsaved, and the believer who hasn't matured in the Lord, will certainly not understand the "ten percent of what I make goes to God" concept. They won't consider giving ten percent, as the Old Testament teaches. "I can't afford it," says the undedicated believer, but that is not taking God at His word. Notice verses 9 and 10 once again. The Lord *clearly* says, "honor Me with your money—I'll increase your wealth." A person is not really committed to the Lord until he agrees with the Lord in the area of giving. J. Vernon McGee said, "May I say that genuine spirituality is not the length of the prayer that you pray; it is the amount on the check that you write. That is the way that one can determine spirituality."[8]

If we have honored the Lord with our income, it is amazing how He will stretch the remaining dollars and guide us into wise money handling. Yes, we can trust Him to provide for us, if we will honor Him not with "what's left over," but with the "first fruits," which means the first part of your income. Teach your children and grandchildren the law of sowing and reaping (2 Cor. 9:6–10). Teach them about the two men in Proverbs 11:24. One honored God, and the other was "stingy," and kept the money for himself. Guess which one prospered? Guess which one was headed for poverty?

> ### 4. God provides a commandment for a better self. (vv. 11–13)

My son, despise not the chastening of the Lord, neither be weary of His correction; for whom the Lord loveth he correcteth, even as a father the son in whom he delighteth. Happy is the man that findeth wisdom, and the man that getteth understanding."

Here we see a father instructing his son about chastening that he should expect to receive from the heavenly Father. The writer of Hebrews quotes these verses (Heb. 12:5–6), and then speaks more on the subject of chastening (Heb. 12:7–11). We are reminded in Proverbs 3:12 that we are chastened because we are loved. Hebrews 12:8 teaches us that a person who doesn't experience God's chastening isn't in God's family at all! All of God's children "are partakers" of His chastening. Why does the Lord chastise us? It is not for *His* pleasure (Heb. 12:10), but for *our* profit. It is to make us a holier people (Heb. 12:10). If we obey this commandment to accept God's correction with a proper attitude, He said He would make us happy.

> *Behold, happy is the man whom God correcteth; therefore, despise not thou the chastening of the Almighty.* (Job 5:17)

When the Lord corrects us and we respond with the right attitude, we always grow a little wiser. Proverbs 3:13 encourages us by stating, "Happy is the man that findeth instruction." Verse 13 functions as a transition verse. It not only connects to the verse group that we are now completing, but it also connects to the following verse group, the Lady Wisdom verses.

God provides His wisdom for us (vv. 14–20). Lady Wisdom is back on the scene in the next few verses. This is her third appearance in Proverbs. As we study the next few chapters of Proverbs, we will see her again and again. Later we will discuss this distinguished lady in detail, but for now, let's just remember that she represents some of the things God has for obedient children.

> *For the merchandise of it is better than the merchandise of silver, and the gain thereof than fine gold. She is more precious than rubies; and all the things that thou canst desire are not to be compared unto her.* (3:14–15)

Lady Wisdom's Worth

- More profitable than silver (v. 14).
- Better than gold (v. 14).
- Worth more than rubies (v. 15).
- Worth more than all the things that one could desire (v. 15).

There are many things that money can't buy. Money cannot secure a place in heaven for anyone, although millions have been deceived into believing that they could "buy" their way into that celestial city. There is not enough wealth in the entire world for you to purchase your own salvation. Your soul is worth more than the whole world. Jesus said: "For what is a man profited; if he should gain the whole world, and lose his own soul? Or what shall a man give in exchange for his soul?" (Matt. 16:26). There is nothing that you can give Almighty God for the salvation of your soul. He made this world and all that is in it and above it. It is His. He holds the title deed to earth. You and I really don't "own" anything. All of our possessions are on loan to us from God. When we die, what do we leave behind? Everything! We are paupers in the sight of God. We are, however, paupers whom God loves, and paupers whom Christ died for. The price for our salvation was paid for by God's Son, Jesus Christ. He shed His blood on the cross for our sins. The apostle Peter wrote these words:

> *Forasmuch as ye know that ye were not redeemed with corruptible things, like silver and gold, from your vain manner of life received by tradition from your fathers, but with the precious blood of Christ, as of a lamb without blemish and without spot.* (1 Pet. 1:18–19)

The apostle John recorded these words of Christ for us:

> *For God so loved the world, that He gave us His only begotten Son, that whosoever believeth in Him should not perish, but have everlasting life. For God sent not His Son into the world to condemn the world, but that the world through Him might be saved. He that believeth in Him is not condemned; but he that believeth*

not is condemned already, because he hath not believed in the name of the only begotten Son of God. (John 3:16–18)

The apostle Paul gave us these words:

But God commended His love towards us in that, while we were yet sinners, Christ died for us. Much more then, being now justified by His blood, we shall be saved from wrath through Him. (Rom. 5:8–9)

Whenever an unsaved person sees his need for salvation and calls on the name of Jesus Christ to save him, the Lord will do exactly that. The following words penned by the apostle Paul explain this. If you do not have salvation, I urge you to read these verses and act upon them! Call on His name in faith, and He will do for you what you could never do for yourself: He will save your soul.

If thou shalt confess with thy mouth the Lord Jesus Christ, and shalt believe in thine heart that God hath raised Him from the dead, thou shalt be saved. (Rom. 10:9)

For whosoever shall call upon the name of the Lord shall be saved. (Rom. 10:13)

Picture a poor, broken down pauper reaching up and receiving a great gift from a king. That is a picture of salvation. Unsaved millionaires, billionaires, kings, queens, presidents, celebrities, as well as common people will all appear before Christ to be judged (Rev. 20:11–12). Be sure that you have accepted Christ as your Savior! The Lord enters a person's life at the moment of salvation. This sets up a relationship whereby the new believer can grow in wisdom. All of us can continue to grow in wisdom by obeying God. When a person takes the Word of the Lord seriously, and calls on Him for salvation, he has indeed feared the Lord, and "the fear of the Lord is the beginning of knowledge . . ." (Prov. 1:7).

Length of days is in her right hand, and in her left hand riches and honor. Her ways are the ways of pleasantness, and all her paths are peace. She is a tree of life to those who lay hold upon her, and happy is everyone that retaineth her. (3:16–18)

Here stands this beautiful heavenly creature, Lady Wisdom, with incredible gifts to offer those who will embrace her. Long life is in her right hand, and riches and honor in her left. Here is a list of the specific benefits that God offers us through this lady named Wisdom:

Lady Wisdom's Specific Benefits (vv. 16–18)

1. A longer life v. 16.

2. A more prosperous life v. 16.

3. Honor v. 16.

4. Pleasantness (the Hebrew word means "agreeableness." This is the opposite of conflict) v. 17.

5. Peace v. 17.

6. Eternal salvation v. 18.

7. Happiness v. 18.

What a great list of benefits we see here from the great God of heaven. Look carefully at this list. Is there any need not covered here? Our loving God delights in providing all the needs of His children when they are walking with Him. "But my God shall supply all your need according to His riches in glory by Christ Jesus" (Phil. 4:19).

The "tree of life" mentioned in Proverbs 3:18 is a clear reference to eternal life. In Proverbs 11:30, the tree of life is called the "fruit of the righteous." This same verse speaks of soul winning with these words: "He that winneth souls is wise." Rev. A. R. Fausset said, "Wisdom brings life to her possessors, as the tree of life in Paradise would have done to our first parents, but that they forfeited it (Gen. 2:9, 3:22–24)."[9]

Lady Wisdom's Power (vv. 19–20)

The Lord by wisdom hath founded the earth; by understanding hath He established the heavens. By His knowledge the depths are broken up, and the clouds drop down the dew. (3:19–20)

By wisdom, the Lord:

1. Founded the earth (v. 19).
2. Established the heavens (v. 19).
3. Broke up the depths (v. 20) (Gen. 7:11).
4. Established the water-vapor cycle (v. 20).

Our God is truly awesome. David, one of Israel's favorite sons, looked up into the beautiful starlit sky one night. He thought about what he saw. He thought about the knowledge and power it took to create it all. He wondered why the Creator, the one with all this power and knowledge, would ever think of us. I have often wondered the same thing. Here are David's words:

> When I consider thy heavens, the works of thy fingers, the moon and the stars, which thou hast ordained, what is man, that thou art mindful of him? And the son of man, that thou visitest him? (Ps. 8:3–4)

One of David's praises to the Creator is found in Psalm 8:9, and another in Psalm 9:1. Let us praise Him with the same words:

> O Lord, our Lord, how excellent is thy name in all the earth! (Ps. 8:9)
>
> I will praise thee, O Lord, with my whole heart; I will show forth all thy marvelous works. (Ps. 9:1)

God Provides Himself for Our Confidence (vv. 21–26)

> My son, let not them depart from thine eyes; keep sound wisdom and discretion; so shall they be life unto thy soul, and grace to thy neck. Then shall thou walk in thy way safely, and thy foot shall not stumble. When thou liest down, thou shalt not be afraid; yea, thou shalt lie down, and thy sleep shall be sweet. Be not afraid of sudden fear, neither of the desolation of the wicked, when it cometh; for the Lord shall be thy confidence, and shall keep thy foot from being taken. (3:21–26)

Solomon returns now to the subject of his commandments (v. 1), and urges his son to not let them "depart from thine eyes . . ." (v. 21). Earlier, he had told his son to "bind them about thy neck" (3:3). Here, he tells his son that they would be life to his soul, and "grace to thy neck" (3:22).

Solomon tells his son he can go through life without fear because the Lord would be his confidence and would be with him (23–26). I'm reminded of the little girl who was attempting to quote the Twenty-Third Psalm. She got the words a little confused and said: "The Lord is my shepherd, why should I worry?" That may not be a good translation, but it sure is good theology. Incidentally, later in that same psalm, David said, "I will fear no evil, for thou art with me" (v. 4). It is truly wonderful to have the presence of the Lord in your life. Put your trust in the Lord, and your confidence will soar, "for the Lord shall be your confidence . . ." (Prov. 3:26).

Group B Commandments

We come now to the second set of commandments in this chapter, group B. These commandments all deal with our relationships to our fellow man. It is interesting that God places these commandments last. Most religions would place these in front of group A (these deal with our relationship to God). Many religions emphasize "do good to our fellow man," and, in varying degrees, they de-emphasize the idea of submission and obedience to a holy, Almighty God. Is it not important to do good to our fellow man? Of course it is, but a look at history will show that man has not done a very good job of this. The place to begin is not with the commandments that deal with person-to-person relationships. The place to begin is with the commandments that deal with the man-to-God relationship: "Trust Me," "Fear Me," "Honor Me," "Submit to Me." If a person starts with these and gets these right, the others will follow. When we are obeying the Lord in these, His love flows through us, and we reach out to do good to all that we can.

As we have, therefore, opportunity, let us do good unto all men, especially unto them who are of the household of faith. (Gal. 6:10)

Here are the other six commandments of Proverbs 3:

> *Withhold not good from them to whom it is due, when it is in the power of thy hand to do it. Say not unto thy neighbor, Go, and come again, and tomorrow I will give, when thou hast it by thee. Devise not evil against thy neighbor, seeing he dwelleth securely by thee. Strive not with a man without cause, if he hath done thee no harm. Envy thou not the oppressor, and choose none of his ways.* (vv. 27–31)

Here is a list of the six commandments using a "thou shalt not" format:

- Thou shalt not withhold good from the person who has earned it (v. 27).
- Thou shalt not delay good to thy neighbor (v. 28).
- Thou shalt not devise evil against thy neighbor (v. 29).
- Thou shalt not strive with anyone without reason (v. 30).
- Thou shalt not envy a man of violence (v. 31).
- Thou shalt not choose any of his ways (v. 31).

God Provides True Justice (vv. 32–35)

The Lord is called "the righteous judge" (2 Tim. 4:8), and it is a sobering thought to realize that everyone will one day bow before Him and will confess that He is Lord (Phil. 2:10–11). In these, the closing verses of this chapter, we see blessings for the believers and curses on the unbelievers.

> *For the perverse is an abomination to the Lord, but His secret is with the righteous. The curse of the Lord is in the house of the wicked, but He blesseth the habitation of the just. Surely He scoffeth at scoffers, but He giveth grace unto the lowly. The wise shall inherit glory, but shame shall be the promotion of fools.* (3:32–35)

The Unbelievers

They are called:	Their curse is:
The "perverse" (v. 32)	They are an abomination to the Lord (v. 32).
The "wicked" (v. 33)	Their homes are cursed (v. 33).
The "scoffers" (v. 34)	He scoffs at them (v. 34).
The "fools" (v. 35)	They will come to shame (v. 35).

The Believers

They are called:	Their blessing is
The "just" (v. 33)	Their homes are blessed (v. 33).
The "lowly" (or humble) (v. 34)	He gives them His grace (v. 34).
The "wise" (v. 35)	They shall inherit glory (v. 35).

Take a moment now and review all the wonderful things mentioned in this chapter that God provides for His people. Truly, He is the God that provides abundantly.

4 | Wisdom – The Principal Thing

The Command in Deuteronomy

God ordained the home to be the place where children are taught the things of God. His command is given in Deuteronomy 6:7, as we have previously mentioned. Listen to His words once again: "And thou shalt teach them diligently unto thy children . . . when thou sittest in thy house. . . ." Deuteronomy is where we learn of the Lord's command to teach His ways to the children in our homes.

The Example in Proverbs

God gave us the command in Deuteronomy. He gave us the example in Proverbs. The Proverbs picture godly parents obeying the Lord's commandment of Deuteronomy 6. God gives us in Proverbs picture after picture after picture of parents teaching their children to love the Lord, to obey Him, and to live right. We will go inside the home in Proverbs 4 now to observe, to listen, and to learn. Upon entering the home, we will see a family gathered together, seated and listening to the instruction of the father. It is probably evening. The day's work is done, the evening meal is finished, and the family members are relaxing. The minds of the children are focused on the things of God, as the father begins to speak:

Get Wisdom — Get Understanding

Hear, ye children, the instruction of a father, and attend to know understanding; for I give you good doctrine; forsake ye not my law. For I was my father's son, tender and only beloved in the sight of my
• *mother. He taught me also, and said unto me, Let thine heart retain my words, keep my commandments, and live. Get wisdom, get understanding; forget it not, neither decline from the words of my mouth.* (4:1–5)

Notice the father is addressing the "children." This is different from the first three chapters. There he addresses a singular son (1:8, 2:1, 3:1). Here he addresses not one, but we suppose, all of the children of the household. He begins by overcoming the "listening gap." He tells the children that he too was a child, he too had a mother and a father, and he too was taught the important things of life by his father (vv. 3–4).

Solomon now begins (v. 4) to quote his famous father, David ("He taught me also and said unto me . . ."). From this scene on, we will see a father instructing his children by teaching them the very things that his father taught him. Basically he tells his children here: "My father taught me about wisdom. The things he taught me, I will now share with you."

The passion of the father in this home school setting is expressed with these words in verse 5: "Get wisdom, get understanding. . . ." The idea behind these words seems to be: "Do whatever you have to do, spare no expense or effort, but get wisdom and understanding."

The Hebrew word translated "get" here is *qânâh*. Repeatedly in Scripture, qânâh is translated "buy," "purchase," "bought," or "possessed." A. R. Fausset comments on this word in this scripture as follows: "Acquire or buy, like a merchant, sparing neither toil nor cost to make thyself possessor of the one pearl of great price."[1] Proverbs 23:23 states:

Buy the truth, and sell it not; also wisdom, and instruction, and understanding. (23:23)

78

Instructions from Father

Forsake her not, and she shall preserve thee; love her, and she shall keep thee. Wisdom is the principal thing; therefore, get wisdom; and with all thy getting, get understanding. Exalt her, and she shall promote thee, she shall bring thee to honor when thou dost embrace her. She shall give to thine head an ornament of grace; a crown of glory she shall deliver to thee. Hear, O my son, and receive my sayings, and the years of thy life shall be many. (4:6–10)

Lady Wisdom makes another appearance. This is her third appearance so far in Proverbs. Once again, she is praised. She is exalted and praised each time she makes an appearance in Proverbs.

What wonderful instruction David gave Solomon! What wonderful instruction Solomon's children are receiving as he recalls his father's words. The lack of godly training in the homes of believers today is abominable! Family time is precious and should be used wisely to teach, train, mold, and disciple our children. Potentially, the best school on earth is "Mom and Dad University." The father here exhorts the son with these thought provoking words: "Get wisdom, get understanding. . . . Forsake them not. . . ." We can feel the force and conviction behind the father's words. We can sense the urgency and the importance of the father's instruction. This is a serious moment. It is a moment for the children to think and think deeply. The father speaks with fervent passion. His eyes gaze intently upon the precious children that God has blessed him with. This is their time with their father for instruction, and they are keenly aware of it. He quotes the words of his father David: "Wisdom is the principal thing; therefore, get wisdom; and with all thy getting, get understanding (v. 7). Hear, O my son, and receive my sayings . . . (v. 10)." Charles Bridges describes what this father is feeling as follows: "This is not the style of a cold pleader, enforcing with decent seriousness some unimportant truth. It is the father feeling that his child's soul is perishing unless it be taught and led in wisdom's ways. Parents! Do we know this stirring concern, anxiously looking out for the first dawn of light upon our child's soul? Do we eagerly point out to him 'wisdom is the principal thing,' to be gotten first?"[2] Mother, father, you will not have those children very long. You will wake up one morning (it will come a lot sooner than you can now imagine), and they will be grown and gone. Your most important ministry is the children in your home. Teach them daily at "Mom and Dad University." Teach them Scripture, morals, values, and godliness.

Lady Wisdom and the Children

Solomon passed on to his children the instruction on wisdom that he received from his father, David. He was told by David that if he would pursue Lady Wisdom and treat her a certain way, she would in return bless him. The following is a paraphrase of Solomon's talk with his children.

The things my father taught me about wisdom:

He told me I should:
1. Get her (wisdom) (v. 5).
2. Forsake her not (v. 6).
3. Love her (v. 6).
4. Exalt her (v. 8).
5. Embrace her (v. 8).

He told me that if I do these things, she would:
1. Preserve me (v. 6).
2. Keep me (v. 6).
3. Promote me (v. 8).
4. Bring me to honor (vv. 8–9).
5. Give me long life (v. 10).

What is Wisdom?

As we read the Proverbs, we read much about wisdom and find that this is a difficult subject. In many verses wisdom is described but is not revealed. Wisdom, it seems, is always partially concealed. We have found that wisdom has personality. Wisdom is feminine. "Who is this lady named Wisdom?" we ask. "What is Wisdom exactly?" we wonder. At first glance, the whole subject seems to be beyond our comprehension. Here is a subject in Scripture that must be studied diligently to achieve a correct understanding. Once we have studied some word meanings, looked into the ancient Near East cultures of Solomon's day, and compared scripture with scripture, the mysteries surrounding the subject of wisdom will disappear. Lady Wisdom herself will be discussed separately in another chapter.

Ancient Near East Wisdom Literature

So called "wisdom literature" was produced extensively by many of the ancient Near East cultures. Social values and rules for success in business and politics were taught in wisdom literature. Into this setting, God placed His chosen people Israel. A Gentile man by the name of Abraham was selected by God to be the father of the Jewish nation. Abraham was converted to the Lord while living in his native Mesopotamia (Acts 7:2). YHWH (the self-existent, or Eternal One, the God of Israel) made a promise to Abraham. The promise was: "And I will make of thee a great nation, and I will bless thee, and make thy name great; and thou shalt be a blessing" (Gen. 12:2). YHWH called Abraham out of Mesopotamia and into the land of Canaan. Later, his descendants would spend 430 years in Egypt and afterwards would return to the land of the Canaanites. YHWH placed His chosen people right smack in the center of these Near East cultures. There is a great deal of similarity between the Jewish Book of Proverbs and the wisdom literature produced in other ancient Near East cultures. Even Scripture compares Solomon's superior wisdom to the wisdom of those in surrounding cultures (1 Kings 4:30, 31, 34).

The similarities between Israel's wisdom literature and the wisdom literature of the surrounding nations is indeed intriguing. There are, however, some differences, one of which is major. The focus of other ancient Near East literature is primarily on social

81

issues, not on "the gods." Proverbs focus not on social graces but on YHWH, Israel's God. Right from the beginning of Proverbs we are told that "the fear of YHWH is the beginning of wisdom."

Another important difference is discovered when we compare the words translated as "wisdom." The Hebrew word for wisdom is *chokmâh*. It means "skillful." It comes from the root word *châkâm* ("to be wise in mind, word, or act"). In the Hebrew writings of "wisdom," emphasis is placed upon a reverence for Almighty God (YHWH). Professor John Walton tells us that "In Egypt, there is no term used that is parallel to the Hebrew term. The Egyptian word *sboyet* (instruction)," Walton tells us, "does not place any emphasis on reverence for deity as hokmah (or chokmâh) does. . . ."[3]

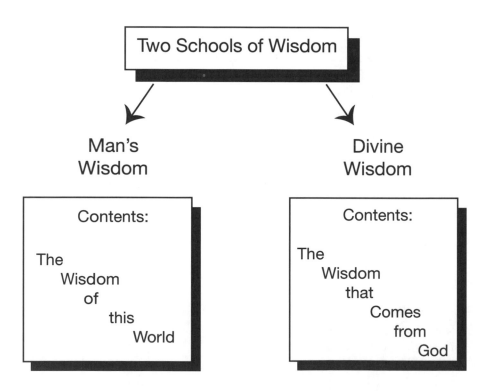

Two Schools of Wisdom

Man's Wisdom

Contents:

The Wisdom of this World

Divine Wisdom

Contents:

The Wisdom that Comes from God

Two distinctive schools of wisdom are found in the Bible. Both schools are mentioned in 1 Corinthians 2, where they are shown in contrast. The two schools of wisdom are: Man's wisdom (vv. 1, 4, 5) and divine wisdom (vv. 4, 5, 6–8). Let's take a closer look at these two schools of "wisdom."

1. The Wisdom of This World—Man's Wisdom

The Hebrew word for wisdom (chokmâh), mentioned earlier, is often used elsewhere in the Old Testament and denotes a physical skill. Here are some examples where chokmâh is referred to as a physical skill:

Exodus 28:3	—	Tailoring
Exodus 31:3–6	—	Metalworking, woodworking
Exodus 35:25–26	—	Spinning
Exodus 35:30–35	—	Engraving, embroidering, weaving, designing

A. THE HUMAN BRAIN: "THE MIRACLE ORGAN."

In the above examples, the skills were given by God to His people that they might serve Him by building and decorating the tabernacle. On a larger scale, however, God has designed the whole human race in such a way that whenever anyone is born into this world, he/she is born with some natural gifts, abilities, and skills. As we grow into childhood and adulthood, we are able to develop these skills through study, practice, and hard work. That is about all that is required. Faith in God is not required. Keeping the commandments is not required. About all that is required for an individual to excel in some designated field is much study, practice, and hard work. Natural man (man without God's Spirit) is capable of great wisdom. We have yet to discover the marvelous possibilities of the human brain, created and fashioned by Almighty God.

The brain of an average adult weighs about three pounds. It is a mass of a pink-gray jelly-like substance. It is composed of billions of cells, called neurons (nerve cells) and glial cells. Information is transferred in the brain along chains of interconnected neurons. It is an electrochemical process called neurotransmission. The brain receives, analyzes, and transmits information through this process of electrochemical exchanges between neurons. The human brain is so marvelous, so complex, and so incredible it is called the "miracle" organ by brain specialists. We are, as David said, "fearfully and wonderfully made" (Ps. 139:14). Man is capable of achieving great earthly wisdom because he was created in the image of God (Gen. 1:27).

How does the brain produce thoughts? Process information? Arrive at logical conclusions? We do not really understand these things. They are a mystery. What does a mind look like? The brain is a physical organ, but the "mind" is man's mental ability. Have you ever thought about it? Consider the following: "No one has ever seen a mind. A surgeon cutting into the brain sees only nerves and blood vessels; to know what is going on in the brain he must ask the patient. . . . Only through language can we get any sort of direct picture of the working of the mind."[4]

In ways that we do not fully understand, man is able to think, reason, remember, and expand his knowledge. He can become very skillful in some art or occupation. This is human wisdom. All knowledge that we can attain by traditional ways is human wisdom.

B. MAN'S KNOWLEDGE IS LIMITED.

Man is capable of obtaining much knowledge, but his capabilities are extremely limited when compared to God, who possesses all knowledge. Come with me (by imagination) to the seashore, if you will, and very carefully pick up just one grain of sand. Look at how tiny that one grain of sand is. Think now about the billions of grains of sand on the seashores of earth. Let that tiny grain of sand that you are holding in your hand represent the total sum of man's wisdom. Let all the grains of sand on all the beaches in all the world represent God's wisdom. If you will do this, you will begin to get just an idea of God's unfathomable knowledge. For example, just in recent years we have discovered that our own galaxy, "the Milky Way," has roughly one hundred billion stars, and that there are, beyond our "Milky Way," at least a billion more galaxies, each having approximately as many stars as our galaxy! God not only made them all; He knows all there is to know about each one! God connects the number of stars with the grains of sand on the seashore in Scripture:

> *I will multiply thy seed as the stars of the heaven, and as the sand which is upon the seashore. . . .* (Gen. 22:17)
>
> *As the host of heaven cannot be numbered, neither the sand of the sea measured. . . .* (Jer. 33:22)

Noted astronomer Sir James Jeans was once asked how many stars he thought were in the universe. He answered, "There must be as many stars in the universe as there are grains of sand on all the seashores of the world."[5] Jeans, an evolutionist, no doubt was unaware that he was quoting sacred Scripture. Long before man had any idea of the vast number of stars in the heavens, God recorded it in ancient Scripture. This awesome God made the stars (by the billions!), He named each one, and He calls each one by name. He tells us this in Isaiah 40:

> *Lift up your eyes on high, and behold who hath created these things, who bringest out their host by number; He **calleth them all by names** by the greatness of His might; for He is strong in power. Not one faileth.* (v. 26)

The infinite God brings finite man to reality with some questions in Job 38. One of these questions is found in verse 4. I paraphrased the verse as follows: "Where were you when I laid the foundations of the earth? Tell me if you know."

There is
a God

Man has
a God
consciousness

The Creator put within us a "God consciousness." People from all over the world, from hundreds of different countries and tribes, practice some form of religion. Travel to any spot on earth where there are people, and you will find men and women with the inner belief that there is a supreme being. Closely related to this is man's conscience, which is able to help him distinguish between right and wrong. Even the most primitive tribes of earth have this "God consciousness" and the belief that they will one day be forced to give an account of themselves to this higher power. Man cannot know God through his own wisdom, but he does know that there is a God, because he possesses a "God consciousness."

What's wrong? I'm not happy. There's something missing in *my* life! What is it?

Natural man can't figure it out— but without God, he's unfulfilled, empty, searching.

2. The Wisdom That Comes from God

However, we speak wisdom among them that are perfect; yet not the wisdom of this age, nor of the princes of this age, that come to nothing. But we speak the wisdom of God in a mystery, even the hidden wisdom, which God ordained before the ages unto our glory; which none of the princes of this age knew; for had they known it, they would not have crucified the Lord of glory. (1Cor. 2:6–8)

IT IS FOOLISHNESS TO THE NATURAL MAN.

A human mind is needed to understand human things. In like fashion, a person must have God's Spirit in order to understand the things of God. Notice in the following verses what God says on these subjects:

For what man knoweth the things of a man, except the spirit of a man which is in him? Even so the things of God knoweth no man, but the Spirit of God. Now we have received, not the spirit of this world, but the Spirit who is of God; that we might know the things that are freely given to us of God. (1Cor. 2:11–12)

Although we are born with a "God consciousness," we are not born with God's Spirit. The natural man or woman ("natural" meaning without God's Spirit) will never understand much spiritual truth. The reason for this is basic: It is God's Spirit that teaches us. We must have His Spirit if we are to be taught His wisdom. We cannot understand the things of God without a teacher. The Spirit is the teacher. The divine wisdom of which I speak is simply foolishness to the natural man. These facts are pointed out in the following verses. Notice also that both schools of wisdom are clearly mentioned:

Which things also we speak, not in the words which man's wisdom teacheth, but which the Holy Spirit teacheth, comparing spiritual things with spiritual. But the natural man receiveth not the things of the Spirit of God; for they are foolishness unto him, neither can he know them, because they are spiritually discerned. (1Cor. 2:13–14)

87

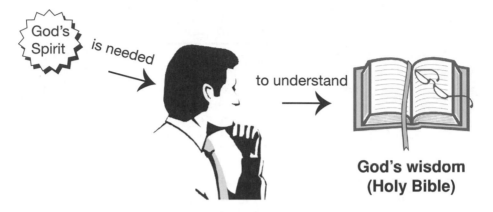

**God's wisdom
(Holy Bible)**

It is clear in Holy Scripture that natural man cannot understand, receive, or "see" spiritual truth. Natural man must have a spiritual birth in order to see the things of God. Here is what Jesus said about it:

> *Jesus answered and said unto him, Verily, verily, I say unto thee, except a man be born again, he cannot see the kingdom of God.* (John 3:3)

> *That which is born of the flesh is flesh; and that which is born of the Spirit is spirit. Marvel not that I said unto thee, Ye must be born again.* (John 3:6–7)

One day, I watched an interesting television talk show. The hostess and her panel of three were discussing some contemporary issues. The panel consisted of an attorney, a psychologist, and a well-known evangelical minister. All three men were well educated. The discussions were friendly, but there was a great deal of difference in the views of the evangelical minister and the other two men. The minister spoke of divine law and based his convictions on Holy Scripture. The other two men based their beliefs strictly on "the wisdom of this world." Their views were obviously shaped by the culture. The minister's views were shaped by the things he had been taught by the Holy Spirit. The hostess was obviously not a believer in Christ. She appeared to be uncomfortable when conversing with the minister. It was apparent that the other two men and the hostess did not agree with the minister's views. Two schools of wisdom were presented on the talk show: 1. The wisdom of this world, and 2. A higher wisdom, one that is not of this world. The hostess and the other two participants did not relate to the spiritual truth that was presented by the minister. They were polite, but it appeared that the minister's views were just "foolishness" to them. I couldn't help but think of the natural man in 1 Corinthians 2:14 who does not receive the things of the Spirit of God and can't know them because he does not have God's Spirit.

Jesus made it clear that God's Spirit cannot be seen. He compared it to the wind. Although we cannot see the wind, there is abundant evidence that it exists. Here are His words on the subject:

> *The wind bloweth where it willeth, and thou hearest the sound of it, but canst not tell from where it cometh, and where it goeth; so is every one that is born of the Spirit.* (John 3:8)

We have never seen the wind, but we know it exists. We have never seen a human mind, but we know everybody has one. We have never seen a thought, but we all have them. We have never seen God's Spirit, but we have all known people whose lives have been changed after receiving Him.

THE PROPER ATTITUDE OF THE "HAVES" TO THE "HAVE NOTS."

Those of us who have received God's Spirit are the "haves." Those who have not received God's Spirit are the "have nots." God expects us to be patient and loving toward the "have nots." We need to always remember that they cannot understand the things of God because they are "have nots." We need to lovingly, but persistently, witness to those "have nots" about what we "have" (God's Spirit in our lives). We need to explain to them again and again how they may receive God's Spirit. Until they are willing to listen to God, however, keep in mind that "The preaching of the cross is to them that perish, foolishness . . ." (1 Cor. 1:18).

What is the Key to Receiving God's Spirit?

Jesus spoke of being "born again," and being "born of the Spirit" (John 3:3–8). He was speaking to a natural man about his greatest need: the need to receive God's Spirit. Later in the conversation, Jesus gave the key whereby any natural man or woman could be born again of God's Spirit and have eternal life:

> *For God so loved the world, that He gave His only begotten Son, that whosoever believeth in Him should not perish, but have **everlasting life**. (John 3:16)*

The key is given again in I John 5:

> *Whosoever believeth that Jesus is the Christ, is born of God. . . .* (v. 1a)

> *He that believeth on the son of God hath the witness in himself. . . .* (v. 10a)

| The Key is | ⟶ | **Faith in Jesus Christ*** |

* That is, faith in Jesus Christ as He is presented in the Bible. This involves the following:

Acknowledging: The individual must acknowledge that he/she is separated from God because of his/her sin.

Believing: The individual must believe that God came to earth in the person of Jesus Christ, that He willingly died on the cross to pay for our sins, that He was buried, rose again on the third day, is alive forevermore, and offers eternal life to all those who believe.

Confessing: The individual must then confess his or her need of Christ and trust Him as Savior.

90

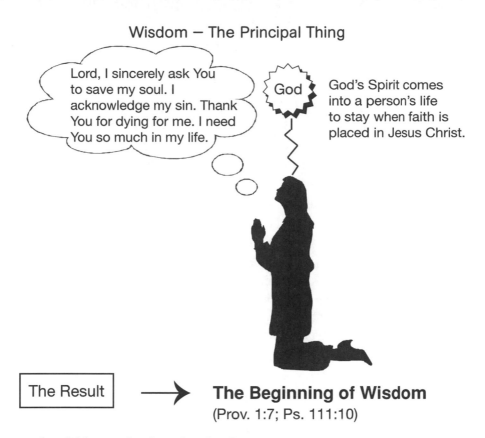

The Result ——→ **The Beginning of Wisdom**
(Prov. 1:7; Ps. 111:10)

It should be made abundantly clear:
Faith in Jesus Christ does not make one wise.

It does, however, bring God's Spirit into one's life. Receiving God's Spirit is simply the *beginning* of the wisdom that is spoken of throughout the Bible, including Proverbs. When natural man places his faith in Jesus Christ, he is, at the moment, "fearing the Lord." This is the first step in a long process of acquiring divine wisdom. As the new believer reads the Bible, meets regularly with other Christians for Bible study, and obeys the Lord as additional truth is revealed to him, he will grow in the "principal thing:" Wisdom (Prov. 4:7). The place of beginning, however, is the fear of the Lord.

* Or faith in the Lord

Dr. R.C. Sproul came to faith as a young man. His fiancée could not understand. She thought that they both had always been "Christians." They had been baptized and confirmed in the same church, had sung in the choir together, and had attended youth fellowship together. She clearly could not understand his newfound "religion," and a severe strain was placed on their relationship. Many months later, reluctantly, she attended a prayer meeting with R.C. She clearly did not want to go to "this religious thing." In the meeting that night, however, she heard of the Lord's love for her, heard of His sacrifice for her, she saw her need of Him, and she came to Him by faith. She received God's Spirit that night. R.C. recalls that "after the meeting, with an excitement that exceeded my own, she said these exact words: 'Now I know who the Holy Spirit is.'"[6]

Wisdom: A Summary

There are two schools of wisdom: 1. Man's, and 2. God's. The Book of Proverbs deals with both schools of wisdom, but emphasis is placed upon God's school of wisdom. Here are some interesting facts about divine wisdom:

1. The fear of the Lord in a person's life is the beginning of wisdom (Prov. 1:7, 9:10, Ps. 111:10).

2. We should ask for wisdom and seek it (Prov. 2:1–7, 4:5–7, James 1:5–6).

3. Wisdom comes from God's Word. We should, therefore, study the Bible diligently (Prov. 2:6, 2 Tim. 2:15, Ps. 119:97–104).

4. God sometimes gives wisdom as a gift (Dan. 1:17, 1 Cor. 12:8, 1 Kings 3:5–12, 4:29, 10:24).

5. We may have many different Christian teachers that help us understand God's wisdom, but the real teacher is God's Spirit (I Cor. 2:6–16, note especially v. 13).

6. Wisdom in our children is the result of godly training, including discipline in the home (Prov. 1:7–8, 4:11, 29:15).

7. Wisdom is given to those who obey God (Deut. 4:5–6, Ps. 119:100–101).

8. Wisdom, once obtained, can be neglected, rejected, and lost (Prov. 3:21, 4:5–6).

9. Christ was God in the flesh. He was, therefore, wisdom personified. He is called:

   The wisdom of God   — 1 Cor. 1:24
   Our wisdom   — I Cor. 1:30

   In addition, we learn that in Christ "are hidden all the treasures of wisdom and knowledge" (Col. 2:3).

10. Obtaining wisdom is a process. We should be growing in wisdom all life long. One may trust Christ as Savior in a moment and experience the new birth, but growing in wisdom is a life long process (2 Pet. 3:18, Ps. 1).

Once You Have Found Her, Never Let Her Go

I have taught thee in the way of wisdom; I have led thee in right paths. When thou goest, thy steps shall not be hindered; and when thou runnest, thou shall not stumble. Take fast hold of instruction; let her not go. Keep her; for she is thy life. (4:11–13)

Read verse eleven from your Bible and ask yourself the question: "What has happened to our homes?" The home used to be a place of learning values. The home was the place where parents would teach the basic issues of life to their children. The home was a place where the entire family enjoyed wholesome recreation together. The home was also a place of daily worship. God was honored. His Word was revered. The father in verse 11 states, "I have taught thee in the way of wisdom." Teaching the children in the way of wisdom is a responsibility that God has given to the father (Eph. 6:4). Where are the godly fathers of today? They are few in number, indeed, and our society is suffering because of it. The main reason our culture is a mess is the fact that we have not taught our children to love the Lord. We have neglected the great

Two Simple Tests

The Glory Test

Ask yourself this question: "Will my child's spirit be glorifying God as he/she uses this item?" If you can before God answer "yes," then that item passes the test. All of the entertainment that fails this simple test should be removed and not allowed in the home thereafter. If you are in doubt about an item, you should consult some Christian parent whose judgment you respect.

The Doubt Test

Having done that, you should now put the item to the Doubt Test. Romans 14:23 states, "And he that doubteth is condemned if he eat, because he eateth not of faith; for whatever is not of faith is sin." If it fails the Doubt Test," the Lord said it is wrong. Any items that fail the Glory Test or the Doubt Test should be removed from the home.

Your children may argue with you, and other parents may disagree with you. This is not a world where people normally put God first in their lives. It is a world that is filled with sin, rebellion, and faulty thinking. If God has shown you that something is wrong, you should cleanse your home of that item without delay. Failure to do this would be disobedience to God. When He shows us that something is wrong in the home and we do not act upon it, our families will eventually suffer because we failed to follow the One who is truly wise. Remember this: Our loving and holy God always wants what is best for us and our families. As a parent, you will make mistakes. There are no perfect parents. We are all human. There are, however, only two kinds of mistakes that we can make as parents: intentional and unintentional. If you have decided to live the Spirit-filled life, you have already eliminated the intentional mistakes. You are well on your way to becoming a better parent. The only other kind of mistake you can make as a parent is the unintentional mistake. The unintentional mistake is a mistake of ignorance. As you grow in the

Lord and in His wisdom, you will make fewer and fewer parenting mistakes. When wisdom comes in, ignorance goes out. May God help you to cleanse your home.

3. Seek Advice.

Seek out a few parents that are doing well in training their children in the Lord's wisdom. Ask them questions. Ask them to give you some pointers. If family devotions are something you are unfamiliar with, perhaps they would allow your family to join them for devotions some evening so that you and your family could see "how it's done."

4. Pray.

Daily ask God to guide you as a parent, and to help you in this all-important role. Pray that you will say the right things, make the right decisions, and teach the right things to your children each day. John Wesley, England's great evangelist of the eighteenth century, one day was reminiscing on the godly training he had received as a child in the home. He is quoted as saying, "I learned more about Christianity from my mother than from all the theologians of England." His mother was a woman of prayer.

5. Establish a regular time for family devotions.

Family devotions are very important. This is where you really teach wisdom (the Bible) in the home. The evening is the best time to have family devotions. Devotional materials are normally available from Christian publishers and bookstores. One of the reasons that I wrote this commentary was to give parents a way of teaching Proverbs to their children in the home. Devotions should not be very long. They should be fairly short and very crisp. They should not be boring. Here's a suggested time frame.

Pre-schoolers to Grade 3 ———— 5–7 minutes.
Grades 4–6 ———————— 10 minutes.
Grades 7–9 ———————— 15 minutes.
Grades 10–12 ——————— 20–30 minutes.

6. Emphasize faith in Christ.

Evangelist Billy Graham told the story of the new pastor who had made a visit to a home. That evening, the husband asked his wife what the pastor had said. "He asked a very strange question," she replied. "He asked," she continued, "does Christ live here?" The husband replied, "Didn't you tell him that we are respectable people who read the Bible and pray and go to church every Sunday?" "He didn't ask those questions," she said; "he only asked, 'Does Christ live here?'" Commenting on this story, Billy Graham said, "That is the question that we must answer for ourselves if our homes are to be the bulwark of the nation." Graham went on to say, "Faith in Christ is the most important of all the principles in the building of a well ordered home."[8]

7. Make devotions enjoyable.

Family devotions are not a time to scold or preach. You do not want to "turn your children off" to God. It should be a fun time for children. Put some thought into devotional time. Maybe do something different each night of the week. Treats, surprises, and regular things the children look forward to can really "turn them on" to family devotions.

If the children dread devotion time, something is wrong! When done properly, devotions are a time the children will look forward to each day. They will quickly learn that it's their "special time" with you and with the Lord. Keep it positive! Resist the temptation to preach. Just teach them in a positive way, using a children's devotional book as your guide, and let them participate.

8. Set a few basic rules.

You will probably need to have a few basic rules for devotions. You will probably need rules concerning talking, "fooling around," lying down, and noises. That's pretty much it. A few basic rules—and remember—keep it positive. No preaching! Your children will listen, they will learn, and they will grow.

9. Let the children participate.

Here's a few things that the children can do during family devotions:

> Read Scripture
> Pray
> Give prayer requests
> Ask questions
> Share their thoughts

A child might be asked to open or close the devotional time in prayer. Have you ever noticed that few teenagers ever pray publicly at church? I sense that they don't know how. Prayer should be taught at "Mom and Dad's University."

10. Get started now!

Start immediately while you are inspired to do so! Satan does not want you to have family devotions. He will do all that he can to keep you from teaching your family the wisdom of God. It is important that you start right away, or you will probably never do it. May God bless as you begin this important undertaking.

Just think of the satisfaction that you will feel one day when you are able to say to that young man or that young woman that lives in your home: "I have taught thee in the way of wisdom, I have led thee in right paths" (v. 11). At that point you'll be able to say to that young adult whom you love so much: "As long as you stay on this path, you will not stumble, or fall (v. 12). Continue in your pursuit of Lady Wisdom (vv. 5, 7), and once you have found her, never let her go, for she is to you life" (v. 13).

Two Paths (vv. 14–19)

As we read the "my son" poems of Proverbs, we see Dad training the son and training the children. We see Dad teaching the wisdom of God again and again in these poems. He instructs his offspring over and over again. What a picture the heavenly Father gives us here of the role of an earthly father. We learn that the earthly father is not only to be the ***provider for*** the home, and the ***protector of*** the home, but he is also to be the ***propagator*** of the wisdom of God ***within*** the home. In the verses that follow, we see once again a godly father instructing his son. Here, as in chapter two, the dad contrasts two very different paths.

> *Enter not into the path of the wicked, and go not in the way of evil men. Avoid it, pass not by it, turn from it, and pass away. For they sleep not, except they have done mischief; and their sleep is taken away, unless they cause some to fall. For they eat the bread of wickedness, and drink the wine of violence. But the path of the just is like the shining light, that shineth more and more unto the perfect day. The way of the wicked is like darkness; they know not at what they stumble.* (4:14–19)

The Path of the Wicked (v. 14)

It is the path of darkness. (v. 19)
Avoid it! (v. 15)
Pass not by it! (v. 15)
Turn away from it! (v. 15)

The Path of the Just (v. 18)

It is the path of light. (v. 18)

All of us have a fallen Adamic nature, and that is why we tend to gravitate toward the sins of the flesh. Godly fathers should instruct their children not to listen to the dirty jokes and the sinful conversations of the ungodly. In verses 14–15, the father issues six commands to his son. All six of the commands deal with avoiding the path of the wicked. The Hebrew word for "wicked" here means "morally wrong." The author of the Bible, the Holy Spirit, warns us in Scripture repeatedly of the danger of running with the wrong crowd. "Enter not into the path of the wicked" commands the father. Commenting on this verse, Charles Bridges said, "Their path (the wicked) is so contrary to the way of instruction that the very 'entrance into it' is forsaking the way of God."[9] "Be not deceived," we are told in 1 Corinthians chapter fifteen, "evil company corrupts good morals" (v. 33). He that travels with skunks shall never smell like a rose. A wise father will instruct his son to avoid those who harm his walk with the Lord. He will also instruct his son to be "a companion of all those who fear" God (Ps. 119:63). The Word of the Lord declares that "He that walketh with wise men shall be wise, but a companion of fools shall be destroyed" (Prov. 13:20).

Hear the Word of the Lord

My son, attend to my words; incline thine ear unto my sayings. Let them not depart from thine eyes; keep them in the midst of thine heart. For they are life unto those that find them, and health to all their flesh. Keep thy heart with all diligence; for out of it are the issues of life. Put away from thee a crooked mouth, and perverse lips put far from thee. Let thine eyes look right on, and let thine eyelids look straight before thee. Ponder the path of thy feet, and let all thy ways be established. Turn not to the right hand nor to the left; remove thy foot from evil. (4:20–27)

This chapter opens with Solomon addressing his children (v. 1). He proceeds to inform his children what David, his father, taught him (vv. 3–4). He continues to quote his father throughout this chapter. It was David who said to Solomon, "My son, attend to my words; incline thine ear unto my sayings" (v. 20). Whereas Solomon got these words from his earthly father, David received them from his heavenly Father. ("All scripture is given by inspiration of God . . ." 2 Tim. 3:16.) So who is really speaking to us here? It is our heavenly Father. He has some instruction for us to keep us from the "way of the wicked" (v. 19). His instruction focuses on these two things: 1. His words. 2. Man's heart.

His Words:

1. **"Listen to my words with your ear." (v. 20)**
   Examples: Family devotions, sermons at church, Bible studies, etc.

2. **"Read my words with your eyes." (v. 21)**
   Personal private devotions, time alone with God.

3. **"Keep my words in your heart." (v. 21)**
   Memorizing Scripture was emphasized a lot more in the days of David and Solomon than it is today. It was David who said, "Thy word have I hidden in my heart, that I might not sin against thee" (Ps. 119:11).

4. **"My words are life to all those that find them." (v. 22)**
   The Bible teaches that natural man has no spiritual life. He is without God's Spirit. The Bible says that man in this condition is "dead" (Eph. 2:1, Col. 2:13). When the natural man **hears** the Word of God and believes in Christ, God's Spirit comes to live within him. He is no longer dead, for he had been "made alive" (Eph. 1:12–14, 2:1). We were once dead spiritually, but His words have made us alive. His words indeed bring life to all them that find them.

5. **"My words are health to the flesh of the believers." (v. 22)**
   Indeed, volumes could be written about the mental and physical health benefits that believers have received because they read the Word of God, believed it, and obeyed it.

The Heart of Man

In verse 23, the subject shifts to "the heart of man." The heart (*lêb* in Hebrew) of man is the will, the intellect. It is the mind of man. I asked the question earlier in this chapter, "What does a mind look like?" No one has ever seen one. Somehow we are able to process information, produce thoughts, and store millions of facts and details into something we call a "memory bank." These facts and details can be brought forth to the conscious mind at any time upon demand.

Almighty God gives us some serious instruction here: "Keep thy heart," and to do it he continues, "with all diligence." The Hebrew word for keep (*nâcar*) means to guard or to protect. Having told us to keep His words in our hearts (v. 21), now he cautions us to "guard" or "protect" the heart. "Keeping" the heart is a mental discipline. We have the ability to choose right thoughts or wrong thoughts, good thoughts or bad thoughts, godly thoughts or ungodly thoughts. These decisions are made "in the heart." The words, the pictures, and the thoughts that we allow into our minds have a very strong influence upon our decision making. We must "guard" our hearts because out of them come the issues of life.

In the following verses (24–27), God instructs us concerning our mouths, lips, eyes, and our feet. These are all servants of the mind. They will only do what the "heart" or mind tells them to do. What we say and what we do are determined by the words, pictures, thoughts, and ideas that we deposit in the "treasury of the heart." Jesus said, "Out of the abundance of the heart, the mouth speaketh. A good man, out of the good treasure of the heart bringeth forth good things, and an evil man out of the evil treasure bringeth forth evil things" (Matt. 12:34b–35).

There was a time when the human race became so godless and so evil that the thoughts, purposes, and desires of men's hearts were *totally* evil:

*And God saw that the wickedness of man was great in the earth, and every imagination of the **thoughts of his heart** was only evil continually. Gen. 6:5*

The time had come when a holy God must act. The Lord then sent the great flood and destroyed all people of the earth with the exception of Noah and his family.

It seems that once again the human race is rapidly approaching a day that will fit the description of Noah's time. Sin is running wild in our society. It seems that most of the restraints on sin have been eliminated. It's like a giant avalanche in progress. Listen carefully and you can hear the rumble in the distance. Here it comes: A great mass of dirt and filth tumbling down the mountain side! Hear it roar! It threatens all of us, like an untamed beast of the wild. It's gathering up speed and momentum as it approaches. Faster and faster it comes. No human being can stop this monstrous avalanche! The weird thing about it is this: The people that caused it to happen see it coming; but alas, they are powerless to stop it! And now the roar is deafening and this monstrous avalanche of filth and wickedness seems to shout: "Get out of my way! I'm coming. Stand against me, and I'll crush you. I'll wipe out anything or anyone who stands in my path!" We cannot stop this avalanche of ungodliness that is even now falling upon us, but there is one thing we can do: We can "keep our hearts."

Purifying the Heart

I am convinced that God's people have not kept their hearts pure for God as they should. We have let down our guard. We have allowed the wrong words, the wrong thoughts, the wrong pictures, and the wrong ideas into our hearts. These have marred our fellowship with Almighty God. They have hindered our ability to make godly decisions. They have tainted our testimonies with the stench of worldly pollution.

The early church also had "heart problems," we find in James 4. The first verse of this chapter reveals that these early Christians had not "kept" their hearts. They had become friends of the world. James rebuked them. They needed to repent, to change their minds about their sin. They were trying to embrace God and the world at the same time. They had become "double minded." James instructed them to submit to God, to resist the devil, and to **purify** their **hearts** (4:7–8).

Thank God, our hearts can be purified. We can be cleansed by confessing our sins to Him (1 John 1:9). Once cleansed, we must be careful to "keep our hearts." We do this by submitting our will to Him fully each and every day.

In this chapter, Almighty God has told us that His wisdom is the *principal* thing. He exhorts us to "get wisdom." The key to growing in wisdom is the heart. He therefore tells us: "Keep thy heart with all diligence; for out of it are the issues of life."

5 | Sex Education in the Home

We all agree that sex education is important. The Bible shows us that sex education should be taught in the home. Holy Scripture does not present the home as *one* place where sex education might be taught, but rather it presents the home as *the* place for sex education. Many parents are trying hard to bring up their children properly but fall flat on their faces in the area of sex education. It's not that parents necessarily lack the desire to provide the proper information to their children. They simply don't know how to tell their children, so they leave this big job up to others. Great problems are caused in the lives of multitudes of people because of a *wrong* view of sex, which ultimately results in the *wrong* use of sex. Think about it—most people today do not have a correct view of sex. Reason? They were taught by people who also had a wrong view of sex. The student takes on the views of the teacher. It's the old adage of "the blind leading the blind." As a concerned follower of Christ, I am now going to ask you a very important question: How can you expect that your children will grow up to have the proper view of sex if you allow others with unbiblical views of sex to teach your children?

"But how," say some, "shall we teach our children about sex?" We should read to our children the words of the one who created sex. God gave us the Bible as a guide for every area of our lives. We should study it and share with our children what He, the creator of sex, has to say to the human race on this very important subject.

The Bible is not a sex manual. Children do not need a sex manual. God tells us in His Word what children need to know about sex. Proverbs is one of the books of the Bible that parents should teach their children in the home. Did you know that it is virtually impossible for parents to cover the Book of Proverbs with their children verse by verse without teaching them most of the things that God wants them to know about sex? There is only one right view of sex, and that is God's view, for He created it. There is only one way that anybody is going to end up with a correct view of sex, and that one way is exposure to and submission to the Word of God.

Verse Groups of Chapter Five

In this chapter, the father gives his son helpful information, godly instruction, and warns him twice about the consequences of immoral living. The father also asks the son a very thought provoking question.

"Learn From Me"

Instructional 1–2 "Learn from me"	Instructional 15–19 The right sexual relationship for life
Informational 3–6 "The lure of sexual sin"	The Question 20 "Why?"
Instructional 7–8 "Stay away from Sexual temptation"	Informational 21 "His eyes are upon us"
Consequential 9–14 The consequences of sex outside of marriage	Consequential 22–23 The consequences of living a godless life

Repentance takes place in these verses, but for the individual described here it is too late. This individual is "at the last" (v. 11). His life is over.

Sex Education in the Home

My son, attend unto my wisdom, and bow thine ear unto my under-standing, that thou mayest regard discretion, and that thy lips may keep knowledge. (5:1–2)

The two main reasons why so many of our sons and daughters grow up and live ungodly lives are: 1. Parents fail to teach their children the ways of God by example and 2. Parents fail to teach their children the Word of God in the home. Sexual sin is destroying multitudes of young lives today! Our boys and girls are growing up without the training and the knowledge that they need to make the right decisions about sex. We would not want to face an enemy on the battlefield if we did not have a proper defensive protection, even if our cause was just. Why, then, are so many believers willing to send their sons and daughters out to Satan's battlefield (the world) without first protecting them with proper armor? One of the most important commands in the New Testament is "put on the whole armor of God, that you may be able to stand against the wiles of the devil" (Eph. 6:11). If our sons and daughters are to be "strong in the Lord, and in the power of His might" (v. 10), then we must equip them with the "whole armor of God" (v. 11), which is the Word of God. Our sons and daughters are wrestling against "principalities, against powers, against the rulers of darkness of this world, against spiritual wickedness in high places" (v. 12). It is crucial, therefore, that we equip our sons and daughters with the "whole armor of God" so that they "may be able to stand in the evil day" (v. 13).

Parents are sending their sons and daughters out onto Satan's battlefield without proper armor (i.e. a good understanding of the Word of God). This is like putting a helpless lamb into a canyon full of wild, vicious, ravenous wolves. The results are predictable. The lamb will not survive. That poor little defenseless lamb will quickly be surrounded by those savage wolves. Those salivating beasts of the wild will be totally obsessed with one thought as they gaze hungrily at the lamb: "Attack! Kill! Devour!" Can you picture the scene? What an ugly, gruesome scene it is. The little lamb, defenseless against the vicious wolves, is quickly destroyed.

A young boy or girl who is not taught God's Word and godly living in the home is like a helpless little lamb that is placed in the canyon filled with hungry, savage canines. Let your sons and your daughters go out into this world without the armor of God's Word and they will face demonic foes as vicious as the beasts that destroyed the little lamb. These invisible foes are powerful and numerous. They are full of hate. We cannot see Satan and his demons, but they are out there everywhere. These rulers of darkness are obsessed with their work of spiritual wickedness! They are out to cause as much confusion, sorrow, grief, pain, and death as they can. They hate God. Since we are made in the image of God, they hate us too. They hate the whole human race. We are at war and we are losing simply because we have not "put on the whole armor of God." Who can best protect a young man from the wiles of the devil? A godly father. Who can best protect a young woman from ungodly forces? A godly mother. We should tackle this God-given task diligently from infancy until the grown child leaves home properly trained and wearing "the whole armor of God."

The Lure of Sexual Sin

For the lips of a strange woman drop as an honeycomb, and her mouth is smoother than oil. (5:3)

The "strange" woman makes her second appearance in Proverbs in verse 3. We will see her appearing on the pages of Proverbs again and again, and so it is in real life. Proverbs deals with the big issues including the temptations, the dangers, and the pitfalls that we face on this life's journey. As I mentioned earlier (see my comments on Proverbs 2:16), the "strange" woman represents all immoral, wicked women. The subject of the unclean woman is not one that we are comfortable with. We would rather avoid it, but like this ancient father of the Near East, we can't. She appears in real life as she does in Scripture and must, therefore, be dealt with. The "strange" woman has ruined multitudes of men down through the ages and has multitudes more in her clutches today. Her goals are to seduce and entrap men. Her goals never change, but her methods do. In addition to using all of her ancient ways to enslave men, she has some "modern" ways, the most powerful one of which is pornography. By the use of pornography, she can make her devilish appeals to hundreds or even thousands of men at the same time. This greatly increases her effectiveness in seducing and entrapping men.

More than likely she will make her first appeal to a young man today through pornography. Pornography comes in many forms. It is addictive, progressive, and abundant. It attacks the dignity of men and women created in the image of God (Gen. 1:27). The strange woman has millions of men in her filthy grip today through pornography. It is an evil scourge that has polluted our land. She has cast aside God's holy commandments, especially His commandment "thou shall not commit adultery." She has grossly distorted God's beautiful gift of sex and has skillfully weaved her web of deception. Her bait is sexual pleasure. Her sales pitch is "don't be afraid. No one will know. You can enjoy me in secret."

> But her end is bitter as wormwood, sharp as a two-edged sword. Her feet go down to death; her steps take hold on sheol. (5:4–5)

She draws men into her deadly clutches and takes them captive. They are like flies caught in the web of the spider. They struggle to get free, but they cannot. They are trapped. Deceived by her honey-like lips (v. 3), now they face an end as bitter as the poison of "wormwood." They listened to her smooth words: "Come, boys, follow me," and they followed. Where will she lead them? She will lead them where she has led all the others: unto death, and the fires of hell that follow.

The Way of Escape

The situation in verses 4 and 5 looks hopeless, and without the God of hope, it is. These captive men, like millions that have preceded them, are facing the two-edged sword of the strange woman (v. 4). She holds the sword that has seen blood again and again. Millions of times it has dripped with the blood of captive men. She ruthlessly slays her captives, but a loving God offers men a way of escape. There is only one thing that can set these captives free. It is the powerful Word of God. "But," one of the captives shouts, "she has a two-edged sword." It is true that she wields a deadly sword, but our God has told us that "the Word of God is quick and powerful and **sharper** than **any** two-edged sword . . ." (Heb. 4:12). In the "battle of the swords," the Word of God is the victor. If you, the reader, are being held in bondage by sexual sin, I encourage you to seek godly counsel. The Word of God can set you free. Seek out a servant of God. He or she will direct you to a biblical counselor who can show you the way to be released from your bondage. The Spirit of God uses the Word of God to empower men and women and set them free from whatever binds them.

"No Time to Think"

> *Lest thou shouldest ponder the path of life, her ways are unstable, that thou canst not know them.* (5:6)

Commenting on this verse in 1846, Charles Bridges, the English minister, said:

> One feature of the tempter's witness is most remarkable. She winds herself in a thousand movable ways to meet the varying humours and circumstances (chapter 7:21); she works upon every weakness; seizes every unguarded moment—all with one deeply hidden object—'lest thou shouldest ponder the path of life.' The checks of conscience must be diverted. No time must be given for reflection. The intrusion of one serious thought might break the spell, and open the way of escape. (See Ps. 119:59, Ezek. 18:28, Luke 15:17.)[1]

"She often changes her disguise," commented Matthew Henry, "and puts on a great variety of false colors, because if she be rightly known, she is certainly hated."[2] Her desire is really Satan's desire: to keep men from the path of life, to keep them from God and His heaven. Her ways are so varied captive men can't figure her out.

The word "mystery" would be fitting on her forehead as it is on the forehead of the harlot in Revelation chapter seventeen.

Stay Away from Sexual Temptation

Hear me now therefore, O ye children, and depart not from the words of my mouth. Remove thy way far from her, and come not near the door of her house. (5:7–8)

Solomon has been sharing with his children the instruction that his father David had given him as a boy. Beginning in verse seven, Solomon now speaks directly to his children. As David instructed his son Solomon to "retain my words" (Prov. 4:4), Solomon instructs his children "depart not from the words of my mouth" (Prov. 5:7). Verse eight could be paraphrased: "Don't come near her, stay far away from her." The best protection is to "flee" temptation (2 Tim. 2:22). Stay away from the fire and you will not get burned. The wise father will share these verses with his sons and warn them that as they go through life they will be confronted in a variety of ways by the strange woman. She is to be avoided at all costs, not only physically but mentally. Jesus warned us that if a man looks at a woman to "lust after her," he "hath committed adultery with her already in his heart" (Matt. 5:28). Proverbs 23:7 warns us that as a man "thinketh in his heart, so is he." Sons should be taught that "heart adultery" is sin. It should be confessed, and forsaken.

Immorality Has Negative Consequences

lest thou give thine honor unto others, and thy years unto the cruel; lest strangers be filled with thy wealth, and thy labors be in the house of an alien, and thou mourn at the last, when thy flesh and thy body are consumed. (5:9–11)

When a man, struggling to provide for his family, runs into trouble, others will normally help. If his friends see that he's doing his best to pay the bills and just needs a little temporary help, they will probably rush to his aid. It is a different story, however, when a man has fallen into sexual sin and because of foolish living finds himself in a financial mess. His friends will not bail him out. They consider him a poor risk. They label him "Loser." He is a loser. He has lost his once precious family, and because of his foolish escapade with a "strange woman," he's about to lose most of his assets. He needs some money. His real estate goes up for sale. The vehicles are next and then the jewelry. Here come the "bargain hunters" with cash in hand. They will purchase his assets as cheaply as they can. They know he needs money, and he needs it now. They will, therefore, pay him only a fraction of what his assets are worth. They are as heartless as he is foolish. "If we don't buy it cheap, somebody else will," they reason. "It's his problem, not ours," they continue. "It's his own dumb fault he's a loser," they tell themselves.

Solomon is giving the children some important and serious instruction in these verses. We could paraphrase his conversation to them as follows: "Listen to me, children, and do what I'm telling you to do. Don't go anywhere near the strange woman (vv. 7–8) because she is a real threat to you. If you do, it is possible that you will lose everything that is worth anything: your worth of self (v. 9), your personal wealth (v. 10), and your physical health (v. 11)."

There is a picture of a man dying a terrible death in verse eleven. His flesh is affected, his body is affected. He is in great pain. He "mourns." The Hebrew word for mourn means to "roar" or "growl." We see a man here whose flesh and body are infected with some sexually transmitted disease. He growls with pain. He's still alive, but his life is over. The error of his ways has caught him. The Bible teaches that sex outside of marriage is always wrong. It does not always result in death, but it always pulls a man or woman down spiritually, emotionally, and mentally.

We Reap What We Sow

and say, how have I hated instruction, and my heart despised re-proof; and have not obeyed the voice of my teachers, nor inclined mine ear unto them that instructed me! I was almost in all evil in the midst of the congregation and assembly. (5:12–14)

People living ungodly lives almost always make excuses for their sinful behavior. When confronted, they will often make statements such as "you just don't understand," and "it's really not my fault." As we read these verses, we find that this man had finally stopped making excuses for his ungodly behavior. He admits that he has hated instruction (v. 12), and didn't listen to his teachers. In a contemporary setting, the teachers of godly things would be the parents, the Sunday school teachers, perhaps a youth worker, and the pastor. In this scripture, the son had rejected the godly instruction of the teachers. He came to the assembly because he had no choice. He sat with the family in the home during devotions, only because there were no options. This man recalls that as a youth he "hated instruction." He had rejected all the things of God that his teachers had tried to instill in him. In the eyes of God, he had been a fool (Prov. 1:7). There is a law of sowing and reaping. Those that don't understand it are deceived. The law states that a person can't live a godless life and get away with it. God will not be mocked by foolish man. "Be not deceived, God is not mocked, for whatsoever a man soweth, that shall he also reap. For he that soweth to his flesh shall of the flesh reap corruption, but he that soweth to the Spirit shall of the Spirit reap life everlasting" (Gal. 6:7–8).

I have paraphrased Proverbs 5:14 as follows: "In the midst of all the people, I have come to the verge of utter ruin. I have become a public disgrace." With his body destroyed by a sexually transmitted disease, he growls in pain and repents of the ungodly life-style that has brought him to an early and miserable death. Those of us in ministry have witnessed this scene over and over again. We have been to the hospitals, and we have stood with open Bibles by the sick bed and have tried to comfort both patient and family. The stories that we could tell are all different, but the theme is always the same. Sometimes the sin is of a sexual nature, sometimes it is alcohol, sometimes it is drug related, and sometimes it is other things. The theme, however, is always the same: Rebellion against God followed by a sin caused disaster. It is God's law of sowing and reaping. At this stage, if the individual is a real believer in Christ, repentance normally occurs.

I wish we had a recording of the many voices of repentance that ministers hear in hospitals all across our land. I think perhaps it would cause scores of people to think deeply on the issues of life and stimulate many to change from a destructive life-style, and to begin a fresh walk with the Lord. The voices would include men and women of all ages. We would hear the voices of the young, and our hearts would break. We would, in fact, hear some very young voices. We would hear from some in their early twenties, and some still in their teens, and our hearts would break again. From this mixed choir of voices, we would hear great cries of repentance. "What a fool I was," mourns a twenty-seven-year-old man. "I have no one to blame but myself," admits another. "Oh, why didn't I listen," cries a teenager. "I see it so clearly now," says a teary-eyed nineteen-year-old woman, "But I just wanted my own way." "Don't be foolish like we were," warns another. There would arise from this strange choir of voices a unified theme: "Don't live like we have lived. Don't be a rebel. It's not worth it. Live for the Lord! Oh, don't throw your life away like we have!" Wise and godly parents will teach their children (as the father in Proverbs 5 did) that they will reap what they sow in this life and in eternity.

The Right Sexual Relationship for Life

Drink waters out of thine own cistern, and running waters out of thine own well. Let thine fountains be dispersed abroad, and rivers of waters in the streets. Let them be only thine own, and not for strangers with thee. Let thy fountain be blessed, and rejoice with the wife of thy youth. Let her be as the loving hind and the pleasant roe; let her breasts satisfy thee at all times, and be thou ravished always with her love. (5:15–19)

These verses speak of sex in marriage and the children that result from that union. Almost everyone would agree that there is a wrong use of sex, and there is a right use of sex. The big question today is:

"Who decides what is right and what is wrong?" Government planners? Public school textbook writers? Doctors? Parents? The church? Those of us who believe that we were created by a holy God, and that the Bible is His inspired Word, should base our sexual morality only on His spoken Word. Any other "would be" authority on sexual matters that disagrees with the Bible, regardless of its source, should be rejected by the Bible-believing Christian. If any so called "authority" disagrees with the Bible, it therefore disagrees with Almighty God, the author of the Bible. Those who reject the biblical view of sex are at odds with the great God who created them. Many Christians today have embraced humanistic views of sex. They are in conflict with the Creator in this area, and are in need of repentance. By repentance, I mean that they need to read the scriptures that deal with this subject, change their minds, and embrace the teachings that the holy God has given us on sexual matters. "Woe to the one who quarrels with his Maker . . .", the Lord states in Isaiah 45:9, and then He asks: "Will the clay say to the potter, 'What are you doing?'" (NAS).

"Drink waters out of thine own cistern," instructs the father (v. 15). A cistern was a receptacle for holding water. When one was thirsty, he could go to either his cistern or to his well and drink good, fresh water, free from contamination until his thirst was quenched. This is a picture of sexual fulfillment in marriage as planned by the loving God that designed us. The Word of the Lord instructs husbands to love their wives (Eph. 4:25), and here in Proverbs 5:19, the man is commanded to be "ravished always with her love." A godly husband will focus all of his sexual desire upon his wife. He should be enraptured by her kisses and exhilarated by her love. She should be the delight of his heart.

Keep in mind that these words were given first not to married men but to young sons. Earlier in the chapter, Solomon, quoting his father David, warned against sex with the *wrong* person (the "strange woman") and against sex at the *wrong* time (outside of marriage). Here, he speaks very favorably of sex with the *right* person ("the wife of thy youth") and sex at the *right* time (in marriage: "wife"). It was the same man of wisdom who said—

"To everything there is a season, and a time to every purpose under the sun" (Eccl. 3:1).

This father taught his children the right use of sex. Parents today should do the same. Parents should also protect their children from sexual sin during their teenage years. They should instruct their teens to "flee also youthful lusts" (2 Tim. 2:22). Joseph is a great model of sexual purity. When Potiphar's wife grabbed Joseph's garment in such a way that it came off and seductively said to him, "Lie with me," Joseph, knowing he was vulnerable, didn't stay around. He got out of that house quickly! Scripture states that "he left his garment in her hand and fled and got out" (Gen. 39:12). He knew the power of the male sex drive, and he didn't want to fail the God whom he had loved and served. In our liberal society, most parents give their teenagers too much freedom. They allow them to be alone with the opposite sex. These naive parents often say, "I trust my teenager." These parents are sending the wrong message to their sons and daughters. The message that they are sending is "sexual purity is no big deal. You can handle it." That is a totally irresponsible message to send to teenagers who desperately need biblical training, guidance, and protection in the area of sex.

Kissing and hugging stimulate both the male and the female. God designed this stimulation to prepare both the husband and the wife for sex. Here's what the hugs and kisses do: 1. They produce a physical change in both the man and the woman; 2. They create a desire in both for sexual fulfillment.

A good and loving God designed this process. Rightfully used, sex is a powerful force for good. When this powerful force is wrongfully used, it is not only sinful but destructive. The wrong use of sex is destroying lives in our society at an alarming rate.

> *Flee also youthful lusts. 2 Tim. 2:22*

Kissing and hugging stimulate both the male and the female. God designed this stimulation to prepare both the husband and the wife for sex.

Here's what hugs and kisses do:

1. They produce a physical change in both the man and the woman.
2. They create a desire in both for sexual fulfillment.

When parents allow their teenager to be alone with another teenager of the opposite sex, they are putting both teens in a place of great temptation. Teens left alone are normally tempted to hug and kiss. Stimulation then occurs quickly. Suddenly, they are in trouble. This "hug, kiss, stimulation" process was designed by God for married people, not for singles!

When teens fail morally, it is normally because their parents did not protect them with good training in the home and with chaperones on *all* dates. Teach your teens that they should never

Why teenagers fail morally:

When teens fail morally it is normally because their parents did not provide adequate moral protection. Parents can protect their teens with:

1. Good Bible based sex education in the home.
2. Adult chaperones on *all* dates.

Teens should be taught:

"Never allow anyone to stimulate you and prepare your body for sex. God *reserved* this for married people."

— Heb. 13:4
— 1 Cor. 6:19–20

allow anyone to stimulate them and prepare their body for sex because God reserved this for married people. "Marriage is honorable in all, and the marriage bed undefiled, but fornicators and adulterers God will judge" (Heb. 13:4). If a young man or woman makes it to the wedding altar pure and undefiled, it will normally not be by accident.

It will normally be the result of one or two godly parents who held a biblical view of sex, took their God-given roles of parenting seriously, and dedicated themselves to bring up their child in the "nurture and admonition of the Lord" (Eph. 6:4).

The Big Question: "Why?"

And why wilt thou, my son, be ravished with a strange woman, and embrace the bosom of a foreigner? (5:20)

Timing is very important in sports, in sales, in speeches, and in just about everything else as well. What an example of perfect timing we have with the father's question to his son in this verse.

Earlier in this training session, the father has given the son much valuable instruction and much good information. He has shown that sex with the wrong person can cause men to mourn (v. 11), and that sex with the right person can bring rejoicing (v. 18). Having explained both the bad and the good, he now proceeds with perfect timing to ask the question. We could paraphrase the father's thoughts as follows: "Son, since you may legitimately enjoy the pleasures of a good wife's love, why would you want to take a chance of missing out on that by getting involved with an unclean woman who will surely mess up your whole life?"

The father very wisely is leading the son to come to a decision. He does not just give him good information and end the training session. He makes his son think of sin's consequences so that he will reject the strange woman: "Why would you want to drink from a polluted cistern?"

His Eyes Are Upon Us

For the ways of man are before the eyes of the Lord, and He pondereth all his goings. (5:21)

Now the father reminds the son of another great truth: We do not do anything in secret. The eyes of the Lord see it all. "The eyes of the Lord are in every place, beholding the evil and the good" (Prov. 15:3). It was Job who said, "Doth not He see my ways, and count all my steps?" (Job 30:4).

The Results of Living a Godless Life

His own iniquities shall take the wicked himself, and he shall be held with the cords of his sins. He shall die without instruction, and in the greatness of his folly he shall go away. (5:22–23)

The father tells his son what it is like to live a life apart from God. He shows his son that the sinner gets all wrapped up in sin. What are these cords that are holding him? They are the "cords of his own sins." The eighteenth century English evangelist John Wesley described this man as follows: "He is in perfect bondage to his lusts, and is neither able nor willing to set himself at liberty."[3]

What a tremendously valuable training session on sex education this father has given his son. The son will never be quite the same after this godly instruction from father. Placed into his mind are godly truths that time will never erase. These precious and valuable truths, placed into the mind of the son by a loving father, shall remain there for life.

6 | The Harvest

A s mentioned previously, the short, witty sayings known as proverbs were common among the nations of the ancient Near East. There were four main settings in these cultures where Proverbs were collected and used. These four settings were: the family, the royal court, schools, and scribal circles. Author Ted Hildebrand states that:

> The family is the most explicit proverbial setting. From the Sumerian "Instructions of Suruppak," to the Babylonian "Counsels of Wisdom," and the Ugaritic "Counsel of Shubeawilum," ancient fathers instructed their sons using the literary forms of wisdom. In Egypt, Ptah-hotep and Ka-gem-ni were aged masters who gathered their children to give them instruction. In Israel, the instructions repeatedly use the formula "Listen, my son." While the term "father" may be a technical term, the father was the one who taught his children his trade, his faith, and his wisdom. The mother was also frequently involved in teaching. King Lemuel tells of wisdom that "his mother taught him" (Prov. 31:1–3) . . . The topics of many of the Proverbs also confirm an original familial setting.[1]

Planning for the Harvest

I was raised on a farm in Chenango County in upstate New York. My parents' farm was located on the top of a hill a few miles outside the picturesque city of Norwich. My brother and I helped with the various harvests each year on the farm. In the spring of the year, the harvest was the gathering of sap from the maple trees. My grandfather would tap the trees and attach two buckets to each tree. The sap would drain from inside the tree into the spigot and would then drip into the bucket. Once a day, we would empty the buckets into large containers and proceed to the sap house where the sap would be boiled down. The end result was delicious New York State maple syrup, which we enjoyed all year long.

The spring was also a time to plant the garden. First we would prepare the ground by plowing. Next we would go over the plowed ground by hand and pick out the grass, weeds, and rocks. We would then stake out rows for planting using wooden stakes and string. We would space the rows one to three feet apart, depending on what we were planting. The seeds were then placed in the rows and covered with soil. The next few months required a lot of work to ensure a good harvest. Autumn found us gathering the annual crop of sweet potatoes, carrots, squash, turnip, pumpkin, onions, etc. These would all be placed into a "vegetable" bin in the cellar. The refrigerator-like temperature of the cellar kept the vegetables fresh and assured us of a good food supply all winter long. Other vegetables from the garden such as tomatoes, beets, corn, peas, etc. would be cooked and stored in glass jars for consumption during the winter months. This procedure was commonly referred to as canning vegetables. A cute saying that was often heard during harvest time was: "We'll eat what we can, and what we can't eat we'll 'can.'" Apples were gathered from the trees and were placed in the vegetable bin. Blackberries, raspberries, and blueberries were also canned and placed on storage shelves in the cellar.

As a child, I discovered that some people had a good harvest, some had a poor harvest, and some had no harvest at all. I noticed that some people didn't plant anything. Others went through the process of preparing the ground and planting the seed, but failed to keep the weeds out of the garden during the growing season. This resulted in a greatly diminished fall harvest. Then, there were others that didn't seem to notice when their gardens were drying up because of a lack of water. Still others didn't deal swiftly with invading insects that can do great damage to a garden in a short time.

I learned some very valuable lessons from my boyhood days on the farm. Here's what I learned about harvests:

1. Harvests don't "just happen."
2. It takes planning to produce a harvest.
3. It takes work to produce a harvest.
4. If you want a good harvest, you must pay attention to the details.

In this session, the wise father speaks to the son on the subject of the harvest. The son receives invaluable training that he can use every day of his life. John Phillips said, "The Book of Proverbs is intended to do for our *daily life* what the Book of Psalms is intended to do for our *devotional life*. They (the Proverbs) are filled with practical wisdom for all ages but, in a special way perhaps, should be taught to our young people."[2]

Warning Against Co-signing

My son, if thou be surety for thy neighbor, if thou hast struck thy hand with a stranger, thou art snared with the words of thy mouth, thou art taken with the words of thy mouth. Do this now, my son, and deliver thyself, when thou art come into the hand of thy neighbor: go, humble thyself, and importune thy neighbor. Give not sleep to thine eyes, nor slumber to thine eyelids. Deliver thyself like a roe from the hand of the hunter, and like a bird from the hand of the fowler. (6:1–5)

"Striking the Hand"

In ancient times, a man could go on record that he was willing to cover the debt of another by striking the hand (v. 1, 17:28, 22:26, Job 17:23). Rev. A.R. Fausset explains that verse one is alluding to "the custom of the surety putting his hand with a quick movement and a clap into the hand of the creditor."[3] To give surety was to insure against loss, damage, or failure to do something. When one co-signs a note, for example, he has become surety. By co-signing, he agrees to be legally responsible for the debt of the other person. This dangerous prospect has always been a menace to one's economic health. Horror stories by the thousands have been told by those who have taken upon themselves this unbiblical yoke. The Word of God issues warning against this practice. It is such a serious matter that the father tells his son that if he finds himself in this situation, he should get out of it without delay (vv. 2–4). He must take care of this at once. He must get out of this financial arrangement before he goes to bed. The impression that the father is giving the son is: "As important as sleep is, here is something that is more important. Don't go to sleep until you've got this matter settled!" (vv. 3–4)

To illustrate the danger, the father proceeds to paint vivid pictures with words. I've paraphrased his words in verse five as follows: "Deliver yourself! You are like a deer, stalked by the hunter! You are like a bird caught in a net!" This wise father, with his carefully chosen words, has placed unforgettable images into the memory bank of the son. Here is another example of unchanging truth. Although the words of Proverbs were penned thousands of years ago, they are needed by people today as much as they were needed by the ancients. Times change, and cultures change—but truth does not.

Consider the Ways of the Ant

Go to the ant, thou sluggard; consider her ways, and be wise, which, having no guide, overseer, or ruler, provideth her food in the summer, and gathereth her food in the harvest. (6:6–8)

1. She is self-motivated (v. 7).
2. She is productive (v. 8).
3. She is harvest-minded (v. 8).

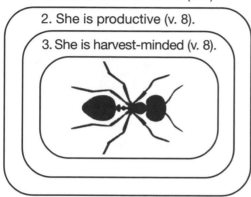

The father focuses the son's attention now on the lazy man ("sluggard") and the ambitious ant. He addresses a lazy man who is not present, but the father is really speaking to his son. The father tells the sluggard to go find an ant and "consider her ways."

I used to study ants on the farm. They were always working. They would carry dirt, one tiny piece at a time, until they had built a mound. Their living quarters would be inside the mound, which is called an "anthill." It was fascinating to watch the activity of the ants around the anthill. They were forever on the move. All summer long, they would gather food and store it for winter. They were "harvest minded."

What lessons we can learn from nature! Solomon here is teaching his son another valuable lesson about sowing and reaping. We see him giving a few simple facts about the ant as he trains his son to be *harvest minded*. He proceeds to tell his son about three men who will miss the harvest.

Three Men Who Will Miss the Harvest

The First Man Who Will Miss the Harvest:
The Lazy Man

"Consider her (the ant's) ways," Solomon declares to the lazy man, "and be wise" (v. 6). The thoughts that occupy the lazy man's mind are not wise thoughts. He is told to consider the ant because he needs a mental adjustment. His thinking is faulty. The thoughts of his mind have held him down like heavy, burdensome weights. He is not growing in knowledge nor wealth. He is not producing anything for his family or for society. There is no mention in our text of a physical problem. The lazy man's problem is a sin problem. None of us like to take responsibility for our sins. Rather than face them, we prefer to cover them up, make excuses for them, or pretend that they don't exist. When we do wrong, often we are heard to say, "It wasn't really my fault; I am not to blame." The lazy man is no exception. He will always have his "reasons" (or "excuses") why he doesn't have a job. In many cases, he has even convinced himself: "I can't work." The lazy man in Scripture is the man who could work, should work, but won't work.

> How long wilt thou sleep, O sluggard? When wilt thou arise out of thy sleep? Yet a little sleep, a little slumber, a little folding of the hands to sleep, so shall thy poverty come like one that traveleth, and thy want like an armed man. (6:9–11)

REASONS FOR THE LAZY MAN

The lazy man is asked two questions in verse 9. These two questions could easily lead to other questions such as: "What is your problem? Are you sick? Did you go to bed late? Why? What are you thinking? Why don't you get up and go to work?" The sluggards of this world have dozens of excuses why they "can't work." There are many excuses, but only one reason: wrong thinking. God states that man is to work. "Six days shalt thou labor, and do all thy work" (Exod. 20:9). If a man won't work, he is in conflict with his Creator. God designed man to work and told him to work.

In 2 Thessalonians 3, the Word of God addresses the problem of some who "would not work." Scripture does not state that they "could not" work, but only that they "would not work." The problem here again was not a physical one, but a mental one. It was another case of wrong thinking! What treatment did God prescribe for those who suffered from the "won't work" syndrome? The treatment was to "command" them and to "exhort" them to work (v. 12). The goal was to get those men and women to repent (change their minds) and go to work. If any of those with the "won't work syndrome" still refused to work, Paul said:

1. Don't give them your food (v. 10).

2. Don't give them your company (v. 14).

RESPONSE OF THE LAZY MAN
Solomon asks this lazy man two questions, but he gets no reply. The lazy man lacks some very important things: Vision! Dreams! A plan! Everybody should have these. Perhaps this man had all these in the past but let them go and embraced instead "wrong thinking." Solomon asks his questions, but he gets no response. Solomon tried to get the man's mind on the harvest (vv. 6–8), but this man is not harvest minded. He is "handout" minded. His "hands refused to labor" (Prov. 21:25).

RESULT OF THE LAZY MAN
The lazy man will miss the **harvest.** He will end up in poverty (v. 11). Proverbs 20:4 states that "the sluggard will not plow by reason of the cold; therefore shall he **beg in harvest,** and have nothing."

Here are some other verses in Proverbs that speak of the lazy man: 10:4–5, 12:24, 27, 13:4, 15:19, 18:9, 19:15, 20:4, 21:25, 24:30–34.

Parents would do well to teach their children these simple harvest truths:

1. Harvests don't **"just happen."**

2. It takes *planning* to produce a harvest.

3. It takes *work* to produce a harvest.

4. If you want a good harvest, you must *pay attention* to the *details.*

The "10–10–80" Plan

In contrast to the lazy man, who is at odds with God, concerned parents should teach their children how to plan, how to dream, and how to actively pursue goals. Children should be taught at a young age that work is desirable, and that it is beneficial. They should contribute to the household by performing small assigned tasks. Parents should teach their children to "consider the ant," and to be "harvest minded." Parents should teach their children to work hard and to save a piece of every dollar that they earn. The "10–10–80" plan outlined below is one sample plan that has worked for many.

The first 10 percent of each dollar — Give to the Lord

The second 10 percent of each dollar — Save for "the harvest"

The remaining 80 percent —
1. Pray for wisdom in purchases
2. Spend accordingly

Harvest Minded Summary for Parents:

Parents who want their children to be harvest minded should teach them:

1. To think, dream, plan, and to pursue good goals.
2. To enjoy work:
    A. God commanded that we work. It is, therefore, good.
    B. Work brings financial benefits.
    C. Work brings personal benefits:
1. Helps us to have a healthy self-image.
2. When we do "good work," we earn the respect of others.
3. To honor the Lord with the "first fruits" of their labors (Prov. 3:9).
4. To save a part of every earned dollar (Prov. 21:5, 20, 30:24–25).

The Second Man Who Will Miss the Harvest: The Ungodly Man

God loves good and He hates evil. Some people have had a hard time accepting the fact that "God is love," or to be more specific, that God loves them. Other people have a different view of God. They have a hard time comprehending the fact that God hates anything. The Bible, however, clearly teaches that our holy God loves good and hates evil. In the following verses, Solomon introduces his son to an ungodly man. Unlike the lazy man just discussed, this man is ambitious. He is filled with ambition to do ungodly and evil deeds. He is called worthless, wicked, and perverse. He is pictured as a man who is up to no good continually.

A worthless person, a wicked man, walketh with a perverse mouth. He winketh with his eyes, he speaketh with his feet, he teacheth with his fingers. Perversity is in his heart; he deviseth mischief continually, he soweth discord. Therefore shall his calamity come suddenly; suddenly shall he be broken without remedy. These six things doth the Lord hate; yea, seven are an abomination unto Him: A proud look, a lying tongue, and hands that shed innocent blood, an heart that deviseth wicked imaginations, feet that are swift in running to mischief, a false witness that speaketh lies, and he that soweth discord among brethren. (6:12–19)

This man has God's attention, but for all of the wrong reasons. He has made himself an enemy of God. He embraces the very things that God hates. The Hebrew word for "abomination" in verse 16 denotes "something disgusting." Scripture tells us of seven things that God hates and finds disgusting. Let us identify these things, study them, and then reject them lest our personal walk with God be hindered. Many will be surprised to learn that all of these disgusting things are in our hearts. They are part of the Adamic nature that we inherited from Adam and Eve. Their natures became corrupted because they listened to Satan and disobeyed God. Our propensity toward evil is better understood when we consider Jesus' words on the subject of the human heart: "For from within, **out of the heart of men,** proceed evil thoughts, adulteries, fornications, murders, thefts, covetousness, wickedness, deceit, lasciviousness, an evil eye, blasphemy, pride, foolishness. All of these things come from within, and defile the man" (Mark 7:21–23). If all of these disgusting things are within us, how then can we have victory and please God? We can have victory and please God by submitting to Him every day. It's called "walking in the Spirit." Galatians 5:16 says: "Walk in the Spirit, and ye shall not fulfill the lust of the flesh."

Seven Things That God Hates

Seven Things That God Hates
1. Pride.

Isn't it interesting that the first sin on God's hate list is pride? Pride was the original sin of the universe. Lucifer, the anointed cherub (Ezek. 28:14), said in his heart (the place where sin always begins) *"I* will ascend into heaven, *I* will exalt my throne *above* the stars of God, *I* will sit also upon the mount of the congregation, in the sides of the north, *I* will ascend above the heights of the clouds, *I will be like the most high."* Dr. C.I. Scofield wrote that "when Lucifer said, *'I will,'* sin began."[4] Pride was also the sin that brought condemnation to the human race. Satan, previously known as Lucifer (Ezek. 28) made his deadly pitch to Eve with these alluring words: "and *ye* shall be as God. . . ."

The "proud look" (v. 17) that our Creator detests is that look of arrogance that conveys a superior attitude. It is the "I am better" look. The Lord commands us in Romans 12:3 not to think of ourselves more highly than we ought to think. In Romans 12:16, He instructs us not to be proud and not to think of ourselves as having all the answers.

Pride Keeps People from Christ

The Word of God declares that "the wicked through the pride of his countenance, will not seek after God, God is not in all his thoughts" (Ps. 10:4). The pride of this wicked man causes him to say: "There is no such thing as God." Here is one major reason why God hates pride: man's pride keeps him from facing the truth. As the pride in an unbeliever's heart grows, it has a distinct tendency to numb the "God consciousness" that the Creator put within us. As his pride grows, a man becomes less aware of God. He may reach the stage where he will proudly say, "I don't need God, and I don't want God." He may even reach the stage where he will say, "There is no God." At this stage the unbeliever has taken himself captive. He is trapped inside his self-created world of fantasy. He has created a make-believe world where there is no God to answer to. He is free to indulge in whatever gross sins he desires because he has convinced himself that there are no eternal consequences for his behavior. "There is no judgment to come, and no hell to avoid," he tells himself. "Christ is not going to return to earth," he confidently states. The Bible declares that this man, walking after his own lusts, is "willingly ignorant" (2 Pet. 3:3–5). He is like one of the unbelievers found in Romans 1:21–22. These pagans are described as follows: "because when they knew God, they glorified Him not as God, neither were thankful, but became vain in their imaginations, and their foolish heart was darkened. Professing themselves to be wise, they became fools."

God is love (1 John 4:8). He desires that none should perish (2 Pet. 3:9). It is, however, difficult (not impossible, but difficult) for a man or a woman to see the light of salvation after embracing darkness in the mind. This is one big reason why God hates pride. It keeps people from coming to Christ.

Pride Exalts Self

Believers also face the problem of pride. It is indeed a serious sin within our churches. Pastors and church leaders are especially susceptible to the sin of pride due to their status and the favorable attention and praise that they often receive. There is a warning issued in 1 Timothy that a man relatively new in the faith should not be a bishop (pastor) "lest being lifted up with *pride* he fall into the condemnation of the devil" (1 Tim. 3:6).

Pride elevates self. We are told to elevate the Lord, not self. In the following verses, the same Hebrew word (*rûwm*) that is translated "proud" in Proverbs 6:17 is translated "exalt" or "exalted." You will notice it is not man that is to be exalted, or lifted up, but God. "O magnify the Lord with me, and *exalt* His name together" (Ps. 34:3). "Be still and know that I am God: I will be *exalted* among the heathen, I will be *exalted* in the earth" (Ps. 46:10). "Be thou *exalted,* O God, above the heavens; let thy glory be above all the earth" (Ps. 57:5).

135

Pride in the heart of church members often causes harm to the Body of Christ. Have you ever thought about it? It is never the humble, self-abased believer who causes trouble in the local assembly. His focus is on obtaining a closer walk with God. Like the psalmist of old, he encourages people to lift up the Lord. "O magnify the Lord with me," he pleads. "Let us *exalt* His name together," he continues (Ps. 34:3). If we are always exalting the Lord from our hearts, as well as our lips, we will be known as peacemakers, not strife causers. It is the proud man who causes harm in Christ's body. "He that is of a *proud* heart stirreth up strife . . ." (Prov. 28:25). Prideful men and women are often unaware of their sin because they have deceived themselves. Jeremiah 17:9 states that "the heart is deceitful above all things and desperately wicked; who can know it?"

Pride Can Keep Us from a Closer Walk With God

Pride is sinful man elevating himself in his own mind. The exaltation of self and the exaltation of God are like opposite ends of a teeter-totter. When one side is exalted, the opposite side is lowered. God is not properly elevated and exalted in a man's life that is dominated by pride.

Pride hinders our walk with God. Humility helps our walk with God. "God resisteth the proud and giveth grace to the humble. Humble yourselves, therefore, under the mighty hand of God, that He may exalt you in due time" (1 Pet. 5:5b–6). A proud heart says, "I can handle this. I'm good." A humble heart says, "Oh, God, this is Your holy work. I am not worthy, and I am not capable. Without You, I can do nothing. Please work through me, or I will fail You." Similar words of instruction are given to us in James 4:6–10. "God resisteth the proud, but giveth grace to the humble," we are told in verse 6. The following instructions are then given: "Submit yourselves, therefore, to God. Resist the devil, and he will flee from you. Draw near to God, and He will draw near to you. Cleanse your hands, ye sinners, and purify your hearts, ye double minded. Be afflicted, and mourn, and weep; let your laughter be turned to mourning, and your joy to heaviness. Humble yourselves in the sight of the Lord, and He shall lift you up" (vv. 9–10). Let the pride in your heart represent one seat, and your exaltation of God represent the opposite seat on a teeter-totter. What does your teeter-totter look like? Who is on the high end? God or self?

Pride Diminishes Our Spiritual Power

The pride that is spoken of in Holy Scripture is a great sin. It is a much greater sin in God's eyes than any of us realize. "Everyone who is **proud** in heart is an abomination to the Lord . . ." states the Word (Prov. 16:5).

God had a big job for the apostle Paul to do. It was, therefore, very important that Paul have God's strength for the task. Pride not only keeps us from a closer walk with the Lord; it also greatly diminishes our spiritual power. God gave Paul an unidentified "thorn in the flesh" to keep him humble so that he might not lose the spiritual power he needed for his historic task. Paul tells us twice in 2 Corinthians 12:7 that the thorn in the flesh was given to him "lest I should be exalted above measure." Paul asked the Lord three times to remove it. God's answer to Paul was: "My grace is sufficient for thee; for *my strength is made perfect in weakness*" (2 Corin. 12:9). Paul then responded as follows: "I will gladly, therefore, brag about my weaknesses so *that Christ's great power might work through me*" (my paraphrase 12:9b). If a believer is to have great spiritual power flowing through him as he serves the Lord, he must regularly empty himself of pride.

Pride Can Come as a Result of Success

Success in sports or academics will sometimes cause a young person to "get a big head." I remember introducing my young sons to the exciting world of amateur wrestling. I told my boys: "You are getting a head start in wrestling because you are so young. You will both be very good. There will come a day when time after time the referee will raise your arm in victory. That will be great; however, I want you to remember something: You are not to get proud. I don't care how good you become, if you get conceited and walk around school like a 'big shot,' your wrestling days will be over!" Our sons did well in sports, and I don't think pride was ever much of a problem with them because we addressed it early. So did the father in Proverbs.

Many things can cause a person to be self-exalted. A handsome or pretty face will sometimes cause pride. Lucifer's beauty is an example of this. He is described in Ezekiel 28:17 as follows: "Thine heart was lifted up because of thy beauty; thou hast corrupted thy wisdom by reason of thy brightness. . . ."

Financial success is a major cause of pride in man. A man works hard, does quite well financially, and begins to think: "Man, I'm really something. Look at what *I* have done. *I* have made it in this world." It was Agur who prayed "give me neither poverty nor riches; feed me with food convenient for me, lest I be full and deny thee, and say, Who is the Lord?" (Prov. 30:8b–9a).

God destroyed the city of Sodom because of the wickedness of the people. They too had prospered. They had plenty to eat, plenty of life's goods, and an abundance of idle time. The Sodomites then became full of pride, which is often the result of prosperity (see Ezek. 16:49–50). Psalm 73 deals with the subject: "The prosperity of the wicked." The people in this psalm are described as a corrupt and wicked people full of pride.

Pride Can Bring Disaster

A person may get away with a prideful heart for a time. The Bible warns us, however, that the God who hates pride will also deal with those who are guilty of it. The great and awesome God declares in Psalm 101:5: "Him that hath an high look and a proud heart will not I tolerate." Proverbs 18:12 states that "Before destruction the heart of man is haughty, and before honor is humility." Perhaps the most sobering verse on this subject is Proverbs 16:18. Here, God says, "Pride goeth before destruction, and an haughty spirit before a fall."

Seven Things That God Hates
2. A lying tongue.

Our God is called the Lord God of Truth (Ps. 31:5, Isa. 65:16). A lie is against the very nature of God! Not one lie will be allowed into the holy city (Rev. 21:27). If man is going to worship God, he "must worship Him in Spirit and in truth" (John 4:24). Lying is an evil that we have all been guilty of. We need to recognize how much God hates this sin. Satan introduced the lie to the human race, and has used it for his evil purposes for thousands of years (John 8:44).

> Satan's biggest purpose with the lie
> is to keep people from heaven

    A. People are lost because they received not the truth (2 Thess. 2:12).

    B. Our salvation is a result of believing the truth (2 Thess. 2:13).

Most of us tend to take lying lightly. "How did you get out of that one?" somebody asks. "Well, I had to tell a little white lie" is often the reply. Let us realize that lies are *never* white. When we tell a lie, we use a tool of Satan. We do not show forth the glory of God in our lives when we speak the lie (1 Cor. 10:31). We grieve the Lord whenever we do not tell the truth.

    A good scripture to memorize on this important subject is Ephesians 4:29: "Let no corrupt communication proceed out of your mouth, but that which is good to the use of edifying, that it may minister grace unto the hearers."

Seven Things That God Hates
3. Hands that shed innocent blood.

Murder has always been recognized as one of man's greatest crimes. The death penalty for murder that God initiated to Noah and his sons has never been rescinded. Human life is to be considered sacred because the Lord made us in His image. "Whoso sheddeth man's blood, by man shall his blood be shed; for in the image of God made He man" (Gen. 9:6). Commandment number six is: "Thou shalt not kill" (Exod. 20:13). Jesus told us that the devil "was a murderer from the beginning, and abode not in the truth . . ." (John 8:44). He was successful in introducing sin into the human race. He continually and aggressively promotes the breaking of all of God's commandments. He has made himself God's enemy. He is, as Paul said, "the enemy of all righteousness . . ." (Acts 13:10). Since it was the devil that brought sin into the human race, we conclude that he plays a role in every sin, and that his bloody hands play a part in every murder.

Seven Things That God Hates
4. A mind that produces wicked plans.

The fourth thing on God's hate list is a "heart that deviseth wicked imaginations . . ." (v. 18). A more contemporary wording of this verse portion would be: "A mind that produces wicked plans." (See my comments on the "heart of man" in Prov. 4:23.) Previously, I mentioned (in chapter 4) the time when, with the exception of Noah and his family, man became so evil in his thinking that "every imagination of the thoughts of his heart was only evil continually" (Gen. 6:5). God sent the great flood to destroy that wicked generation but spared Noah and his family because "Noah was a just man . . . and . . . walked with the Lord" (Gen. 6:9).

Although not all of man's plans are evil today, they are all, at best, "flawed." They are flawed because man has a "flawed planner." Man's planner (his mind) is often referred to in Scripture as his "heart." The Bible teaches that man has a serious "heart problem." How bad is the human heart? It is a lot worse than we think it is. We fool people all the time by saying one thing and having something totally different in our hearts. Such is the deceitfulness of the human heart. We are even fooled by our own hearts. We have heard people say things like: "I can't believe I did that," or "I was so confused, I don't know what I was thinking," or "I just wasn't thinking right." I suppose that all of us could look back on our lives with regret for some things that we have thought, and some things that we have read, and some things that we have done. We pay psychiatrists, counselors, and other professionals large sums of money to help us figure out our own minds! The Lord stated that "the heart is deceitful above all things, and desperately wicked," and then He asked this question: "Who can know it?"

The only one who knows all there is to know about your heart is the Lord. ***"For I know the things that come into your mind, every one of them,"*** said the Lord (Ezek. 11:5). "Shall not God search this out? For he knoweth the secrets of the heart" (Ps. 44:21). (See also: 1 Sam. 16:7, 1 Chron. 28:9, Jer. 17:10, Matt. 9:4, 1 Kings 8:39.) Many people do not like to hear the Bible preached because they feel convicted. God's Word tells us what we really are, and many of us just don't want to face the truth. The Living Bible translates Hebrews 4:12 as follows: "For whatever God says to us is full of living power: it is sharper than the sharpest dagger, cutting swift and deep into our innermost thoughts and desires with all their parts, exposing us for what we really are." God knows all there is to know about us for it is "He that searcheth the hearts" (Rom. 8:27). The God that knows our hearts uses His Word to expose us for what we really are.

The following prayer expressed in verse by J. Edwin Orr ought to be prayed (in our own words) to the Lord each day:

> Search me, O God, and know my heart today;
> Try me, O Savior, know my thoughts I pray.
> See if there be some wicked way in me;
> Cleanse me from every sin and set me free.[5]

> Seven Things That God Hates
>
> **5. Feet that eagerly run to do bad things.**

The person described in verse 18 is a person that is determined to do bad deeds. "The heart blazes the trail," says J. Vernon McGee, "that the feet will follow."[6] These are individuals that are determined to do evil. They pursue evil with vigor and enthusiasm. They are rebels against God and against their own consciences, which they have seared by their determination.

Swift punishment for criminals is an effective deterrent to crime. Whenever a nation's judicial system becomes lax, crime increases. As our nation has drifted further and further from God, we have become weaker and weaker in our resolve to punish lawbreakers. The consequences are obvious. All kinds of crimes against our citizens are flourishing. (Murder, rape, thefts, assaults, etc.) God addresses this subject in Ecclesiastes 8:11: "Because sentence against an evil work is not executed speedily, therefore the heart of the sons of man is fully set in them to do evil." Our blasé judicial system has actually encouraged the feet of the wicked to pursue ungodly life styles.

> Seven Things That God Hates
>
> **6. A slanderer.**

A slanderer is one who tells lies meant to do harm to the good name and reputation of another. The slanderer is identified in verse 19 as a "false witness that speaketh lies." The Lord has already told us (vv. 16–17) that He hates lies and that they are disgusting to Him. The sin of slander is even worse. It is a lie designed to hurt another. The ninth commandment is "thou shalt not bear false witness against thy neighbor" (Exod. 20:16). The God of truth (Ps. 31:5) hates the lie, and the God who is just (Rev. 15:3) hates the injustice of slander. Zechariah 8:17 states: "And let none of you imagine evil in your hearts against his neighbor; and love no false oath; for all these are things that I hate, saith the Lord."

Our Lord was slandered by the Jewish religionists during His earthly mission. When He performed those wonderful miracles of healing the sick and raising the dead, the Pharisees sneered: "He casteth out demons by the prince of demons" (Matt. 9:34). When Jesus ate with the tax collectors and sinners in Matthew's house, the Jews accused Him of being "gluttonous, and a winebibber, a friend of tax collectors and sinners" (Matt. 11:19). They slandered Him when He appeared before Caiphas, the high priest (Matt. 26:57–68). Again and again, they spoke lies against Him. I have a hunch that the self-righteous religionists slandered Jesus daily during His earthly ministry.

Followers of Jesus are often slandered. The first martyr in the New Testament was Stephen. He is described in Acts 6:5 as "a man full of faith and of the Holy Spirit. . . ." Scripture testifies that he "did great wonders and miracles among the people" (Acts 6:8). Whenever a genuine movement of God takes place, the religionists always turn against the man God has raised up. The "salvation is by works" ministers strongly oppose the message that "Jesus paid it all," and normally will seize any opportunity they can find to "silence the messenger." Stephen was no exception. They couldn't "resist the wisdom and the Spirit by which he spoke" (Acts 6:10), so they "set up false witnesses" against him (v. 13), and a short time later they murdered him (vv. 54–60).

Slander is a horrible sin. God's choicest servants have suffered slander all through the ages. We could continue on the subject of slander for an extended period of time. Scripture has a lot to say on this subject. Let us conclude, however, with the words of our Savior on the subject: "Blessed are ye, when men shall revile you, and persecute you, and **shall say all manner of evil against you falsely, for my sake.** Rejoice, and be exceedingly glad; for great is your reward in heaven; for so persecuted they the prophets who were before you" (Matt. 5:11–12).

> Seven Things That God Hates
> ### 7. A person that sows discord among the brethren.

The last sin on this infamous list in Proverbs 6 is the sin of sowing discord. The God of peace delights in unity (Rom. 15:33, 16:20, Phil. 4:9, 1 Thess. 5:23, Heb. 13:20). The subject of Psalm 133 is the unity of brethren. In this diminutive psalm of only three verses, God shares with us His thoughts on unity. I encourage you to read these words carefully:

> *Behold, how good and how pleasant it is for brethren to dwell together in unity! It is like the precious ointment upon the head, that ran down upon the beard . . . that went down to the skirts of his garments, like the dew of Hermon, and like the dew that descended upon the mountains of Zion; for there the Lord commanded the blessing, even life for evermore.*

The great English preacher Charles Spurgeon said, "When love reigns, God reigns."[7] We experience a little bit of heaven on earth when the brethren are dwelling together in unity. The Lord tells us that unity is "like the precious ointment upon the head" (v. 2). Spurgeon said:

> It has a **sweet perfume** about it, comparable to that precious ointment with which the first high priest was anointed at his ordination. It is a **holy thing,** and so again is the Lord's service. What a sacred thing must brotherly love be when it can be likened to an oil which must never be poured on any man but on the Lord's high priest alone! It is a **diffusive thing:** being poured on his head the fragrant oil flowed down upon Aaron's beard, and thence dropped upon his garments till the utmost hem was anointed therewith; and even so doth brotherly love extend its benign power and bless all who are beneath its influence. . . . It has a **special use** about it; for as by the anointing oil Aaron was set apart for the special service of Jehovah, even so those who dwell in love are the better fitted to glorify God in His church. The Lord is not likely to use for His glory those who are devoid

of love; they lack the anointing needed to make them priests unto the Lord.[8]

The Sower of Discord is a Thief

I remember from my childhood a historic church in my home county of Chenango in New York state. The church is in the country and sits on a small hill overlooking the main road. The area is simply known as White Store. Although regular services weren't held, the church was left open for prayer and for sightseers. A donation box was attached to the wall in the entry. There was always at least one service a year held at the White Store Church. I was there on one of those special occasions. How shocked everyone was upon entering the church that day. It was discovered that someone had gone into the church, ripped the donation box off the wall, and stole the donations. I was not yet a Christian, but I remember thinking: "Who would steal from God? Boy, I wouldn't want to be in that man's shoes! He's in big trouble! He stole from God!"

The man or woman who sows discord among God's people is also guilty of thievery. When sown seeds of discord germinate, they produce indescribable things and will quickly rob the saints of their peace and joy. The people of God then begin to think on fleshly things instead of on godly things (Phil. 4:7–8). When there is peace in a congregation, people can focus on the Lord and "let the peace of God rule" in their hearts (Col. 3:15). This is God's plan for His people. When discord comes into a congregation, it kicks out peace. When discord comes into the church, people are forced to shift their attention from the Lord to the carnal problems that have risen within the congregation. God is then robbed of the people's devotion, thoughts, attention, and as we have already mentioned, the people are robbed of their peace and joy. This kind of theft is far worse than someone breaking into a church and stealing the donation box or the sound system. It is always a shocking blow to a church when a break-in and a theft occur, but stolen items can often be replaced within a few days. Things can get back to normal quickly. It's not that easy to replace stolen peace and stolen joy in a congregation. After the thief has sown his dirty seeds of discord, it often takes years for a congregation to recover its peace, its joy, and its focus on the Lord. No wonder the Lord told us that a person who sows seeds of discord among brethren is an abomination to Him.

Two Reasons Why People Sow Seeds of Discord

People who cause division within a congregation are not being driven by the Lord but by their own sinful natures. It is the old nature that produces strife and discord (Gal. 5:20). It is the new nature that produces love and joy and peace (Gal. 5:20). The reasons why people sow seeds of discord will vary from person to person. All of these people, however, have a **common problem:** they are "walking in the flesh," not in "the Spirit."

1. THE LACK OF THE NEW BIRTH.

One reason why some people sow seeds of discord is the fact that they have never experienced the new birth. In Proverbs 4 we covered the fact that a person must have God's Spirit in order to understand the "things of God." Many times a lost church member will not be sympathetic towards the "things of God." He simply doesn't understand them!

2. UNRESOLVED SIN.

Another reason why some people sow seeds of discord is the fact that there is some unresolved sin in their life. It is often some deep seated sin that has been growing (many times secretly) in the person's heart for years. A believer with some unresolved sin issue in his life may (depending upon his personality traits) be a candidate for the office of "discord seed sower." The "opposition party boss" (Satan) has a long standing reputation of promoting this type of individual. He often propels this type of person into some position of influence and then uses him as his agent, encouraging him to sow his wicked seeds. Later when the problems of discord begin to bring forth corrupt fruit, God's people often realize as the householder in Matthew 13 did—"An enemy hath done this" (Matt. 13:28).

The Proper Action to Take When Someone "Shares" His "Seeds of Discord" with You

Those who sow their "seeds of discord" often do so under false pretense. They often approach people secretly. They may make statements that sound similar to the following: "I'm only telling you this because I wanted you to pray about the matter," or "I think something should be done, but don't let anybody know that I said anything."

What to Do:

1. *Refuse to listen to gossip.*

2. *Refuse to take a vow of silence.*

   If the person asks you to promise that you will not reveal the source of the information that you are about to receive: Refuse.

   If the person asks you to promise not to repeat the conversation to the individual(s) that he is about to disparage: Refuse. Always keep these options open.

3. *Confront him.* (Eph. 4:14–15, Prov. 6:19)

   If someone is guilty of sowing seeds of discord to you, you should confront that person with his sin. You should lovingly rebuke that person with Scripture, and with total honesty. If the person repents of his sin, that should be the end of the matter.

4. *Meet with the pastor.*

   If, however, you are aware that this person, having been rebuked in love by you, is persisting in sowing seeds of discord, it is your duty to act. You should set up an appointment with the pastor and update him on the whole incident. This is as far as you go. You have confronted the person biblically, truthfully, and with love. The person persisted in his sin, so you took the incident to the proper person: the shepherd of the sheep. You have handled a negative situation in a biblical and positive manner. There is, however, one more thing that you can do: you can pray.

5. Pray.

Pray for the sower of bad seed, pray for the pastor, and pray for the spiritual health of the entire congregation. We need to remember that "the effectual, fervent prayer of a righteous man availeth much" (James 5:16b).

A Biblical Response by the Pastor

The proper steps to be taken concerning confrontation, forgiveness and church discipline are given to us in Matthew 18:15–17. This passage of Scripture tells the servant of the Lord *what* to do. Another key passage on this subject is 2 Timothy 2:24–26. This passage tells the servant of the Lord *how* to do it.

> *And the servant of the Lord must not strive, but be gentle unto all men, apt to teach, patient; in meekness instructing those that oppose him, if God, perhaps, will give them repentance to the acknowledging of the truth; and that they may recover themselves out of the snare of the devil, who are taken captive by him at his will. 2 Tim. 2:24–26*

These verses contain valuable leadership principles for handling conflict. These leadership principles are directly from the Lord. They are, therefore, a pattern for the servant of the Lord to follow when conflict arises within the church.

Six Leadership Principles—Dealing with Conflict
(2 Tim. 2:24–26)

1. Do not argue.

And the servant of the Lord must not strive. . . . (v. 24)

2. Be gentle to all.

but be gentle to all . . . (v. 24)

3. Teach them.

apt to teach . . . (v. 24)

4. Be patient.

patient . . . (v. 24)

5. Discipline them with the hope that God will change their minds.

In meekness instructing those that oppose him, if God, perhaps, will give them repentance to the acknowledging of the truth. (v. 25)

The Greek word translated "instructing" is *paideuo*. In the following verses of the King James Bible paideuo is translated "chastise," "chastened," "chasteneth," or "chasten": Luke 22:16, 23:22, 1 Corinthians 11:32, 2 Corinthians 6:9, Hebrews 12:6, 7, 10; Revelation 3:19. The following meaning of paideuo comes from "Notes on Galatians" by Hogg and Vine: "It is clear that not the impartation of knowledge but severe discipline is intended."[9] Commenting on the use of paideuo in 2 Timothy 2:25, Joseph Thayer tells us that the meaning is "to chastise or castigate with words, to correct: of those who are molding the character of others by reproof and admonition."[10]

6. Be aware that the devil is influencing their thoughts.

and that they may recover themselves out of the snare of the devil. . . . (v. 26)

The people described in 2 Timothy 2:25–26 are people whose thinking is faulty. Their thoughts are full of error. This certainly fits the description of those who sow discord in the church. When discord arises in the church, pastors should follow the leadership principles that our Lord gave us in these verses and pray that the Lord will help the sowers of discord to see their error, to change their minds (repentance), and to acknowledge the truth (v. 25).

Seven Things That God Hates: Summary

Now that we have discussed the seven things that God hates from Proverbs 6, let's review them one more time. As we do, let us ask the Lord to reveal to us any of those things that might be present in our hearts. J. Vernon McGee said: "This list of seven sins is like a mirror. We look into it, and we squirm because we see ourselves."[11]

Seven Things That God Hates
—these are an abomination unto Him—
1. Pride
2. A lying tongue
3. Hands that shed innocent blood
4. A mind that produces wicked plans
5. Feet that run to do bad things
6. A slanderer
7. A person that sows discord

Cleanse me, Lord,
From all my sin.
I want a closer
walk with You.

We should
- Identify our weak areas
- Add those to our prayer list
- Ask God for victory

The Final Chapter in the Life of the Ungodly Man

We have looked at the ungodly man that God describes in Proverbs 6. We have found that his mind is consistently on evil things (v. 14). He is guilty of embracing the things that God hates. He spends his years thumbing his nose at God and appears to get away with it. He even has found ways of justifying his actions. He has told himself: "I'm *right*. The things I think are *right*, and the things that I do are *right*." Proverbs 14:12 states: "There is a way which seemeth *right* unto a man, but the end thereof is the way of death." Proverbs 12:15 says: "The way of a fool is *right* in his own eyes."

His calamity, however, comes "suddenly" (Prov. 6:15). He has no warning. Like the rich man in Luke 12, he's prepared to enjoy his harvest "for many years" to come (v. 19). He is going to "take it easy." He's going to "eat, drink, and be merry." It's harvest time! "Suddenly," however, the God he has avoided all these years speaks and says, "Thou fool, this night shall thy soul be required of thee . . ." (v. 20). In an instant, his life is over. He has left this earth and all of his possessions behind. He is in hell, suffering the penalty of his sins. He has missed the harvest, and he has missed heaven. "So is he that layeth up treasure for himself, and is not rich toward God" (v. :21).

The Third Man Who Will Miss the Harvest: The Adulterous Man

The third man in this chapter who misses the harvest is the adulterous man. Once again, we find the father instructing his son to avoid wrong sexual activity. Many fathers have lectured their sons about staying pure, but the power of a lecture is limited. This father gives the son something more than a lecture. He gives him something that has the power to keep him clean. He gives him *a plan*. It is crucial that we give our sons and daughters a *plan* for staying clean. If we fail at this, they will dishonor themselves, their parents, and the Lord with their bodies. Thus God shows us a picture of a father giving his son a plan for staying clean.

"Son, Here is God's Plan for You"

My son, keep thy father's commandment, and forsake not the law of thy mother: Bind them continually upon thine heart, and tie them about thy neck. When thou goest, it shall lead thee; when thou sleepest, it shall keep thee; and when thou awakest, it shall talk with thee; for the commandment is a lamp, and the law is light, and reproofs of instruction are the way of life, to keep thee from the evil woman, from the flattery of the tongue of a foreign woman. Lust not after her beauty in thine heart, neither let her take thee with her eyelids. (6:20–25)

This young man is again being instructed to stay in the Word of God. The Word of God in verse 20 is referred to as the father's commandment, and also as the law of the mother. In verse 23, the father's commandment is called a "lamp," and the mother's law is "light." Compare this with Psalm 119:105: **"Thy word** is a lamp unto my feet, and a light unto my path." Spurgeon said:

> We are walkers through the city of this world, and we are often called to go out into its darkness; let us never venture there without the light-giving Word, lest we slip with our feet. Each man should use the Word of God personally, practically, and habitually, that he may see his way and see what lies in it. . . . He who walks in darkness is sure, sooner or later, to stumble; while he who walks by the light of day, or by the lamp of night, stumbleth not, but keeps his uprightness.[12]

Charles Bridges reminds us that godly parents "will bring you God's Word, not their own."[13] Matthew Henry, commenting on verse 20, said:

> It is God's commandment and His law. But our parents directed us to it, put it into our hands, trained us up in the knowledge and observance of it . . . the cautions, counsels, and commands which our parents gave us agree with the Word of God, and therefore we must hold them fast. Children, when they are grown up, must remember the law of a good mother as well as the commandment of a good father.[14]

Solomon passes on to his son a plan for staying clean. Solomon got the plan from his father David. It was David who said, "Wherewithal shall a young man cleanse his way? By taking heed thereto according to thy word" (Ps. 119:9). Solomon tells his son to "bind" the words of God "continually" upon his heart (Prov. 6:21). He was telling his son to memorize Scripture. When we memorize Scripture, we are "tying" it into our "heart" (mind). The battle for godliness is won or lost in the mind (Prov. 4:23). Solomon knew the importance of memorizing Scripture. His father had taught him to "hide" the word in his heart, so he would not sin against God (Ps. 119:11). No doubt, he had heard and read his father's words "I will not forget thy word" (Ps. 119:16).

The word "continually" in verse 20 reminds us that memorizing Scripture is an ongoing task. All of us that know the Lord should be "binding" His words "continually" in our minds. As we "bind" the Word of God into our minds, it will, bit by bit, force out of our minds wrong ideas and wrong desires. Are you "binding" the Word into your mind? Are you, in other words, memorizing Scripture? Parents, grandparents, and Sunday School teachers, are you training the children to memorize Scripture? Pastors, are you encouraging your church families to hide the Word in their hearts? We need to remember that this plan originally was not Solomon's plan or David's plan. It *was* and *is* God's plan. The heavenly father gives the plan to the children to keep them from all kinds of evil.

The Human Race is Sinful and Weak

When it comes to sin, all of us are weak. There are no exceptions. There are no "strong" men or women who can, by their own power, live righteously. "He that is without sin among you, let him first cast a stone . . ." said Jesus on one occasion (John 8:7). No one threw a stone that day. No one even picked one up. Although none of us is strong, there is an abundance of power available to us. There is the power of the Holy Spirit (Acts 1:8), and there is the power of the Word. Proverbs 6:22–24 deals with the power of the Word.

The Power of the Word of God
(Prov. 6:22–25)

1. It has power to *lead* you. (vv. 22, 23)

"Thou shalt guide me with thy counsel. . . ." (Psalm 73:24)

2. It has power to *keep* you. (v. 22)

The meaning of the Hebrew word translated here as "keep" is to hedge about (as with thorns), to guard, or protect. The Word of God has power to protect you against "all of the fiery darts of the wicked" (Eph. 6:16).

3. It has power to *talk* to you. (v. 22)

"The Word of God," commented Matthew Henry, "has something to say to us upon all occasions, if we would but enter into discourse with it, would ask it what it has to say, and give it the hearing."[15]

4. It has the power to *convict* you of sin in your life. (v. 23)

Before we can change and be more like Christ, we must see our need for change. It is the Word that convicts us and shows us our need to change (Acts 2:37, Heb. 4:12).

5. It has power to help you *avoid* sexual sin. (vv. 24, 25)

Notice that lust is a sin of the heart. Jesus taught that adultery has already been committed in the heart when a person lusts after someone else (Matt. 5:28). Lust is not a big problem for people who fill their minds with Scripture.

Jay Adams tells us that "Biblical teaching protects one from evil women with their smooth tongues (v. 24). How? By both prohibitions and warnings. By pointing to the true source of sexual happiness (cf. 5:18 ff.)."[15]

There is plenty of power available for any believer to have victory over sin. We are weak, but God has given us something powerful (Heb. 4:12) to keep us from evil: The Word of God.

The Costly Sin of Adultery

For by means of an unchaste woman a man is brought to a piece of bread; and the adulteress will hunt for the precious life. Can a man take fire in his bosom, and his clothes not be burned? Can one go upon hot coals, and his feet not be burned? So he that goeth in to his neighbor's wife; whosoever toucheth her shall not be innocent. Men do not despise a thief, if he steal to satisfy his soul when he is hungry; but if he be found, he shall restore sevenfold; he shall give all the substance of the house. But whoso committeth adultery with a woman lacketh understanding; he that doeth it destroyeth his own soul. A wound and dishonor shall he get; and his reproach shall not be wiped away. For jealousy is the rage of a man; therefore he will not spare in the day of vengeance. He will not regard any ransom, neither will he rest content, though thou givest many gifts. (6:26–35)

Many a man's downfall can be traced to an initial act of adultery. Satan has used this trap on men for thousands of years. Even though it has caused men great pain and suffering, somehow men still think they can fornicate without consequences. Scripture warns, however: "Be not deceived, God is not mocked, for whatsoever a man soweth, that shall he also reap. For he that soweth to the flesh shall of the flesh reap corruption . . ." (Gal. 6:7–8a). There are huge and terrible consequences for the breaking of this commandment. Some of the consequences are: confusion, a growing lust, poverty, disease, and death. Jay Adams writes: "'It won't happen to me,' you say? Well, read verses 27 and 28. In one way or another, sexual evil will turn back on you. You *will* be burned by it. Incidentally, these two verses would be ideal for counselees to memorize as portable truth to use in the hour of temptation. At that time these verses will *talk* to them, speaking volumes!"[16]

In verse 26, we see the third and final man in the chapter who will miss the harvest. All of his wealth and possessions are gone. He lost it all because of adultery. People laugh and tell dirty jokes about the sin of adultery. *Wise* men and women do not laugh at these jokes, however. They know something of the misery that this sin causes the human race. How many children are out there in our society who are suffering mentally because one or both parents are missing from the home due to a sin called adultery? How many do *you* know? Have you heard a little boy sob and say, "Where's Daddy? Why doesn't he come to see me?" Let me tell you about some innocent young children. They haven't had much to be happy about for quite a while. They miss their mother. She found another man. She hasn't been around for weeks. Today, however, the children are excited. Mother promised that she would come and visit! The children wait, and wait, and wait. It gets late. It's dark. She didn't come! She promised! The children are crushed. Their spirits are broken. They are hurt and confused. They feel so helpless. You ask yourself with great concern, "What will ever become of these poor, heartbroken children?", but you have no answer. Then you ask yourself, "What is the reason behind this broken home?" This time you have an answer. The answer is adultery. Everybody loses with this sin. The biggest losers, however, are the innocent children.

The adulterous man in verse 26 has lost any hope of a harvest. He's lost everything. He has learned too late that immorality carries a high price tag. The time finally comes in life when he should be enjoying the fruits of all of his labor, but he's broke. His net worth is a "piece of bread" (v. 26). The sin of adultery started him on a downhill slide that left him with an empty bank account in his older age.

Solomon wisely taught his son these solemn truths. With a thousand immoral voices in our pagan society aimed at seducing the morals of our youth, it is crucial that we give them God's plan to keep them from immorality. If parents want their children to grow up morally clean and to love God, they should help them to memorize key portions of Holy Scripture that deal with this subject. Verses about the evil woman, her beauty, her flattering tongue, and her enticing ways should be memorized. "Bind them continually upon thy heart . . ." the heavenly Father tells us through Solomon. God's Word has the power to keep the individual on track throughout life. When harvest time comes, the individual who was faithful to God's warnings, commandments, and exhortations will not be empty handed. He will have some assets paid for and the love and respect of family.

A Comparison of the Three Types of Men in Proverbs 6 Who Missed the Harvest

Type	Outstanding Characteristic	Result
The Lazy Man	No Ambition	Poverty (v. 11)
The Ungodly Man	No God	Early Death (v. 15)
The Adulterous Man	No Morals	Poverty, Dishonor (vv. 26,33)

Each experienced unfulfilled desires:	
The Lazy Man	Had desires that were not met (Prov. 13:4)
The Ungodly Man	Had desires that knew no ending (Prov. 6:14)
The Adulterous Man	Had desires that could not be satisfied

Each failed to consider the age-old law of sowing and reaping:

Be not deceived, God is not mocked, for whatsoever a man soweth, that shall he also reap.

— Galatians 6:7

7 | The Young Man Who Lacked Wisdom

Say It Over and Over Again

My son, keep my words, and lay my commandments with thee. Keep my commandments, and live, and my law as the apple of thine eye. Bind them upon thy fingers, write them upon the table of thine heart. Say unto wisdom, Thou art my sister, and call understanding thy kinswoman, that they may keep thee from the strange woman, from the foreigner who flattereth with her words. (7:1–5)

N otice how quickly here in chapter seven the Holy Spirit (the author of the Word) focuses our attention on training the youth. We can open our Bibles to any one of these early chapters in Proverbs, read a few words, and without any introduction or explanation, find ourselves *immediately* in the midst of a parent-child training session.

Once you have discovered this important truth, you will probably never be able to open your Bible to these chapters again without being aware of it. When the Holy Spirit emphasizes something, you can be sure that He has a specific reason for doing so. Why in these chapters does the Holy Spirit so quickly and so definitely draw our attention to a parent teaching a child godly values? It is because the task of godly training (or "wisdom" training) in the home is absolutely crucial in raising children. Without this godly training, it is almost certain that as the child grows into a young adult, he or she will be engulfed in, wrapped up with, and indoctrinated by the prevailing godless culture of the day with all of its evils.

Many children are exposed to Christian teachings for a few hours each week in a church. This is valuable training for the children but falls short of the mark. If Sunday school and church attendance were all that our children needed, I'm sure that the Holy Spirit would have placed all of His emphasis upon the family worshipping at the temple. But where do we find the Holy Spirit placing the emphasis? He has placed the emphasis on the parents training their children in the home. Although it is true that many of our children attend church for a few hours each week, it is also true that they spend the rest of their week in a culture that is characterized by godlessness. The lyrics of the songs that they listen to, the movies that they watch, the schools that they attend, and the culture in which they live reject the moral teachings of the Word of God, and they reject the God of the Word.

Let us consider a child of God who grows up in the environment just described. He will enter adulthood with very little of God's wisdom in his heart. He will, however, carry into adulthood some Christian beliefs from his earlier training. He will normally believe in the Bible and in heaven and in hell. His Christian beliefs, however, will not affect his life-style very much. These beliefs will not, for the most part, be at the center of his heart but in the peripheral areas. At the center of his heart will be the philosophy of the pagan culture. Instead of being a testimony to the lost and a light to shine in a dark world, his life-style will blend with the life-style of the surrounding pagans. Since he was saved in childhood, God's Spirit will be in him as he goes through life. His parents, however, did not teach him to plant the words of God deep into his heart. He therefore never learned how to walk with God. He will grow up then as many "churched" children do, with a "life focus" on self rather than on Christ. Having adapted the philosophy of the lost world, he finds ways to "excuse" his sin. He knows his life-style is wrong, yet he continually attempts to justify it in his own mind.

What happens when a believer grows up without having God's Word written upon his heart? (Prov. 7:3):

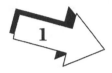

He *will* have the *Spirit* of God in his life. (Eph. 1:13–14)

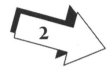

He will *not* have the *sense* of *God's presence* in his life. (1 John 1:6)

His childhood Christian beliefs will be *greatly compromised* (especially in the area of morals). (Compare 2 Pet. 2:7–8)

His sinful life will be *synthetically sanitized.* (He finds ways to excuse his sins) (Compare Prov. 21:2, 28:13, 30:12, Jer. 2:13)

His testimony to a lost world will be *completely neutralized.* (Compare Gen. 19:14, Matt. 5:16, 1 Cor. 15:33, Phil. 2:15)

Do you know any believers like that? Most of us do. This is the reason why, here in Proverbs, the Holy Spirit is emphasizing the fact that parents need to teach Scripture to their children in the home. Furthermore, they need to teach these things to their children not once, not twice, but over and over again, just as this father did. Repetition "makes it stick." Doctor Mark Cambron, speaking at Florida Bible College, once said: "Repetition is theological mucilage."

The godly father knows the importance of getting the Word of God into his son's heart (mind).

Wisdom training includes:

- The Word of God
- Modeling the life
- Repetition

Put God's Word deep into your heart

Repetition is powerful. The ancient Near Eastern father in Proverbs knew this. He spent time going over the key issues with his son again and again.

It is also important that we as parents "practice what we teach." We should be good examples to our children. Children are smarter than we often give them credit for. If we aren't honoring God in some area of our life, they will probably spot it. Children will not take the things of God seriously if they see hypocrisy in our lives. A godly father will model the Christian life to his family. When we are *consistent* in our personal lives, and *persistent* in training our children in the home, the Word of God will find a resting place deep in their minds. They will certainly grow then in wisdom.

The "Heart" Issue

*. . . write them upon the table of **thine heart.** (Prov. 7:3)*

*Keep **thy heart** with all diligence, for out of it are the issues of life. (Prov. 4:23)*

*For from within, **out of the heart** of men, proceed evil thoughts, adulteries, fornications, murders, thefts, covetousness, wickedness, deceit, an evil eye, blasphemy, pride, foolishness. All of these evil things come from within, and defile the man. (Mark 7:21–23)*

The following diagrams should help us to understand the "heart" (mind) issue more clearly.

Human Wisdom

The Black Circle = the mind and views of an average lost person within our "human wisdom-based" culture. Within this culture the "things of God are viewed as foolishness" (1 Cor. 2:13–14).

Divine Wisdom

The White Circle = a value system that is based on God's Word. This is godly wisdom.

A young person's value system is still being formed as he grows from adolescence to adulthood. If he does not have the Lord in his life and receive "wisdom" training from the Bible, he will develop a value system that is in great conflict with his Creator. Since he inherited a corrupt nature from his parents (as all of us did), he will by that nature be drawn toward the wrong things. Ungodliness will grow in his heart (mind).

The mind of the lost person is spiritually dark. (Eph. 4:18)

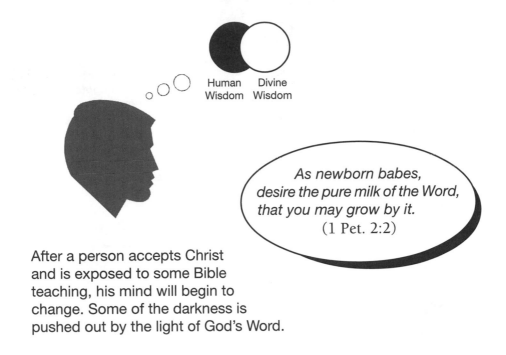

After a person accepts Christ and is exposed to some Bible teaching, his mind will begin to change. Some of the darkness is pushed out by the light of God's Word.

When a young person accepts Christ as Savior and begins to learn some truths from Scripture lessons at the local church, his worldly value system will be challenged. Some of his ideas will quickly change. He will still be living each week, however, in a culture that is radically different from the teachings of the Bible. Unless this young person somehow learns to hide the Word of God in his heart, he will reach adulthood with a value system that is more like the world than it is like Christ. In adulthood, his life-style will not be so very different from the life-style of the unsaved. His thought life will be impure. He may be immoral in his life-style. He may use drugs or alcohol. He may have a string of broken marriages. His parents, if Christians, will no doubt be confused and ask themselves, "Why?" I have known of many such parents who, with breaking hearts, have lamented, "We took our children to Sunday school and church every Sunday, but they have grown up and are living awful lives. What did we do wrong?"

Unfortunately, most of us in ministry have not successfully instilled within our parishioners the importance of "wisdom training" in the home. We have not sounded the alarm. We have not emphasized from our pulpits that the devil is seeking our young people. He walks about this godless, dark culture like a roaring lion "seeking whom he may devour" (1 Pet. 5:8). We have not taught our people that the Lord commands parents to train their children in His Word in the home. Further, we have not taught our people *how* to have family devotions.

There are two possible reasons why we have not done these things. The first reason is a sin called "neglect." The sin of neglect occurs when we know what to do, but we just don't do it. Ignorance is the second reason. Perhaps many of us in ministry have somehow missed the importance of encouraging our church families to establish a family altar. Perhaps we have been ignorant of the model that the Lord has given us in the Book of Proverbs. If we have been ignorant, it is probably because we have not walked as close to the Lord as we should. Surely, the Good Shepherd will direct His pastors to the proper food to feed His sheep, but have we been listening? Have we been sensitive to His leading in this area? Obviously, many of us have not.

We watch in amazement as teenagers and young adults turn away from the Lord and His church and pursue ungodly life-styles. Many of these grew up in our churches from infancy. They heard our Sunday school lessons, and they heard our sermons each Sunday. They lived, however, all week, every week, in a godless culture. If somehow we could have influenced the parents to have had devotions and a Bible memorization program in the home while the children were growing up, many of them never would have strayed from the Lord.

I call upon those of us in ministry who have failed to teach our people this great truth to repent on our faces before God. Let us, with God's help, begin to correct this wrong immediately. There are few issues in our churches as pressing as this one. Let us preach on the importance of family devotions, and let us develop some classes to teach our families how. Let us give public recognition to the families that are consistent with "wisdom training," using them as models for the congregation.

An Encouraging Word to Parents

There is an old Pennsylvania Dutch epigram that says, "We get too soon old, and too late smart." Many Christian parents are walking around feeling defeated because their children have grown up and have left the ways of the Lord. These parents have concluded: "We got too late smart." Their hearts are grieving over the low living of their offspring. These parents should not, however, give up hope for their adult children. Countless wonderful stories can be told of wayward children coming back to the Lord after years of wandering aimlessly in sin. God delights in answering our prayers. I believe that wayward sons and daughters all over America and all over the world could be reclaimed for the Lord if parents and grandparents would begin to "pray without ceasing" (1 Thess. 5:17).

How wonderfully forgiving our Lord is. He is always ready to recover a wayward son or daughter who returns to Him. All that the wayward child of God has to do is turn his or her heart toward God and say, "Lord, I have sinned and I have been away from You, but I am now coming back to You." Whenever a believer who is out of fellowship with the Lord will turn his heart toward God and pray a sincere prayer of repentance, he is forgiven, cleansed, and restored. The loving heavenly Father welcomes the prodigal son or daughter back without exception with open arms.

That son or daughter, cleansed by Almighty God and freshly endued with the power of the Holy Spirit, can have a brand new start in life. Parents sometimes have prayed for years that this very thing would happen. When it does, they often watch in utter amazement as they see their wayward child day by day becoming a totally new person in Christ.

Are you a parent with an adult child who is not walking with the Lord? Although that child may be wrapped up in an ungodly life-style, if he (or she) truly accepted Christ in earlier years, God's Spirit is still residing in the heart (Gal. 4:6, 2 Cor. 1:22) and will ultimately convict him (or her) of the sin that is there (John 16:8–11). May I suggest that you do the following? First, confess your parental shortcomings (all of us have some!). Second, accept the

Lord's forgiveness and put all the mistakes of the past behind you. Third, pray diligently for your child. Pray that God's Spirit will work powerfully in your son's or daughter's life and by his catalytic action bring about a full repentance. It may happen quickly, or it may take years. Keep praying, and keep believing God. I believe your sincere prayers to the Lord will eventually be rewarded.

> God's Spirit still resides in the heart of the disobedient child of God and will ultimately convict him (or her) of the sin that is there. (Gal. 4:6, 2 Cor. 1:22, John16:8–11)

Let us look now at what happens when a young person accepts the Lord into his life and begins to grow in God's wisdom. A few young people will grow on their own; most, however, have to be taught. God has assigned this responsibility to the parents.

What to do if you have an adult child who is not walking with the Lord:

- Confess your shortcomings.

- Accept the Lord's forgiveness and put the mistakes of the past behind you.

- Pray diligently for your child.

Growing in Wisdom

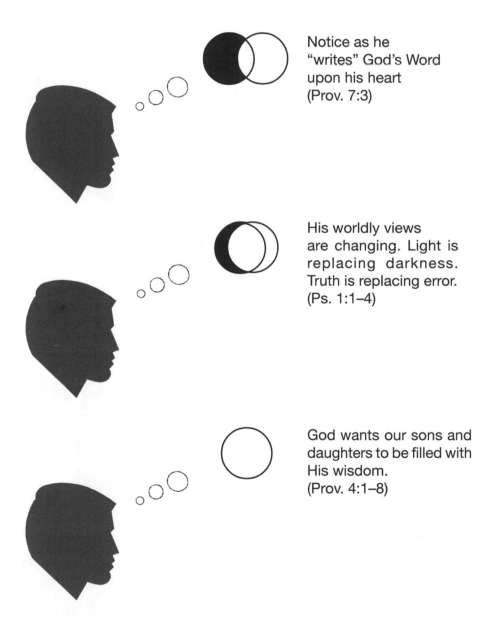

Notice as he "writes" God's Word upon his heart (Prov. 7:3)

His worldly views are changing. Light is replacing darkness. Truth is replacing error. (Ps. 1:1–4)

God wants our sons and daughters to be filled with His wisdom. (Prov. 4:1–8)

Light and Darkness

In these opening verses of Proverbs 7, Solomon has once again proclaimed quite eloquently that God's Word, when placed in the heart, brings wisdom and has the power to keep a young man from sexual immorality. These are the verses of *light* in the chapter. The subject in verses 1–4 is God's Word, and His Word always brings *light*. In verse five, the subject changes from the words of God to the words of the flatterer. There is also a transition from *light* to *twilight*. As we proceed now into the rest of the chapter, the light quickly fades, and the scene dramatically shifts to a *black* and *dark night* (v. 9).

A Young Man Void of Understanding

Solomon is about to relate to his children (v. 24) a story about a young man who was not prepared for life. We know that he did not have God's Word in his heart, for he was "void of understanding." The story begins in verse six.

> *For at the window of my house I looked through my casement, and beheld among the simple ones, I discerned among the youths, a young man void of understanding, passing through the street near her corner; and he went the way to her house.* (7:6–8169)

The Young Man Is Headed in the Wrong Direction

The first thing that we are told about this young man is that he was "void of understanding." He did not know the Lord. He did not know the Word. He did not know that a loving, all-powerful Creator had fashioned him for a purpose. He did not know that he was made to have fellowship with God. Although he was young, his heart was already filling up with the ungodly sins of the surrounding culture. Other men, you see, had been acting unknowingly as agents for "the evil one" in this young man's life. These men, both young and old, were also "void of understanding." They were all glad to corrupt his young mind with their evil thoughts and deeds. Jesus, you remember, told us that "the mouth speaks out of that which fills the heart" (Matt. 12:34 NAS). These men, speaking from their sin-filled hearts, planted wicked, ungodly thoughts into the heart of this youth. The heart of a young man "void of understanding" is fertile ground for the seeds of sinful thoughts to germinate, and germinate they did. This young man had been thinking unclean, lustful thoughts. When we first meet him, he is already heading in the wrong direction. We see him passing through the street near her corner, that is near the corner of the prostitute.

The young man in this story represents young men contemporary with the culture and with the times of the reader. This young man, then, represents young men of our day. Do you know a young man who is headed the wrong direction? Perhaps he hasn't done anything bad yet, but you sense that it is only a question of time before he does. The young man in this story has historically represented young men of any generation who are headed in the wrong direction.

The Outside Force

Sir Isaac Newton developed the "law of inertia." This law states that an object that is moving in a certain direction will continue to move in that direction unless acted upon by some "outside force." Apply Sir Isaac's law to a young man whose mind and feet are headed in the wrong direction. In the absence of an "outside force," he will continue to move in the direction of moral and physical danger. There are many "outside forces" that God can use to bring a young person to salvation and a change of direction. Some of these would be: A mother, a dad, a grandparent, an older brother or sister, an aunt or uncle, a church friend, a pastor, a Sunday school teacher, or a youth worker. The ultimate "outside force" that God uses in a young person's life, however, is the Holy Spirit. Normally, the Holy Spirit works in cooperation with someone who is willing to be a force for good in the young person's life. Working together, a soul is saved or a saint restored, and a young life is brought back from the brink of moral, and possibly physical, disaster.

Are you an "outside force" for God? The young person who you know is headed down the wrong direction will, in the absence of an outside force, continue to move in that same direction. Will you pray and ask God to give you the privilege of working with Him as an outside force in the life of some young person? After you have prayed, take the next appropriate steps, as the Holy Spirit directs. It will mean spending some time with that young person. It will mean showing that person Christian love. It will mean exposing that young man or woman to some key passages that are relative to his or her need. Most of all it will simply mean that you are placing yourself at the Holy Spirit's disposal to use you in the life of that young person anyway He chooses to.

The Young Man Is Going Out at the Wrong Time

In the twilight, in the evening, in the black and dark of night. . . .
(7:9)

It is good for men to be home at night where they will not be tempted to sin. It is especially important for young, single men to be home at night away from the temptations that cause "youthful lusts" (2 Tim. 2:22). I remember very vividly the night that I was lost in the downtown area of a large American city. I had my wife and three children with me. We had never been in the area before. I must have made a wrong turn, for suddenly we had no idea where we were, and we quickly became fearful. My biggest concern was the deviant-looking individuals who were loitering on every corner in the area. When the black of night came, these individuals left their dwelling places and took to the streets. I couldn't help but think of the roaches that hide in the woodwork by day and come out at night. Sexual activity seemed to be the goal of these individuals. With our windows up, and our doors locked, and all five of us praying up a storm, we drove and drove and finally found our way out of the area. "Lust hates the light," said Rev. A.R. Fausset, "being conscious of its own guilt."[1] When the sun goes down, the creatures of darkness come out. "The sinner," said Rev. Fausset, thinks no eye can see him in the dark, but God's eye is upon him

(Ps. 139:120)."[2] Not only is this young man headed in the wrong direction, he is also going out at the wrong time. We find him going out "in the black and dark night" (v. 9). The devil's demons swarm after dark, then quickly dissipate to search for fresh victims and new converts. We have left now the "verses of light" in this chapter (vv. 1–4). In verse nine, we see the light give way to twilight only to be followed quickly by the black and dark night. The rest of this ancient story takes place at night.

> *And behold, there met him a woman with the attire of an harlot, and subtle of heart. (She is loud and stubborn; her feet abide not in her house; now is she outside, now in the streets, and lieth in wait at every corner.) So she caught him, and kissed him, and with an impudent face said unto him, I have peace offerings with me; this day have I paid my vows. Therefore came I forth to meet with thee, diligently to seek thy face, and I have found thee. I have decked my bed with coverings of tapestry, with embroidered works, with fine linen of Egypt. I have perfumed my bed with myrrh, aloes, and cinnamon. Come, let us take our fill of love until the morning; let us solace ourselves with love. For my husband is not at home; he is gone on a long journey. He hath taken a bag of money with him, and will come home at the day appointed. (7:10–20)*

The young man had been traveling down the wrong path, and he had been desiring the wrong things. Traveling down wrong paths will ultimately place a person right smack in the face of temptation. The devil will see to that. This young man went out at night seeking fellowship with darkness, only to discover that darkness was seeking fellowship with him. As he proceeds to the very street the harlot lives on (he shouldn't have done that! Proverbs 5:8), this creature of darkness was there to greet him and to lure him into evil activities.

There is here in verse 10 a shift of focus. The author of Scripture, the Holy Spirit, diverts our attention from the young man and in verses 10–21 focuses on the harlot. There are obviously certain things about the harlot that the Holy Spirit wants young men to know.

Hollywood, television, Broadway, and the rest of the entertainment world regularly glamorize the prostitute. They portray her in such a way that she is to be desired, not shunned. Many people are quick to point out (often with a devilish grin) that "she represents the world's oldest profession, you know." That is not a true statement, but is often repeated by people who haven't thought it through.

The minds of evil men feed eagerly on the perverted theme of the prostitute as a heroine. Let's look now at the thing that the Holy Spirit wants young men to know about her.

The Harlot

1. She is immodest in her dress. (v. 10)

Matthew Henry comments: "The purity of the heart will show itself in the modesty of the dress. . . ."[3] The shameless exposure of her body aroused the young man sexually, creating within him lust, passion, and desire.

2. She is immodest in her speech. (v. 11)

"Instead of the soft and gentle voice of feminine modesty, she is 'loud,' and full of words flowing from assurance. A modest woman shrinks from undue publicity . . ."[4] writes Rev. A.R. Fausset. She is self-willed, and does not want anybody to lecture her. She thinks that she has all the answers.

3. She is immodest with her actions. (v. 13)

Scripture says, "She caught him." The Hebrew word here that is translated "caught" suggests that she "seized him." She put her arms around him, embraced him tightly (as the Hebrew word suggests), and kissed him. The young man was no doubt filled with the mixed emotions of fear and excitement. His God-given conscience was probably screaming at him and warning him, "Get out! Get out while you still can! Danger! Danger!" Sensing what conscience was saying to the young man, she clutched him even tighter, fearing that her human prey may escape. "No! I am not about to let that happen," she tells herself, holding the young man close.

4. She is immodest with her appeals. (vv. 14–20)

This woman (would you believe?) is religious (v. 14). She claims that she has been to the temple and has fulfilled her vows to God. The "varnish of religion," states Charles Bridges, "is often a cover for sin. . . . Beware of any voice, though from the most revered quarter, that manifestly encourages forbidden indulgence."[5] She has used religion to "candy coat" her sin, as millions of people do today. While the young man's conscience is sounding the alarm, the harlot has long ago learned to silence the voice of her conscience with her religious activities. This "religious harlot" has deceived herself concerning her sin (1 John 1:8).

She proceeds to offer the young man the very sinful things he has been fantasizing about. The unclean thoughts that have so often occupied his mind, she now offers to him in the flesh. Many who have read this text have been shocked with her boldness and disgusted with her filthiness. She is brazen and wicked. She, without any sense of shame, encourages the young man to break God's seventh commandment (Exod. 20:14). "Come," she pleads, promising forbidden pleasures. The Savior's invitation to "come" is an invitation to eternal life (Matt. 19:21, John 7:37–38, Rev. 22:17). The harlot's invitation to "come" is an invitation to death and hell (Prov. 7:27).

The Young Man Gives in to Temptation

With her much fair speech she caused him to yield; with the flattering of her lips she forced him. He goeth after straightway, as an ox goeth to the slaughter, or as a fool to the corruption of the stocks, till an arrow strike through his liver—as a bird hasteneth to the snare, and knoweth not that it is for his life. Hearken unto me now, therefore, O ye children, and attend to the words of my mouth. Let not thine heart decline to her ways; go not astray in her paths. For she hath cast down many wounded; yea, many strong men have been slain by her. Her house is the way to sheol, going down to the chambers of death. (7:21–27)

This creature of darkness has spun her web effectively. With her words, her lips, and with her body pressed tightly against this young man, he succumbs to temptation. The burning lust within him is now a more powerful force than the voice of conscience. The wicked woman will be used by Satan tonight, as she introduces the young man to the dark world of sexual immorality.

There is a special communiqué from God to men in v. 21. Here God lets us know, as He does elsewhere, that there is real power in the words of an unclean woman. This power can indeed cause a man to fail morally. As the pure Word of the living Lord is a powerful force for good, so too are the impure words of the loose woman a powerful force for evil. Beware of "flattering lips!"

The focus shifts back to the young man in verses 22–23. We see him going after her "straightway" in verse 22. The Hebrew word translated "straightway" in this verse means "suddenly." We see the young man yielding his will to her in verse 21. Having ignored conscience and being inflamed with lust, he "suddenly" goes after her.

The Young Man Is Ruined Morally

The young man will have his night of pleasure, but the cost to him will be tremendous. As the ox unknowingly goes to be slaughtered, as the fool goes unknowingly to the correction of the stocks, as the bird goes unknowingly to the snare, the foolish young man "goeth after her." He doesn't know "that it is for his life." Matthew Henry said: "It is his life, his precious life, that is thus irrecoverably thrown away, he is perfectly lost to all good, his conscience is debauched; a door is opened to all other vices, and this will certainly end in his endless damnation."[6]

Solomon makes another appeal to the children to beware of the trap of the harlot (vv. 24–27). I want to point out once again that this is a "heart" issue. "Let not *thine heart*," Solomon warns, "decline to her ways." She has, he tells us, wounded many, and she has slain many. That is precisely why this father has warned his sons: "Come not near the door of her house" (Prov. 5:8).

The deceptive ways of Satan are seen throughout this story. The harlot's bed looks beautiful with its coverings of tapestry and the fine Egyptian linen. It's even perfumed with myrrh, aloes, and cinnamon (vv. 16–17). Her house, however, is a "death house" (v. 27). Satan makes sin look so wonderful, but he never shows his victims the end result. "Sin, when it is finished, bringeth forth death" (James 1:15). So how does the story of the young man who lacked wisdom end in Proverbs 7? He dies before his time. The last word of the last verse is "death." The story of the foolish young man ends in death. The message from God to young people in these verses is this: Sexual sin can and often does lead to a premature death.

8 | Winning the Children to Christ

Proclamation vv. 1–5

Exhortation vv. 6–12

Consideration v. 13

Explanation vv. 14–31

Invitation vv. 32–36

This chapter develops like an arrow, pointing the children to the Lord and salvation.

Permit little children, and forbid them not, to come unto me.
(Matt. 19:14)

And He laid His hands on them.
(Matt. 19:15)

Hearken unto me, O ye children; for blessed are they who keep my ways.
(Prov. 8:32)

I am the Way– the Truth– and the Life.
(John 14:6)

In this chapter, Christ addresses the children and invites them to Himself.

We have now studied the first seven chapters of Proverbs. We could not help but notice the great effort that has been put forth in these chapters to win the children to the Lord. David has been involved in this effort. Solomon has been a large part of this effort. Lady Wisdom has also been involved. Behind all of this holy effort, however, is the Lord Himself. He is always the one who motivates willing parents to win the children to faith in the Son of God and to win them to godly living.

We have also discovered in these chapters that there is an opposing force at work behind the scenes. This opposing force seeks to win the hearts of the youth away from the Lord. In Scripture as in life, the force that opposes the work of God is always Satan. We see him in these chapters working his evil through various individuals. Although these individuals are probably not aware of it, their agenda is really Satan's agenda. Ungodliness is their goal. They seek to corrupt and ruin the morals of the young and lead them into sin and folly. They prey especially on the innocent, the weak, and the undecided. We see Satan promoting his dark agenda through "sinners" (1:10–19), "evil" men (2:12–15), "scoffers" (1:22), "fools" (1:22), the "wicked" (2:22, 4:14–17, 19, 6:12), the "transgressors" (2:22), and the unclean woman (2:16–19, 5:3–14, 6:24–26, 7:5–27).

In these early chapters, we have witnessed a concentrated effort put forth to win the children to the Lord and the godly life. Almighty God in chapter after chapter gives us picture after picture of a father teaching godliness in the home. We see the father promoting the good things and warning against the bad things. Time after time, we see him teaching the things of God in the home. The single greatest truth for parents that God is emphasizing in these early chapters of Proverbs is this: If you want your children to grow up and live godly lives and not get messed up by Satan, you must spend time with them night after night. You must show them in the Bible what God has to say about temptation, sin, and all the affairs of life. This training in the home takes a little time and effort each day, but the results are well worth it. God is willing to help any parent succeed with a family altar.

This chapter develops like an arrow pointing the children to the Lord and salvation. We will see in this chapter that Christ addresses the children and invites them to Himself. We will identify five separate sections as the "arrow" of God develops in this chapter.

Section One: Proclamation

Doth not wisdom cry, and understanding put forth her voice? She standeth in the top of high places, by the way in the places of the paths. She crieth at the gates, at the entry of the city, at the entrance of the doors. Unto you, O men, I call, and my voice is to the sons of man. O ye simple, understand wisdom; and, ye fools, be ye of an understanding heart. (8:1–5)

Solomon is the speaker (Prov. 1:1). We see him once again in his now familiar role as a father training his children (v. 32). The setting is yet another "wisdom training" session at "Mom and Dad University."

Solomon once again mentions the mystery woman—"Lady Wisdom" (8:1). The focus is upon her as chapter eight opens. We see her here not in an inactive, passive role, but in a very active one. We see her here as an orator. First we see her standing in a high place at an intersection where two or more paths converge. She cries out from her elevated pulpit, and as the people pass by they hear her message. Then we see her "at the gates," at the very entrance of the city. Here, at the city's entrance, she cries out to the people entering and exiting the city. She has a message to proclaim (1:20–22, 8:3–5). It is a message from God. Take notice that whenever Lady Wisdom speaks, she speaks for God.

Section Two: Exhortation

Hear; for I will speak of excellent things, and the opening of my lips shall be right things. For my mouth shall speak truth, and wickedness is an abomination to my lips. All the words of my mouth are in righteousness; there is nothing crooked or perverse in them. They are all plain to him that understandeth, and right to those who find knowledge. Receive my instruction, and not silver; and knowledge rather than choice gold. For wisdom is better than rubies; and all the things that may be desired are not to be compared to it. I, wisdom, dwell with prudence, and find out knowledge of witty inventions. (8:6–12)

Her exhortation is to "hear." She promises to speak of excellent things. As a spokeswoman for God, her words of "excellent things" are not her words at all, but are God's words. Notice they are without error. There is nothing crooked about them (v. 8). Lady Wisdom cries out that men should "hear" her, because she is about to speak words of truth, wisdom, and righteousness. Jay Adams states that she "describes her instruction as important. What could be more so than God's own words of wisdom? They are important for all of life."[1]

Once again, we are told that wisdom is to be valued above silver, gold, or rubies. Wisdom, we are told, is more valuable than anything that the heart can desire. Absolutely nothing can compare to God's wisdom (v. 11). Matthew Henry said: "Whatever we can sit down and wish for of the wealth of this world would, if we had it, be unworthy to be compared with the advantages that attend serious godliness."[2] Proverbs 16:16 says: "How much better is it to get wisdom than gold! And to get understanding is rather to be chosen than silver." These verses and other similar verses clearly teach that the truths of God's Word are far more important than anything else that one could possibly desire. "More to be desired are they (the words of God) than gold, yea, than much fine gold; sweeter also than honey and the honeycomb" (Ps. 19:10).

Section Three: Consideration

The fear of the Lord is to hate evil; pride, and arrogance, and the evil way, and the perverse mouth, do I hate. (8:13)

Verse 13 stands all by itself on this chapter. The Holy Spirit put it there for a very important reason. The subject of this verse is the fear of the Lord. This is a good place to stop and have a "spiritual check-up." The fear of the Lord is related to our salvation and our personal relationship with Him. Take a moment and read verse 13 again, and as you do, ask yourself, "Do I hate evil, pride, and arrogance in *my* life, as well as in the lives of others?" If your answer is anything other than "yes," then God has just revealed to you that your fear of the Lord is not what it should be. Matthew Henry said, "Everyone hates them (evil, pride, arrogance) in others, but we must hate them in ourselves. . . . Whenever there is an awe of God, there is a dread of sin, as an evil, as only evil."[3]

In the cemetery that surrounds the old church at Plymouth, Massachusetts is a tombstone with a very interesting epitaph. My wife and I discovered it while visiting the many wonderful historic sites in the area. The cemetery dates back to the early years of our country. Here is an approximate quote from the tombstone: "Stop and consider as you pass by, as you are now, so once was I. As I am now, you soon shall be. Prepare your soul for eternity." Reading the epitaph here probably doesn't cause you to think deeply about eternal matters, but it would if you read it on that weathered tombstone in the middle of the oldest cemetery in New England. That thought-provoking statement in that cemetery setting caused me, as a young man in my early twenties, to really think about some important issues. "Stop and consider," the epitaph begins. That is good advice. Proverbs 8:13 is a good place also to "stop and consider." Read the verse again. If your fear of the Lord is not what it should be, the reason is one of two things: 1. You have not really experienced Christ in salvation, or 2. Your personal relationship with the Lord is lacking. If either of these is true in your life, I would like to encourage you to speak to a pastor or a Christian friend.

Section Four: Explanation

Counsel is mine, and sound wisdom. I am understanding; I have strength. By me kings reign, and princes decree justice. By me princes rule, and nobles, even all the judges of the earth. I love those who love me, and those who seek me early shall find me. Riches and honor are with me; yea, durable riches and righteousness. My fruit is better than gold, yea than fine gold; and my revenue than choice silver. I lead in the way of righteousness, in the midst of the paths of justice, that I might cause those who love me to inherit substance; and I will fill their treasuries. The Lord possessed me in the beginning of His way, before His works of old. I was set up from everlasting, from the beginning, or ever the earth was. When there were no depths, I was brought forth—when there were fountains abounding with water. Before the mountains were settled, before the hills, was I brought forth; while as yet He had not made the earth, nor the fields, nor the highest part of the dust of the world. When He prepared the heavens, I was there; when He set a compass upon the face of the depth; when

He established the clouds above; when He strengthened the fountains of the deep; when He gave to the sea its decree, that the waters should not pass His commandment; when He appointed the foundations of the earth, then I was by Him, as one brought up with Him; and I was daily His delight, rejoicing always before Him, rejoicing in the habitable part of His earth; and my delight was with the sons of men." (8:14–31)

Lady Wisdom is first seen in Proverbs chapter one. She can be seen there in a setting similar to the setting here in chapter eight. In chapter one, she is seen "in the streets" (v. 20) and at "the gates" of the city (v. 21). She is seen crying out the divine message to the unsaved. We have already noted that when she speaks, she speaks for God. Actually, it is the Lord speaking through her. The more she speaks, the more we realize that it is really the Lord speaking. For example, it is clearly Lady Wisdom speaking in Proverbs 1:22, but look who is speaking in the next verse (1:23). It is YHWH Himself. "I will pour out my Spirit unto you . . ." He states. So first we see Lady Wisdom speaking, then suddenly the Lord is speaking, and He continues to speak until the chapter ends.

We find Lady Wisdom in an almost identical role in Proverbs chapter eight. Early in this eighth chapter, we see her proclaiming her urgent message to all who pass by. As we continue reading, we suddenly realize: "Why, this is not Lady Wisdom speaking anymore. She was speaking before, but now it is Christ speaking." As we look at the next section, we will discover that indeed it is the Son of God who is speaking. Here in this Old Testament book, Christ Himself tells us who He is.

He Is the All-Knowing One. (v. 14)

Charles Bridges states: "It is not that He *hath understanding* to order and govern the world. But *He is understanding.* All is in Him. All is derivable from Him."[4]

Christ was, as we pointed out earlier, "wisdom" personified (1 Cor. 1:24). He is the counselor in Proverbs 8:14 and in Isaiah 9:6. He knows the thoughts of all men (Ps. 94:11, Matt. 9:4, 12:25, Luke 5:22, 6:8, 11:17).

He Is the All-Powerful One. (vv. 14–16)

"He removeth kings, and setteth up kings" (Dan. 2:21). Kings do indeed reign by Him. Proverbs 21:1 tells us that "the king's heart is in the hand of the Lord, like the rivers of water; He turneth it withersoever He will." Charles Bridges said, "The government of the world is on the shoulders of the Head of the church" (Isa. 9:6).[5] Pilate had no idea when Jesus stood before him, that he would one day *kneel* before Jesus (John 18:28–19:16, Phil. 2:9–11). When the Son of God makes His dramatic return to earth on the white horse described in Revelation 19, He will be followed by an army from heaven also seated upon white horses. On Christ's garment shall be these words: "KING OF KINGS, AND LORD OF LORDS" (Rev. 19:11–16).

YHWH's creation is the subject in verses 24–29. And how did YHWH create the heavens and the earth? He "created all things by Jesus Christ" (Eph. 3:9). The New Testament affirms again and again that Jesus Christ is the all-powerful Creator. John tells us that "*all* things were made *by Him*, and *without Him was not anything made* that was made" (John 1:3). The writer of Hebrews tells us that God "made the worlds by His Son." Paul informs us that "*by Him* were *all things created*, that are in heaven, and that are in earth, visible and invisible, whether they be thrones, or dominions, or principalities, or powers—*all things were created by Him and for Him*" (Col. 1:16).

Christ's work as Creator in verse 30 is not seen as clearly in the King James Version as it is in some of the later translations. The King James Version quotes the Son of God as saying: "Then I was by Him, as one brought up with Him." Here are three other translations of the text:

New King James: "Then I was beside Him as a *master craftsman.*"

New International Version: "Then I was the *craftsman* at His side.

New American Standard: "Then I was beside Him as a *master workman.*"

He Is the One Who Loves Us. (v. 17)

"I love those who love me," He declares (v. 17). The reason why so many people love Him is found in 1 John 4:19, which says: "We love Him, because He first loved us." The very essence of God is love. First John 4:8 states, "God is love." Christ showed His love for us at the cross by giving His very life for us. Hanging on the cross in great physical agony, with His life ebbing from His bruised body, He prayed, "Father forgive them; for they know not what they do" (Luke 23:34). Not only did we not love Him, but the Bible teaches that we were His "enemies" when He died for us (Rom. 5:10).

His transforming love is so great that others will see it in our lives as we grow in Him. Here is an amazing truth: God has given the unsaved the ability to "sense" Christ in us when they see our love. It is not enough that people see in us such things as religion, education, knowledge of Scripture, a strong belief system, well-defined personal convictions, and a separation from sin. They will not know that Christ is in us unless they see our love. Theologian Francis A. Schaeffer brought this to our attention years ago when he said, "The mark of a Christian is love." Jesus said, "By this shall all men *know* that ye are my disciples, if ye have love one to another" (John 13:35).

He Is the One Who Is Always Available to the Seeking Heart. (v. 17)

"Those who seek me early shall find me," He states (Prov. 8:17). This is a wonderful promise from the one who loves us and gave Himself for us. Whenever an individual sincerely searches for the truth, Christ will get the truth to him. Just as men love Him because He *first* loved them, the unsaved *seek* Him because He *first seeks* them. "For the son of man is come to *seek* and to save that which was lost," said Jesus (Luke 19:10). Paul encouraged the pagans of Athens to "seek the Lord." Standing on Mars Hill, he declared to them that "He (the Lord) is not far from every one of us" (Acts 17:27). He is always available in this life to the seeking heart. Even on the very last page of the Bible, we see that His message to mankind through His Spirit is "whosoever will, let him take the water of life freely."

He Is the One Who Offers Riches and Honor. (vv. 18–21)

"They shall have," says Matthew Henry, "as much riches and honor as infinite wisdom sees good for them."[6] Many believers have been blessed with riches and honor here on earth, and many haven't. All of us who know Christ, however, have a great *inheritance* (v. 21) awaiting us in heaven. Even the foundations of the wall of the heavenly city are "garnished with all manner of precious stones" (Rev. 21:19), and the street of the city is made of "pure gold" like "transparent glass" (Rev. 21:21). This incredibly beautiful city described in Revelation 21 is in your future if you have accepted Christ. He said, "I go to prepare a place for you" (John 14:2). The apostle Peter spoke about our *inheritance* in Christ. He said that our *inheritance* is "incorruptible, and undefiled." Futhermore, believer, he said it is "reserved in heaven for you" (1 Pet. 1:4).

He Is the Everlasting One. (vv. 22–30)

Before the world was created, "YHWH possessed me in the beginning of His way," Christ states in verse 22. John 1:1 declares that "In the beginning was the Word, and the Word was with God, and the Word *was* God." John 1:14 testifies that "the *Word* was made flesh and dwelt among us (and we beheld His glory, the glory as of the only begotten of the Father), full of grace and truth." The Son has co-existed with the Father for all eternity. "I and my Father are one," said Jesus (John 10:30). As YHWH has existed for all eternity past, so has Jesus Christ. Even the Old Testament prophet Isaiah, some 700 years before the birth of the Christ child, foresaw His coming and declared Him to be *The Mighty God, The Everlasting Father* (Isa. 9:6). Christ is the "everlasting" one in Proverbs 8:23.

He Is the One Who Rejoiced with the Father in Eternity Past. (vv. 30–31)

The entire chapter of John 17 is a prayer that Jesus prayed when He was on earth. His prayer included these words: "I have glorified Thee on earth; I have finished the work which Thou gavest me to do. And now, O Father, glorify Thou Me with Thine own self with the glory which I had with Thee before the world was" (John 17:4–5).

We know practically nothing about the unique relationship that YHWH and the Son had in eternity past. Here in Proverbs 8, however, for a moment, the curtain that separates our day from eternity past is drawn back, and we are allowed a rare and fascinating look at this divine association. "I was daily His delight," the Son declares. That statement reveals to us that the eternal Father was eternally pleased with the eternal Son. As we continue our glimpse into eternity past, we see the Son "rejoicing always before Him" (the Father). The Son of God has just described something that is difficult for our sinful minds to comprehend: perfect harmony. There has always been perfect harmony and unity among the persons of the Godhead. Our understanding of this great truth is expanded when we focus on some of the divine attributes:

Deity is Wisdom.	Absolute wisdom is always in agreement with absolute wisdom.
Deity is Truth.	When truth faces truth, there can be no debate.
Deity is Light.	When light meets light, all is light.
Deity is Love.	When perfect love meets perfect love, there is absolute accord.
Deity is Perfection.	When perfection meets perfection, there is no imperfection.

Perfect harmony has always existed in the Godhead. In the absence of sin, there is nothing to disrupt harmony. The Son's claim that "I was daily His delight" was confirmed centuries later by the Father at Jesus' baptism. "This is My beloved Son, in whom I am well pleased," said the voice from heaven (Matt. 3:17). Aren't you glad that He gave us this priceless glimpse into their eternal relationship? Do these words of Christ in the Old Testament thrill your heart as they do mine? His words here should fill us with awe, and create within us a desire to know Him better.

He Is the One Who Delights in Us. (v. 31)

The human race was a special creation of God. He gave us special privileges. We were even created in His image. We enjoyed a unique relationship with Him. Adam and Eve's disobedience to the Lord changed our relationship to Him, however, and ruined our standing. We became a fallen race. We willfully rebelled against the word of our Creator. Unless something was done to undo this damage, the race would be banned forever from the presence of the everlasting, holy God. We would suffer the awful consequences of our sin for all time and eternity. We had disobeyed deity. The holy trinity of heaven looked upon our plight. They saw something that the demons of hell did not see. Deity saw not only what we *were*, but what we *could become*. These creatures of sin could become new creatures in Christ!

Christ was, in fact, ordained for His great work of redeeming men "before the foundation of the world" (1 Pet. 1:20). The problem of man's sin had been discussed in the divine counsel of heaven. The persons of the Godhead were in agreement as they always are. The Son would come and pay in full the awful price for our sins that would be required by the holy and just God. There wasn't a hint of hesitation from the Son. It was simply instant agreement. Many centuries later, a man named Isaiah heard deity in counsel ask, "Whom shall I send, and who shall go for Us?" Isaiah, in Christ-like fashion, did not hesitate, but cried out, "Here am I, send me."

Jesus, the Christ, would be anxious to come to earth, anxious to take upon Himself the "form of a servant" (Phil. 2:7), and was perfectly willing to become "obedient unto death, even the death of the cross" (Phil. 2:8). "My *delight* was with the sons of men," He states in Proverbs 8:31. His delight, His desire, His reason for coming was to redeem this poor, lost, struggling race known as man. Have you grasped this incredible statement from the Lord? We are His delight. The Hebrew word translated "delight" in verse 31 is *sha'shua'*. It means enjoyment, delight, or pleasure. We are His pleasure! We are His joy! That is why He was willing to endure the cross and all the shame. We were the "joy that was set before Him" (Heb. 12:2)! The angels in heaven view with great interest the joy that the Father and the Son experience each time a lost sinner turns to Christ (Luke 15:10).

Section Five: Invitation

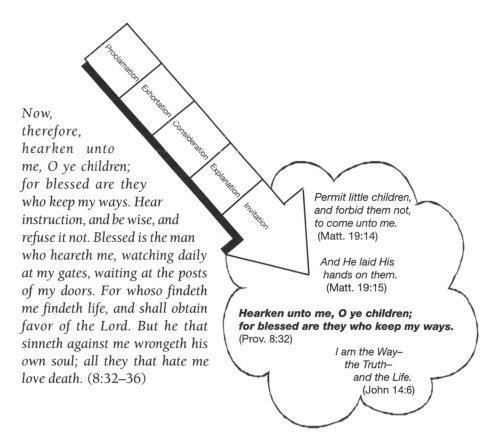

Now, therefore, hearken unto me, O ye children; for blessed are they who keep my ways. Hear instruction, and be wise, and refuse it not. Blessed is the man who heareth me, watching daily at my gates, waiting at the posts of my doors. For whoso findeth me findeth life, and shall obtain favor of the Lord. But he that sinneth against me wrongeth his own soul; all they that hate me love death. (8:32–36)

Proclamation
Exhortation
Consideration
Explanation
Invitation

Permit little children, and forbid them not, to come unto me. (Matt. 19:14)

And He laid His hands on them. (Matt. 19:15)

Hearken unto me, O ye children; for blessed are they who keep my ways. (Prov. 8:32)

I am the Way— the Truth— and the Life. (John 14:6)

Multiple voices sometimes speak to us from a single passage of Scripture. To illustrate this point, let us say that Rev. Smith, one of Christ's ministers, preached from Acts 2:14–41. As Rev. Smith delivered his sermon to the audience, the audience actually heard several speakers. First of course, the audience heard Rev. Smith. He quoted the words from the text. The second speaker that the audience heard was Peter. He is the one who preached the sermon that is found in Acts 2:14–41. As Rev. Smith, therefore, read the text, the audience was hearing Peter, because it was Peter who spoke these words. Third, the audience heard from Luke, for he was the human author of the text. He penned the words. The fourth speaker that the audience heard from is the Holy Spirit. He authored the text. He is the divine author of all Scripture. The audience will also be addressed by Joel, the Old Testament prophet, because Peter quotes him (Acts 2:16–21). The audience will hear from David also. Peter quotes him verses 25–31. This is just one of many examples where multiple voices speak to us from a single passage of Scripture.

As you read Proverbs 8:32–36, ask yourself, "Who is speaking?" If you studied the text and concluded that it is Solomon speaking, you would be correct. If you concluded, however, that it is Lady Wisdom speaking, you would still be correct. Here is another example of multiple voices speaking to us from a single passage of Scripture.

Verse 32 presents one more time the "children" receiving godly admonition from their father. What beautiful pictures of family devotions we have here in Proverbs. In each of the chapters that we have covered so far, we see a father exhorting his children to "hear" his words, to receive them, and to keep them. Here once again sits the father instructing the children about spiritual things. The father is there, the children are there, but wait—who is speaking? It is the Savior! He is speaking to the children through the father! He is seen here in this ancient home because He was invited. When parents have family devotions, Mom and Dad are essentially saying—"Lord, we welcome You. Come." Jesus doesn't turn down invitations. Study the gospels and you will find that

He went everywhere that He was invited. He also promised that when two or three are gathered together in His name, He would be there "in the midst of them" (Matt. 18:20). Thousands of Sunday school teachers have opened their classes by singing this prayer with their students: "Into our class, into our class, come into our class, Lord Jesus. Come in with power, and bless this hour. Come into our class, Lord Jesus." Christian parents should be singing this prayer, or a similar one, in their homes each day. They should "invite" the Lord to come into their home to bless the children and to teach them during the family altar time. "Into our home, into our home. Come into our home, Lord Jesus." We will now go back into this Near Eastern home and see what else the Savior has to say to the children. He has already told them (through the father) who He is (the one who loves them, the one who is available, the one who offers riches and honor, the one who is everlasting, etc., vv. 14–31). We'll go back into the home now and hear what he has to say.

Christ Offers Blessings to the Children. (v. 32)

He says to the children "blessed are they who keep my ways." Centuries later in the New Testament, Christ repeated His promise of a blessing with the following very similar words: "Blessed are they that hear the Word of God, and keep it" (Luke 11:28). Does Jesus really care for our young children? More than you can possibly know! Matthew tells us of a time that Jesus called a little child to Himself and set him in the midst of the assembly. Jesus proceeded to tell the people that "whosoever shall receive one such little child in my name receiveth me. But whosoever shall offend one of these little ones who believe in me, it were better for him that a millstone were hanged about his neck, and that he were drowned in the depth of the sea" (Matt. 18:5–6).

It is a natural thing for children to love Jesus. Children respond to love, and Jesus loves them. What, then, keeps so many children from coming to Christ? Jesus had to correct His own disciples over this issue. They thought that their Master was too busy and too important to be bothered by children. How wrong they were! Some parents had brought their little children to Jesus with a simple request. Would Jesus please just touch them and perhaps pray for them (Matt. 19:13)? The disciples rebuked the adults who brought the children. When Jesus saw what the disciples were doing, He was very displeased and said to them: "Permit the little children to come unto me, and forbid them not, for such is the kingdom of God" (Mark 10:14). Then, Jesus "took them up in His arms, put His hands upon them, and *blessed* them" (Mark 10:16).

Christ Offers Instruction and Wisdom to the Children. (v. 33)

When parents teach their children the things of Christ in the home, He is there "in the midst of them" (Matt. 18:20), aiding the parents in the disciplining process. Unfortunately, His instruction is not available in the homes of many believers because He has not been invited. Just as Christ will not enter into a life unless He is invited, He will not come into a home and conduct wisdom training if He is not invited. Parents, when you establish family devotions in the home, you are inviting Christ into your home. He is as willing to teach your children as He was these children in Proverbs. How did He teach them? He taught them through their father. Establish a family altar in your home, and Christ will teach your children through you. What could be more exciting than to be used of God in the home in the lives of your children?

Christ Offers Life to the Children. (vv. 34–35)

"Whoso findeth me findeth life," He states in verse 35. Centuries later, Jesus, speaking to some hard hearts in Jerusalem, said, "Ye will not come to me, that ye might have life" (John 5:40). Here in Proverbs 8, Christ speaks to the children and teaches them two great truths. The first truth is "Whoso findeth me findeth life." He tells them that the way to have life is through Him. The second truth is that not only will the person who finds Him have life but shall also "obtain favor of YHWH." In other words, the way to be in a right relationship with YHWH is to *know* His Son. In the few short words recorded in verse 35, then, Christ presents Himself to the children as the way to life and the way to favor with the Father

(YHWH). During His New Testament ministry, He taught these truths many times. Here is one example: "Jesus saith unto him, I am the way, the truth, and the life; no man cometh unto the Father but by Me" (John 14:6).

It is a beautiful and wonderful thing when parents establish a family altar in the home. Christ comes into their homes and speaks to the tender, young children. He offers them Himself. He offers them life everlasting. He offers them a way to have the favor of the heavenly Father. The Lord blessed our marriage with three beautiful children. All three of them came to Christ at very young ages. They each made a profession of faith in the home by age five. Christ's Spirit came into our home, showed them their need, and their young, tender hearts responded to His love for them. How wonderful is Christ's offer of life to the children.

Christ Warns the Children of the Consequences of Rejecting. Him (v. 36)

Christ gave them the good news of life in verse 35, and now He shows them the alternative in verse 36. The alternative to receiving Christ is to reject Him. He tells the children that "He that sinneth against me wrongeth his own soul; all they that hate me love death." In 1846, England's Charles Bridges, writing about the man described in verse 36, wrote: "How cruel he is to himself, while he is despising his Savior. Every bait of sin is the temptation to suicide—soul murder. The snatching at it is as if men were in love with damnation. They love that which will be their death, and put that from them which would be their life. Sinners die, because they will die; which leaves them inexcusable, makes their condemnation more intolerable, and will forever justify God when He judges."[7]

Children given the opportunity will normally accept Jesus Christ. Once the children have opened their hearts to Jesus, the foundation for the spiritual growth has been established for "the fear of the Lord is the beginning of knowledge . . ." (Prov. 1:7). Parents should proceed to teach their children the Word of God in family devotions throughout adolescence.

Summary:

We have just completed an incredible chapter in Proverbs! We have heard from Lady Wisdom, from Solomon, and from the Son of God. We have even had a glimpse of the incredible relationship between YHWH and His Son in eternity past. We have seen the Son revealing Himself to the children and offering them the gifts of life, wisdom, and blessings. I hope that God blessed you in the study of this chapter as He did me. It is, indeed, an awesome portion of Holy Scripture.

9 The Lady Named Wisdom
And
A Woman Called Foolish

T he subject of Lady Wisdom comes up again and again as we study Proverbs. She makes her initial appearance in chapter one. As the scene opens here, we see her proclaiming a message to the people of the city. It is a message from God (Prov. 1:20–33). She then makes appearances in several other chapters, as we already noticed. Here in chapter nine, she comes upon the scene immediately. If you will read the first word of the first verse, you will see her name. Since she is the opening subject of this chapter, we will focus our attention on her as we begin.

An Invitation to Life

Wisdom hath builded her house, she hath hewn out her seven pillars; she hath killed her beasts; she hath mixed her wine; she hath also furnished her table. She hath sent forth her maidens; she crieth upon the highest places of the city. Whoso is simple, let him turn in hither; as for him that lacketh understanding, she saith to him, Come, eat of my bread, and drink of the wine which I have mixed. Forsake the foolish, and live, and go in the way of understanding. (9:1–6)

Who Is This Lady Named Wisdom?

When I began my study of Lady Wisdom, I did not know that it would require many long days and nights of research. First and foremost, I read them *carefully*, *prayerfully*, and *repeatedly*. Then, I studied other portions of Scripture that I thought might be germane to the subject. I then researched biblical history, secular history, and mythological history of the ancient Near East. We are told repeatedly in Proverbs to desire wisdom and to seek her. During these long days and nights of research and study, all my energies were directed on discovering exactly who Lady Wisdom is. From the beginning, I had a general idea, but I wanted to know specifically because God places great emphasis upon our association with Lady Wisdom.

The Lady Named Wisdom and a Woman Called Foolish

She is symbolic.
She is *not* a real person.
She does *not* have flesh and bones.
Neither is she deity in spirit form.
She is a symbol.

She speaks only for YHWH, Israel's God.
She acts as His messenger and His
representative.

Lady Wisdom represents the Word of God
and the God of the Word.

Lady Wisdom Described:

- She is to be sought after like we would seek after valuable treasures (2:4).

- We are encouraged to search for her like we would a hidden treasure (2:4).

- Through her, we can understand the way of salvation (2:5).

- She brings happiness to those who find her (3:13).

- She is more valuable than silver or fine gold, and more precious than rubies (3:14–15, 8:11).

- She is so valuable, nothing can be compared to her (3:15, 8:11).

- She brings long life and riches (3:6, 4:9, 9:11).

- Follow her, and experience pleasantness and peace (3:17).

- She can preserve those who don't forsake her (4:6).

- She keeps those who love her (4:6).

- She is the principal thing (4:7).

- She will promote those who exalt her (4:8).

- She will bring honor to those who will embrace her (4:8).

- She can keep the young man from the unclean woman (7:4–5).

- She speaks of excellent things (8:6).

- She speaks truth (8:6).

- She abhors wickedness (8:7).

Lady Wisdom Observed

Study the passages in the Book of Proverbs where she speaks, and you will observe the following:

- She is a messenger of God.

- She speaks for God only.

- She offers good things: salvation and blessing.

- She warns of bad things to those who reject her: judgment, death, etc.

- God speaks through her.

(1:20–33, 8:1–36, 9:1–18).

All of the cultures of the ancient Near East embraced mythological gods and goddesses, some of which were similar in authority to Lady Wisdom. The most important example of this would be Egypt's Ma'at, goddess of law, truth, and justice. Ma'at was the daughter of the sun god Re, and wife of Thoth, the god of wisdom. Ma'at represented "a standard for acceptable behavior."[1] She played an important role in the judgment after death. The heart of the deceased was weighed in a scale balanced by Ma'at as a test of truthfulness.

The Israelites had previously lived in Egypt for over 400 years, and would have been familiar with Egypt's Ma'at. Because of their exposure to Egypt's goddess of law, truth and justice, the Israelites would be able to identify with Lady Wisdom, representing the Word of YHWH (their God), and YHWH Himself, author of the Word. This is, no doubt, one reason why the Lord chose Lady Wisdom as a symbol for His Word.

Another reason why the Lord might have introduced Lady Wisdom during Solomon's day would be to reach the lost of other surrounding countries. We know that the unsaved from many nations would journey to Jerusalem to hear the teachings of this most famous of all wise men, Solomon. With expectant hearts, they would make the journey to hear this renowned man of knowledge. Solomon would bring them face to face with Lady Wisdom (1 Kings 4:29–34). We are told that "all the kings of the earth sought the presence of Solomon to hear his wisdom, that God had put in his heart (2 Chron. 9:23). Those who came and were diligently seeking truth no doubt found the Lord and His salvation, for He said, "Those who seek me early shall find me (Prov. 8:17). Doesn't it make sense that a loving God who is anxious to save would use a symbol that the lost could identify with? Any pagans who might have come under Holy Spirit conviction would have been able to identify with Lady Wisdom because of their cultural backgrounds. The symbol of Lady Wisdom would actually aid them in understanding the truth. Solomon's words were no doubt used of God to form a mental picture of Lady Wisdom in the minds of "wisdom" seekers. As they sat and listened to this man whom God had blessed with wisdom, they would come to realize that Lady Wisdom is the Word of YHWH, Israel's God. They would then understand the "fear of YHWH, and find the knowledge of God" (Prov. 2:5).

The Son of God repeatedly used mental pictures to help teach truth during His earthly ministry. He used symbols that the people of His day would be able to identify with and understand. He illustrated truth with such things as the sower and the seed, the shepherd, the lost sheep, salt, the tares and wheat, the mustard seed, the sheep among wolves, and the grape vine.

God, in His wisdom, gave Solomon a symbol to use in educating others concerning Himself. He would show the pagans someone who was much more desirable than their mythological gods and goddesses. He would introduce them to Lady Wisdom. They would be confronted with all of the wonderful things that Solomon has to say about her. They would listen with great interest as they discovered that Lady Wisdom represents all that YHWH has said, and all that YHWH is. No doubt, many came to faith in YHWH through Solomon's incredible Spirit-led teaching and writing.

What is Her House? (v. 1)

There was no temple in Jerusalem until Solomon. King David wanted to build a house for the Lord, but the Lord had other plans. David addresses this issue to his son Solomon in the Book of 1 Chronicles.

> But the word of the Lord came to me, saying, Thou hast shed blood abundantly, and hast made great wars; thou shalt not build an house unto my name, because thou hast shed much blood upon the earth in my sight. Behold, a son shall be born to thee, who shall be a man of rest; and I will give him rest from all his enemies round about; for his name shall be Solomon, and I will give peace and quietness unto Israel in his days. He shall build an house for my name; and he shall be my son, and I will be his Father, and I will establish the throne of his kingdom over Israel forever. (1 Chron. 22:8–10)

Notice that God, who is sovereign, chose Solomon before he was even born to build the temple. We are told that in the fourth year of Solomon's reign "he began to build the house of the Lord" (1 Kings 6:1). The project took seven years (1 Kings 6:38). Solomon did a lot of other building as well. He built his own house and the house of the forest of Lebanon. He built the Hall of Pillars and the Hall of the Throne. He also built a house for Pharaoh's daughter, whom he had taken as his wife (1 Kings 7:1–12).

It is difficult to identify with certainty the "seven pillars" mentioned in Proverbs 9:1 since Solomon's temple only had two pillars. Perhaps it is a reference to other pillars in Solomon's government complex. It could also be a reference to the seven chains that graced the top of each of the temple's pillars (1 Kings 7:16–17).

The house that Lady Wisdom built in the Old Testament was the temple. It was the place for God's people to sacrifice and worship. Lady Wisdom has built another house in the New Testament age. If you study carefully Proverbs 9:1–6, you will see both the Old Testament house (the temple) and the New Testament house (the church). We have by careful study determined that Lady Wisdom represents the Word of God and the God of the Word. In the Old Testament, what people were identified with the Word of God? That's an easy question. The answer is Israel. What "house" did the Word of God build in the Old Testament? That is also an easy question. The answer is the temple. Now let's move on to the New Testament age and consider the same two questions. In the New Testament age, what people are identified with the Word of God? That's another fairly easy question. The answer is that diverse body of people who are collectively known as the "believers." The last question is what "house" has the Word of God built in the New Testament? It is certainly not the Jewish temple. The last temple at Jerusalem (Herod's temple) was destroyed in A.D. 70 by Roman soldiers. The "house" or "temple" or dwelling place of the Lord in the New Testament is the body of the believer (1 Cor. 6:19–20). When we accepted Christ as our personal Savior, we received His Spirit and were placed into a select association known as the Body of Christ (1 Cor. 12:12–13). This is the "church" (Eph. 1:22–23, Col. 1:24) that Jesus promised to build (Matt. 16:18). He is building His church through the preaching of the Word of God. He began to build it on the day of Pentecost in Acts 2:41–47 and continues to add to it until this very day. The house that Lady Wisdom has been building these last 2,000 years is the church. We are a "holy temple in the Lord . . . built together for an habitation of God through the Spirit" (Eph. 2:21–22).

Seven Pillars of the Church

There are some doctrinal pillars in the New Testament church that are crucial to its very existence. Remove one of these pillars of truth, and soon the building would crumble. The devil is well aware of this. For 2,000 years, he has been hammering away at these pillars in an attempt to destroy the church of Jesus Christ. There have been times in history when it looked like he would succeed in accomplishing his wicked task, and at times he nearly did! He is still attacking the great pillars of truth today. He never gives up. He is relentless in his efforts to see one or more of the great pillars of the faith shatter and collapse, falling to the earth to rise no more. But the truth is, he can't do it! He can hinder the church. He can distract the church. He can slow down its work. He cannot, however, destroy it because one mightier than he said, "I will build my church, and the gates of hell shall not prevail against it" (Matt. 16:18). We know that Satan is not going to take the church *down* because Jesus is going to take the church *up*. At the rapture of the church, we will "meet the Lord in the air" (1 Thess. 4:17). Let's briefly consider seven paramount pillars of the church.

Pillar #1: The Bible Is the Word of God

Explanation: The Bible in its original documents is the inspired Word of God. It is the written record of His supernatural revelation of Himself to man. It is absolute in its authority, complete in its revelation, final in its context, and without any errors in its statements.

> Scripture:
> 2 Tim. 3:16,
> 2 Pet. 1:19–21
> 2 Pet. 3:16

Comments: Throughout history there has been a satanic attack upon the Holy Scriptures. The main focus of Satan's assault against the church has been on this particular pillar. He has rammed it, butted it, battered it, and pounded it, but the pillar stands. Neither has the Bible lost its power. It still speaks to the hearts of men and women (Heb. 4:12). It is not only the "immovable object," but it is also the "irresistible force," and when the gospel that is found within it is heard, it brings conviction; and when it is believed, its great power brings salvation (Rom. 1:16).

Analysis: Satan knows that the church could not survive without this pillar. If he could destroy everybody's faith in the Bible, the true church would collapse and the purposes of God would be thwarted.

Pillar #2: The Fall of Man

Explanation: Every member of the human race is fallen, sinful, and lost. Adam and Eve were created in innocence but by voluntary transgression fell into sin, thus plunging the whole human race into condemnation and death, so that now, all mankind is born in sin and is without excuse before God. Regeneration by the Holy Spirit, therefore, is absolutely essential for the salvation of man.

Scripture:
Gen. 3, Rom. 3:23,
John 3:7, Rom. 5:10–19,
Rom. 6:23

Comments: Modern man has, by and large, adopted the philosophy of humanism. Humanism is a man-centered philosophy that attempts to solve the problems of man and the world *without* God. Humanism embraces the view of Protagoras, a fifth century B.C. Greek philosopher. He taught that "man is the measure of all things." The concept of sin to a humanist is moot. If Satan could get the church to cease preaching "all have sinned and come short of the glory of God" (Rom. 3:23), and cause it to adopt the big lie of the humanist that "there are no absolutes," the gospel message would become irrelevant and would undergo a process of metamorphosis. No longer would the church proclaim with boldness and authority that "Christ died for *our sins!*" (1 Cor. 15:3). Without that life-giving message, the true church would wither, convulse, and die.

Pillar #3: There Is a Literal Heaven and a Literal Hell

Explanation: God, who has always been, made man in His own image and likeness. Emory Bancroft said, "Unending existence is an inseparable part of man's heritage."[2] The Bible teaches that "the wages of sin is death," but death in Scripture never means "annihilation." Every person will live somewhere forever. It will either be an eternity in heaven or an eternity in hell for every individual. Those who accept Christ as Savior in this life shall inherit eternal life; those who do not, shall face eternity in "the flame." Hebrews 9:27 states: "And as it is appointed unto men once to die, but after this the judgment. . . ."

> Scripture:
> Matt. 25:46,
> Jude 6–7,
> 2 Thess. 1:8–9,
> Rev. 14:11, 20:10

Analysis: Satan is always attacking the doctrine that man is an eternal being, and he especially attacks the part of that doctrine that declares that the punishment for rejecting God's Son is everlasting. If Satan could get God's people to reject the biblical teaching of a literal heaven for the believer and a literal hell for an unbeliever, the church would be left with a powerless message that would be incapable of reaching the lost of our world for Christ. Satan would have modern man believe that man evolved from the animals. His death is no different than a dog's death. There is no life after death, and certainly no judgment.

Pillar #4: Jesus Christ Is God

Explanation: The Lord Jesus Christ is fully God who took on flesh and dwelt on earth (the virgin birth). He was sinless. He has existed from all eternity co-equal with the Father and the Holy Spirit. Jesus Christ was a man, yet He was also truly God. He was the God-man.

> Scripture:
> 2 Cor. 5:21,
> 1 John 3:5,
> Isa. 7:14, 9:6;
> John 14:9,
> 1 Tim. 3:16

Whenever anyone refuses to accept Jesus Christ as his **Lord,** he is guilty of the sin of rejecting God. R.A. Torrey wrote, "But suppose one questions or denies His divinity. That does not change the fact nor lessen his guilt. Questioning or denying a fact never changes it. Suppose that one denies the goodness of a man who is in fact the soul of honor. It would not altar the fact but simply make the questioner guilty of slander. So denying the fact of the deity of Jesus Christ does not make it any less of a fact, but it does make the denier guilty of awful, blasphemous, slander."[3]

Analysis: Satan attacks the deity of Christ because he wants to prevent people from being saved. To be saved, one must believe that Christ is the Lord and that He gave His life to pay for our sin. "The gift of God is eternal life through Jesus Christ our **Lord**" (Rom. 6:23). "That if thou shalt confess with thy mouth the **Lord** Jesus (literally: "Jesus is Lord"), and shalt believe in thine heart that God hath raised Him from the dead, thou shalt be saved."

Pillar #5: Christ Died for Our Sins

Explanation: Jesus Christ gave Himself as a substitutionary sacrifice by shedding His blood and dying on the cross. He died, was buried, and rose again on the third day. Salvation is available to all who will believe. The substitutionary death of Christ for our sins is known in theological circles as the atonement. Atonement is the bringing together of two who previously were enemies into a new relationship of friendship and peace.

Scripture:
1 Cor. 15:3,
2 Cor. 5:21,
Titus 2:14,
Heb. 10:10–14,
1 Pet. 2:24,
1 John 3:5;
Heb. 9:2–28

Analysis: Throughout church history, Satan has attempted to change people's views on the meaning of Christ's death. Mark Cambron assembled the following list of unscriptural theories that have been perpetrated:

1. The death of Christ was a martyr's death.

2. The death of Christ was accidental.

3. The death of Christ was a moral example.

4. The death of Christ was an exhibit of God's displeasure with sin.

5. The death of Christ was to show man that God loves him.

6. The death of Christ was the death of a criminal.[4]

Satan would love for the church to buy into his lie that the death of Christ was really *not* for our sins but for some other reason. He knows Scripture well. He knows that the supernatural new birth cannot take place unless the unsaved individual will trust fully in Christ as the one who died and paid in full the penalty for his sin.

Pillar #6: Jesus Christ Rose from the Dead

Explanation: The word "gospel" means "good news." The following is quoted from 1 Corinthians 15:1–4: "Moreover, brethren, I declare unto you . . . that Christ died for our sins according to the scriptures; and that He was buried, and that He rose again the third day according to the scriptures." The gospel (good news) that we preach is not only that Christ died for our sins but that He was buried and rose again!

Scripture:
1 Co. 15:1–8,
Matt. 28:6–7,
Luke 24:39,
John 20:27,
Mark 16:6,
Luke 24:2–6

Analysis: Cambron states that "if Christ had no resurrection, there is no gospel, and if no gospel, we are not saved. Satan has always been against the Word, and he has many weapons trained on it. The revelation he most despises is that of the resurrection."[5] Even some in the first century were denying this pillar of truth. Paul addressed this important issue in his first letter to the church in Corinth:

Now if Christ be preached that he rose from the dead, how say some among you that there is no resurrection from the dead? But if there be no resurrection from the dead, then is Christ not risen; and if Christ be not risen, then is our preaching in vain, and your faith is also in vain. Yea, and we are found false witnesses of God, because we have testified of God that He raised up Christ, whom He raised not up, if so be that the dead rise not. For if the dead rise not, then is not Christ raised; and if Christ be not raised, your faith is in vain, ye are yet in your sins. (1 Cor. 15:12–17)

What a helpless situation we would be in if our Savior had not risen from the grave. Satan hates this precious doctrine, but it is one of the indispensable pillars of the faith. It is also one of the most important facts of all of history.

> What a difference there would be,
> If Christ had not risen for you and me.
> We'd still be lost and in our sin
> If Jesus had not risen again.
> We'd have no Savior to proclaim,
> All of our preaching would be in vain;
> And death would be loss instead of gain.
> Most miserable we would surely be,
> If Christ had not risen for you and me.
> But Christ arose, now praise His name!
> Our faith and our preaching are not in vain!
> — Don Manley

Pillar #7: We Are Saved by Faith Alone

Explanation: The Bible clearly teaches that man is saved by undeserved mercy through faith, and nothing of man enters into his salvation. It is a free gift. Man's efforts, regardless how well-intended, before or after salvation, have nothing to do with it. Salvation is by the finished work of Christ, and nothing can be added to it.

Scripture:
Eph. 2:8–9,
Gal. 2:16,
Rom. 11:6,
Titus 3:5,
Rom. 3:22, 28;
4:5, 4:22–24;
9:30–32; 10:9, 13

Analysis: The teaching that Christ paid for all sin is the heart of the gospel. Satan is always busy trying to get us to "add" something to the message of "we are saved by faith alone." He knows that if he could accomplish this, the church would end up with a powerless message, for there is only one true gospel (Gal. 1:6–9, 2 Cor. 11:3–4). The common title for this doctrine is "justification by faith." That phrase became the theme of the Christian Reformation. Martin Luther said justification by faith was "the articles of a standing or a falling church."[6] I whole-heartedly agree with Luther that without this pillar of truth, the church would fall. No one can be saved apart from this message from God.

Wisdom's Pillars Still Stand

Satan cannot tear down these pillars that wisdom has built. Does he hinder the work of the Lord? Yes. He cannot, however, remove any of the great pillars of faith, for our Lord said, "I will build my church." He will continue to build it until the heavenly trumpet sounds and the church is caught up to meet the Lord in the air (1 Thess. 4:16–17).

The Old Testament Sacrifice

God has always had a people to represent Him, to love Him, to obey Him, and to worship Him. The people of God have always been a minority group, but He has always found some who, with all of their human faults and frailties, would represent Him. In the Old Testament, Israel, representing the people of God, was often referred to in the feminine gender (Isa. 4:5, 26:17, 40:2, 51:3, 65:18–19, Lam. 1:1–8, Jer. 3:1, 6–9, Ezek. 5:5–6, etc.). "She hath killed her beasts" is no doubt a reference to the Old Testament sacrifices. We see Lady Wisdom working through the Jewish people. When the temple was completed, Solomon held a dedication service that lasted seven days. An incredible number of animals were sacrificed at this time. There were so many, they could not be counted (1 Kings 8:5, 2 Chron. 5:6). After the fire came down from heaven and consumed the burnt offering and the sacrifices, Solomon and the people sacrificed 22,000 oxen and 120,000 sheep (2 Chron. 7:1–11, 1 Kings 8:62–66). Dyson Hague made the following comments about the sacrifices of the Old Testament:

> As we study the Old Testament, we are struck with the fact that in the Old Testament system, without an atoning sacrifice there could be no access for sinful men into the presence of the holy God. The heart and center of the divinely revealed religious system of God's ancient people was that without a propitiatory sacrifice there could be no acceptable approach to God. There must be acceptance before there is worship; there must be atonement before there is acceptance. This atonement consisted in the shedding of blood. The blood shed was the blood of a victim which was to be ceremonially blemishless (Exod. 12:5, 1 Pet. 1:19); and the victim that was slain was a vicarious or substitutionary representative of the worshipper (Lev. 1:4; 3:2, 8, 13; 4:4, 15, 24, 29; 16:21, etc.). The death of the victim was an acknowledgment of the guilt of sin, and its exponent.
>
> In one word: The whole system was designed to teach the holiness and righteousness of God, the sinfulness of men, and the guilt of sin; and above all, to show that it was God's will that forgiveness should be secured, not on account of any works of the sinner or anything that he could do, any act of repentance, or exhibition of penitence, or performance of expiatory or restitutionary works, but solely on account of the undeserved grace of God through the death of a victim guilty of no offence against the divine law, whose shed blood represented the substitution of an innocent for a guilty life. . . . It is obvious that the whole system was transitory and imperfect, as the eighth chapter in Hebrews shows. Not because it was revolting as the modern mind objects, for God intended them thereby to learn how revolting sin was and how deserving of death; but because in its essence it was typical, and prophetical, and intended to familiarize God's people with the great idea of atonement, and at the same time to prepare for the sublime revelation of Him who was to come, the despised and rejected of men who was to be smitten of God and afflicted, who was to be wounded for our transgressions and bruised for our iniquities, whose soul was to be made an offering for sin (Isa. 53:5, 8, 10, 12).[7]

209

Christ's Great Sacrifice

God's people in the New Testament (the church) are also collectively referred to in the feminine gender. Husbands are told to love their wives as Christ loved the church and gave Himself for *her* (Eph. 5:25). He wants to present her to Himself as His bride without any spot or wrinkle (Eph. 5:27). She (the church) is presented to Him as His bride in Revelation 19:7–9.

The animal sacrifices that we see in verse 2 were a prophetic picture of Jesus Christ as the "Lamb of God" that would later be slain for the sins of the world (John 1:29, Rev. 5:8–9). The bread and wine of verse five also picture Christ's sacrifice. Lady Wisdom is quoted as saying, "Come, eat of my bread." The night that Jesus was to be betrayed, He took some bread and gave it to the disciples saying, "Take, eat, this is my body" (Matt. 26:26). Lady Wisdom (v. 5) then offers the wine. "Drink of the wine which I have mixed," she states. Jesus, after He had given the disciples bread, gave them the wine. "Drink ye all of it," He said, "for this is my blood of the New Testament, which is shed for many for the remission of sins" (Matt. 26:27–28). The animal sacrifices, the bread, and the wine were all prophetic pictures of the Lamb of God who would come and die on the cross for our sins.

Lady Wisdom Calls (vv. 3–6)

The Invitation

Once again, we see the Lady calling out to the people who pass by (v. 3). We first saw her speaking openly to the public in chapter one. We saw her again in chapter eight making her appeal to the men of the city. Here in chapter nine, now, we see her once again crying out her invitations.

Who Is Invited?

Lady Wisdom is seen inviting the "simple," those who lack "understanding," and the "foolish" to the table (Prov. 9:4–6). These who hear her may be well educated and have plenty of earthly wisdom. Notice, for example, that they have business to attend to in the city (1:21, 8:3, 9:3). Lady Wisdom's message, however, does not deal with the wisdom of man but with the other school of wisdom: the wisdom of God. She is seen calling out to those who lack that wisdom. These are the ones who have never placed their faith in the Lord. The acquisition of divine wisdom, remember, does not begin until a person fears (places faith in) the Lord (Prov. 1:7). Study all three of the passages in Proverbs where she speaks (chapters 1, 8, 9) and you will see that she is directing her invitation to the unsaved.

What Is the Invitation About?

God's message to the unsaved always deals with their need of salvation. He loves the world and invites this sinful, rebellious race to turn to Him in faith. "Turn to me and be saved, all the ends of the earth; for I am God, and there is no other," He declares (Isa. 45:22 NAS). The Lord's invitation for the lost to come to Him for salvation is clearly seen in Proverbs 1:23. Speaking to the lost through Lady Wisdom, He says, "Turn you at my reproof; behold, I will pour out my Spirit unto you, I will make known my words unto you." Here in Proverbs 9 he first invites the sinner to "come, eat of my bread, and drink of the wine which I have mixed" (v. 5). Centuries later, Jesus, referring to any who would believe in Him, would say: "He who eateth my flesh and drinketh my blood, hath eternal life; and I will raise him up at the last day" (John 6:54). The invitation to the bread and wine in Proverbs 9:5 is an invitation to come by faith to the one that these elements represent: Jesus Christ. It is an invitation for sinful beings to be made righteous by personal identification with Christ.

Whom Does Lady Wisdom Symbolize Here?

Lady Wisdom, we said earlier, represents the Word of God and the God of the Word. What else do we know about her? There is one other very important thing that I have noticed about her. Whenever we see her speaking, she is *preaching* a message of salvation to the lost. God always uses His people to deliver His message of salvation. In her oratorical role, Lady Wisdom is symbolic of those who represent God and proclaim His message of salvation. Her voice is symbolic of all the voices of God throughout history who have proclaimed God's message of salvation to a lost world. We see her crying out the Word of God to lost men, encouraging them to "fear the Lord." Charles Bridges, vicar of Old Newton, in Suffolk, England had this to say about her in 1846:

> Has she not followed thee to thy place of business—of diversion—of sin? Has she *not put forth her voice* in the Bible—in the family—in the preached Word? The loudness—the perseverance of the *cry* betokens earnestness in thy friend, and danger in thy condition. For would she have cried so loud, or continued so long, if she had not loved thy soul; if she not had known the wrath that was hanging over thee—the hell that was before thee?

> The call is unfettered; not to devils; but *to man* not the righteous, but *to the sons of men*. Every child, therefore, of guilty Adam has his name in the warrant. It is the proclamation of the gospel "to every creature" (Mark 16:15). Wherever the Word reaches, the offer is made. Wherever a lost sinner be found on this side of the grave, the free welcome of the gospel meets him. . . .[8]

Lady Wisdom Brings a Message of Joy

Let's go back to Proverbs 1 for a moment and take another look at the first mention of Lady Wisdom preaching. She appears on the scene preaching for the first time in verse 20. This verse states that "Wisdom **crieth** outside; she uttereth her voice in the streets." Several different Hebrew words are translated "cry" and "crieth" in our English Bibles. The Hebrew word that the Holy Spirit selected in verse 20 for "crieth" is *rânan*. This word has a more positive meaning than other Hebrew words translated "crieth." Rânan means "to shout aloud for joy." Lady Wisdom, then, must have a message of "joy," of "good news" to deliver to mankind.

Do you remember the message that the angel brought to the shepherds the night of Jesus' birth? The angels said, "I bring you **good tidings of great joy,** which shall be to all people. For unto you is born this day in the city of David, a Savior who is Christ the

Lord" (Luke 2:10–11). The message of Christ is a message that brings great joy.

Lady Wisdom brings a message of joy, a message that when received causes great rejoicing. Her message is only "bad news" to those who reject Christ's offer of salvation. An example of this is given in Proverbs 1:24–32. Her message to all those who will receive it, however, is indeed "good news."

We are told by our Lord to "Go ye into all the world, and preach the *gospel* to every creature" (Mark 16:15). The word "gospel" is translated from the Greek word *euaggelion,* which means "good news." Those who took the message of salvation to others were called "evangelists," which comes from the Greek word *euaggelistes* (meaning: "a message of good"). Historically, God has delivered his message of salvation to this lost world through others who were willing to serve Him. These are the "evangelicals" of both testaments, old and new. These are the ones who spoke to the people of their respective generations about God, His holy Word, and His great salvation. As they spoke to the lost of this world about Him, God spoke through them. It is no different today. As we witness to the lost, reason with them, and proclaim the good news to them, God speaks to their hearts through us. Lady Wisdom, proclaiming her message of joy to the lost, is a picture of God speaking to mankind through His people.

Lady Wisdom represents God speaking through Noah, who preached for Him in a day when no one would listen (2 Pet. 2:5). She represents God speaking through Jonah as he goes to Nineveh, preaches boldly for God, and sees the heathen city of at least 120,000 people turn to him (Jon. 3:6, 10, 4:11). She represents God speaking through the disciples as they went into the world to proclaim the life-giving message of Christ in obedience to His command (Mark 16:15). She represents God speaking through Martin Luther, the great reformer, as he risked his life by preaching "salvation is by faith alone!"

Lady Wisdom represents God speaking through England's George Whitefield as he stood on that little hill in 1739 and preached to the coal miners as they were making their way home

213

after a day of labor in the mines. They were foul smelling and illiterate. They were known as the colliers of Kingswood. Respectable people were afraid of them. Even hardened sailors were shocked by their actions. They were infamously known as "gin-devils, wife beaters, and sodomites." Whitefield's powerful voice sounded out to them a hundred yards away: "Blessed are the poor in spirit, for they shall see the kingdom of heaven." They stopped and stared. They had never heard a minister before. About 200 of them came closer to see and hear this strange man. Their faces were totally blackened from the grime of the mines. Whitefield preached Christ to them. For the first time, these men heard the message of hope! Forgiveness! Salvation! Author John Pollock tells us what happened next: "Suddenly, he (Whitefield) noticed pale streaks forming on grimy faces, on that of a young man on his right, and an old bent miner on his left, and two scarred, depraved faces in front; more and more of them. Whitefield, still preaching, saw the 'white gutters made by their tears down their black cheeks.'"[9]

Lady Wisdom represents God speaking through all of the voices that have carried His message of joy and of hope and of peace. She also represents God speaking through you and me as we proclaim the "good news" to those of our day who are every bit as lost as the colliers of Kingswood were in the day of George Whitefield.

Who Are Her Maidens? (v. 3)

Lady Wisdom's maidens are yet another expression of God speaking through His people. He speaks through these maidens as they present His holy Word to the lost. These maidens serve Lady Wisdom, the one who represents the Word of God and the God of the Word. To hear her is to hear God. To hear one of her maidens, therefore, is also to hear from God, for He speaks through His Word as His servants proclaim it.

A Symbolic Lady Named Liberty

An impressive figure of a woman stands on Liberty Island in New York Harbor. She is nearly 152 feet tall, and she stands on a 150-

foot tall pedestal. We know her simply as "Liberty." Sometimes we affectionately refer to her as "the lady in the harbor." Most of us are not aware of the official title of this great statue. It is "Liberty Enlightening the World." In her uplifted right hand, Liberty holds a torch that is illuminated by lights on the balcony. In her left hand, she holds a tablet of law.

New York Harbor became known as "the gateway to America." Since 1886, Lady Liberty has "stood at the gate," she has shined forth her light, and she has given hope to millions. She has become a symbol of freedom to oppressed people around the world. A sonnet by Emma Lazarus appears on her pedestal. It says, in part:

> Give me your poor, your huddled masses yearning to breathe free, the wretched refuse of your teeming shore. Send these, the homeless, tempest-tost to me, I lift my lamp beside the golden door!

There are some striking similarities between Lady Liberty and Lady Wisdom. Liberty holds the law in one hand and lifts her lamp with the other hand, and guides the ships teeming with foreigners through the harbor and to the city's entrance. In similar fashion, Lady Wisdom holds the law (the law of God) in her hand. She, too, lifts up a lamp (the Word of God [Ps. 119:105]) to direct the people into a beautiful new world. Through the years, millions of people have found her to be a sure and steady guide on their way to the celestial city. She, too, is a symbol of freedom: Freedom from the penalty of sin and the power of sin! She, too, has a message to proclaim to the masses, and it is similar to Lady Liberty's message. Her message comes from the one she represents. Her message is:

> Come unto me, all ye that labor and are heavy laden, and I will give you rest. Take my yoke upon you, and learn of me; for I am meek and lowly in heart, and ye shall find rest unto your souls. For my yoke is easy, and my burden is light. (Matt. 11:28–30)

Two Responses to Lady Wisdom 14 (vv. 7–12)

He that reproveth a scoffer getteth to himself shame, and he that rebuketh a wicked man getteth himself a blot. Reprove not a scoffer, lest he hate thee; rebuke a wise man, and he will love thee. Give instruction to a wise man, and he will be yet wiser; teach a just man, and he will increase in learning. The fear of the Lord is the beginning of wisdom, and the knowledge of the Holy One is understanding. For by me thy days shall be multiplied, and the years of thy life shall be increased. If thou be wise, thou shalt be wise for thyself; but if thou scoffest, thou alone shalt bear it. (9:7–12)

1. The response of the scoffer and the wicked man. (vv. 7–8)

Jesus tells an interesting story in the New Testament that runs parallel to the one discussed in these early verses in Proverbs 9. In His story, as in Proverbs, the beasts had been slaughtered, and the meal had been prepared. The servants are sent forth, as in Proverbs, inviting people to "come" (Matt. 22:4). The servants, however, were treated badly and were then slain. The king reacted by burning the offender's city and destroying the people. He summoned other servants and instructed them to "go, therefore, into the highways, and as many as ye shall find, bid to the marriage." Jesus said that this is like the kingdom of heaven (v. 2). The Jews rejected God's Son, and so the invitation to "come" to His wedding has gone out for the last 2,000 years to the Gentiles.

There are many in every age that do not want God or His Word. The scoffer and the wicked men of Proverbs 9:7 are examples of those who do not want anything to do with a holy God. "For everyone that doeth evil hateth the light, neither cometh to the light, lest his deeds should be reproved," said Jesus (John 3:20). The maidens are not forbidden to invite these simple ones to Wisdom's house, but Matthew Henry points out that "they are advised not to pursue the invitation by reproving and rebuking them."[10] Jesus, speaking of the Pharisees, told His disciples to "let them alone . . ." (Matt. 15:14).

"The gospel is indeed to be 'preached to every creature' (Mark 16:15)," says A.R. Fausset, "and ministers are to 'reprove, rebuke, exhort, with all long-suffering' (2 Tim. 4:2) . . . But after the hearers of the message have hardened themselves continually against it, and resisted the Holy Ghost, then further admonition would be lost labor, and would only bring increased scorn upon the admonisher."[11] Dr. J. Vernon McGee, speaking on this subject, said the following:

> If you give the Word of God to some people, they will actually hate you for it. This is a pattern that has been true down through the ages. These are people who are so shallow, empty, and ignorant that they will not receive the Word of God at all.

> Regardless of the degree they hold, they are ignorant. . . . The general rule is that the less a man knows, the more he thinks he knows. I have never met a liberal yet who didn't think he was a very smart cookie. He thought that he knew and understood it all, yet he doesn't understand. The more a man really knows, the more he will recognize his ignorance and limitations. One of the truly great preachers whom I have known—and I think he had one of the best minds of any man I have ever met—often said, "The more I study the Bible, the more I recognize how ignorant I am of it." My friend, you cannot study the Bible without realizing how ignorant you are of it. However, the scorner has no interest in learning the Word of God. You waste your time by giving it to him.[12]

2. The repentant sinner's response. (vv. 9–12)

The "scoffer" rejects God's words, but the wise man receives godly instruction readily and "he will be yet wiser," and "will increase in learning" (v. 9). The whole "wisdom" process begins (as we stated earlier) with faith in the Lord, or as it is stated here: "The fear of the Lord" (v. 10). We are told repeatedly in Scripture that the fear of the Lord is the beginning of wisdom. "The repetition of this weighty sentence," says Charles Bridges, "deepens our estimate of its importance."[13] In our conversations, we often emphasize things that are important to us by repeating them. Everything in the Bible has been spoken by God and is therefore important. Bible students should, however, pay close attention to truths that are repeated over and over again in Scripture. This is God's way of emphasizing a truth that is very important. When you come upon one of these repetitions in Scripture, you should automatically think: "There is that truth again. God is emphasizing that this is a very important truth." This "fear of the Lord is the beginning of wisdom" truth is found in Job 28:28, Psalm 111:10, Proverbs 1:7, and Proverbs 9:10.

Unlike the individuals in verse seven, the repentant sinner will listen with interest to Wisdom's invitation to "come and eat of my bread, and drink of the wine which I have mixed" (v. 5). The repentant sinner accepts the invitation and enters Wisdom's house. Jesus tells us how the repentant sinner will act in the house of wisdom:

> *And the tax collector, standing afar off, would not lift up so much as his eyes unto heaven, but smote upon his breast, saying, God be merciful to me a sinner. I tell you this man went down to his house justified.* (Luke 18:13–14a)

An Invitation to Death

> *A foolish woman is clamorous; she is simple, and knoweth nothing. For she sitteth at the door of her house, on a seat in the high places of the city, to call those who pass by, who go right on their way. Whoso is simple, let him turn in hither; and as for him that lacketh understanding, she saith to him, Stolen waters are sweet, and bread eaten in secret is pleasant. But he knoweth not that the dead are there, and that her guests are in the depths of sheol.* (9:13–18)

The subject now shifts from the very desirable lady named Wisdom to the very dangerous woman described as foolish. When we compare these two symbolic women, we will discover that the contrasts are striking. Both women are after the hearts of men. Both invite them to their houses. At this point the similarities stop and the contrasts begin. These two women are opposites. One encourages men to a life of devotion to God, and the other seduces men into lives of sin. Lady Wisdom offers an invitation to life, and the foolish woman extends an invitation that leads to death. If Lady Wisdom speaks only for God and acts as His messenger, who do you think the foolish woman speaks for? Whose messenger is she? The following is a brief comparison of Lady Wisdom and the foolish woman. The list is not exhaustive, and you may wish to expand it.

Lady Wisdom	The Foolish Woman
Represents *Almighty God.* (1:20–33)	Represents the *god of this world* (opposes the message of God). (2 Corin. 4:4)
Represents the God of *truth.* (8:7)	Represents the god of *lies.* (5:3, 11; 7:22–23; John 8:44)
Invites people to her house. (9:4)	*Invites people to her house* (the foolish woman's invitation starts the same as Lady Wisdom's: compare 9:4 and 9:16.)
Her house is the way to *life eternal.* (9:5–6, 8:35)	Her house is the way to *hell.* (2:18–19; 7:27; 9:18)
Offers the *"Bread of Life"* to all. (9:5–6, John 6:48)	Offers the *"bread of death"* to all. (9:17–18)
Offers the *wine to all.* (9:5) (Jesus instructed us to drink of the wine, symbolic of His blood, in remembrance of Him.) (1 Corin. 11:25)	Offers *no wine.* (9:17) (It is interesting that the harlot from Rome in Revelation 17, representing a counterfeit of Christ's church, also offers no wine. There we see her alone clutching "the golden cup in her hand," which is not the cup of the Lord, but only a fake. (Rev. 17:4)
Offers: *Long-term* happiness, wisdom, understanding. (3:13–18; 4:5–8) Obtaining wisdom begins with 1:7, but is a process that takes time and effort. (2:3–5, 4:5–13; Ps. 1; 2 Pet. 3:18)	Offers: *Instant gratification.* (7:8, 9:17) A temporary escape into immorality with long-term, dire consequences. (7:21–27, 9:18)
Speaks of *spiritual things, excellent things.* (8:6–11)	Speaks of *fleshly sins.* (5:3–4, 7:10–21, 9:17)
She is to be *desired* and sought after (3:15–18, 4:5–13)	She is to be *avoided.* (4:15, 5:8)
She *regenerates* men. (1:23)	She *degenerates* men. (5:20–23, 6:32–33, 7:25)
She will *preserve* you. (4:6)	She will *destroy* you. (7:21–26)
She will *give* you wealth. (3:16)	She will *take* your wealth. (5:10, 6:26)
She will bring you *honor.* (4:8)	She will bring you *dishonor.* (6:33)

"In every city, on every street, by every door of opportunity, these two voices of wisdom and folly are appealing to men," states G. Campbell Morgan. "To obey the call of wisdom is to live," he continues; "to yield to the clamor of folly is to die. How shall we discern between the voices? By making the fear of the Lord the central inspiration of the life; by yielding the being at its deepest to Him for correction and guidance."[14] Children and parents alike should be aware of these conflicting invitations. Parents should teach these things diligently to their children during family devotions. Charles R. Bridges wrote:

> Reader—the wisdom of God, and the great deceiver of man—stand before you. Both are wooing thine heart; the one for life—the other for death. Both are intensely anxious for success. *Wisdom crieth. The foolish woman is clamorous* (v. 3 with 13). The one makes the *simple* wise unto eternal life. The other bears away her willing captive into unutterable misery. Which voice arrests thine ear, and allures thine heart? Which feast excites thine appetite? Whose guest art thou? Wilt thou not open thine eyes to the infatuation and pollution of this house of horror and death? . . .[15]

Wisdom –
The Principal Thing

Section Two

This section consists of topical studies
of important subjects found in the Book of Proverbs.

10 | **Wine and Strong Drink**

The Word "Wine"

Wine in the Bible is a generic word that is used to describe the juice of the grape. The word *wine* does not describe the "condition" of the juice, but only the juice itself. On the farm in the fall of the year we would gather apples from our trees, load them onto a vehicle, and take them to a place called the cider mill. The apples would be squeezed under great pressure by a machine that would force the juice out of the apples. We would drive home without any apples, but we would have something else to take home and enjoy: the juice from the apples. It is called *cider.* Like wine, cider is a generic word used to describe the juice from the apple. It does not describe the "condition" of the juice, but only what it is: it is juice from the apple. Cider may be "sweet" or, if left to ferment, may become "hard" and then turn to vinegar. The same word *cider* is used to describe the juice from the apple, regardless of whether it is sweet or hard.

In ancient Near East culture, there were two kinds of wine: unfermented wine and fermented wine. When wine is mentioned in the Bible in a favorable light, the reference is to unfermented wine. When it is spoken of in a negative sense, such as causing misery, sorrow, poverty, etc., the reference is to fermented wine.

In order for the wine to ferment, conditions have to be just right. The temperature must be between 50 and 75 degrees, and the exact proportions of sugar, yeast, and water must be present. In temperatures above 75 degrees, grape juice will naturally turn to vinegar. The summers in the Near East are very hot, with temperatures sometimes exceeding 100 degrees. Count Chaptal, a French chemist, said, "Nature never forms spirituous liquors, she rots the grape upon the branch; but *it is an art* which converts the juice into (alcoholic) wine."[1]

In the hot climate of the Near East, the newly pressed grape juice was often boiled down into a syrup. This would prevent the wine from turning into vinegar and would also prevent fermentation. Thus the valuable fruit of the vine was "preserved." The water would evaporate during this process. The result would be a higher percentage of sugar, making fermentation impossible. The following quotes are taken from William Patton's book *Bible Wines or Laws of Fermentation and Wines of the Ancients*, which was first published in 1871:

Boiling, or Inspissating.

By this process the water is evaporated, thus leaving so large a portion of sugar as to prevent fermentation.

Herman Boerhave, born 1668, in his *Elements of Chemistry*, says, "By boiling, the juice of the richest grapes loses all its aptitude for fermentation, and may afterwards be preserved for years without undergoing any further change."–*Nott*, London Edition, p. 81.

Says Liebig, "The property of organic substances to pass into a state of decay is annihilated in all cases by heating to the boiling point." The grape juice boils at 212 ; but alcohol evaporates at 170, which is 42 below the boiling point. So then, if any possible portion of alcohol was in the juice, this process would expel it. The obvious object of boiling the juice was to preserve it sweet and fit for use during the year. . . .

Archbishop Potter, born A.D. 1674, in his *Grecian Antiquities*, Edinburgh Edition, 1813, says, vol. ii. p. 360, "The Lacedæmonians used to boil their wines upon the fire till the fifth part was consumed; then after four years were expired began to drink them."

He refers to Democritus, a celebrated philosopher, who travelled over the greater part of Europe, Asia, and Africa, and who died 361 B.C., also to Palladius, a Greek physician, as making a similar statement. These ancient authorities called the boiled juice of the grape *wine*, and the learned archbishop brings forward their testimony without the slightest intimation that the boiled juice was not wine in the judgement of the ancients.

Aristotle, born 384 B.C. says, "The wine of Arcadia was so thick that it was necessary to scrape it from the skin bottles in which it was contained, and to dissolve the scrapings in water."—*Bible Commentary* [sic], p. 295, and *Nott*, London Edition, p. 80.

Columella and other writers who were contemporary with the apostles inform us that "in Italy and Greece it was common to boil their wines."—*Dr. Nott*.

Some of the celebrated Opimian wine mentioned by Pliny had, in his day, two centuries after its production, the consistence of honey. Professor Donovan says, "In order to preserve their wines to these ages, the Romans concentrated the must or grape juice, of which they were made, by evaporation, either spontaneous in the air or over a fire, and so much so as to render them thick and syrupy."—*Bible Commentary* [sic], p. 295.

Horace, born 65 B.C., says, "There is no wine sweeter to drink than Lesbian; that it was like nectar, and more resembled ambrosia than wine; that it was perfectly harmless, and would not produce intoxication."—*Anti-Bacchus*, p. 220

"The Mishna states that the Jews were in the habit of using boiled wine."—*Kitto*, vol. ii. p. 477.

W.G. Brown, who travelled extensively in Africa, Egypt, and Syria from A.D. 1792 to 1798, states that "the wines of Syria are most of them prepared by boiling immediately after they are expressed from the grape, till they are considerably reduced in quantity, when they were put into jars or large bottles and preserved for use. He adds, "There is reason to believe that this mode of boiling was a general practice among the ancients."

Cyrus Redding, in his *History of Modern Wines*, says: "On Mount Lebanon, at Kesroan, good wines are made, but they are for the most part *vins cuit* (boiled wines). The wine is preserved in jars."—*Kitto*, ii. 956.

Dr. A. Russell, in his *Natural History of Aleppo*, considers its wine (Helbon) to have been a species of sapa. He says: "the inspissated juice of the grape, sapa vina, in the public markets; it has much the appearance of coarse honey, is of a sweet taste, and in great use among the people of all sorts."—*Kitto*, ii., 956.

Leiber, who visited Crete in 1817, says: "When the Venetians were masters of the island, great quantities of wine were produced at Rettimo and Candia, and it was made by boiling in large coppers, as I myself observed."—*Nott*.

Mr. Robert Alsop, a minister among the Society of Friends, in a letter to Dr. F.R. Lees in 1861, says: "The syrup of grape juice is an article of domestic manufacture in most every house in the vine districts of the south of France. It is simply the juice of grape boiled down to the consistence of treacle."—*Bible Com.* [sic], p. xxxiv.

Rev. Dr. Eli Smith, American missionary to Syria, in the *Bibiotheca Sacra* for November, 1846, describes the methods of making wine in Mount Lebanon as numerous, but reduces them to three classes: 1. The simple juice of the grape is fermented. 2. The juice of the grape is boiled down before fermentation. 3. The grapes are partially dried in the sun before being pressed. With characteristic candor, he states that he "had very little to do with wines all his life, and that his knowledge on the subject was very vague until he entered upon the present investigation for the purpose of writing this article." He further as candidly confesses that the "statements contained in this article are not full in every point"; that "it was written in a country where it was very difficult to obtain authentic and exact information." Of the vineyards, he further states that in "an unbroken space, about two miles long by half a mile wide, only a few gallons of intoxicating wines were made. The wine made is an item of no consideration; it is not the most important, but rather the least so, of all the objects for which the vine is cultivated." He also states that "the only form in which the juice of the grape is preserved is that of dibbs, which may be called *grape-molasses*." Dr. E. Smith here confirms the ancient usage of boiling the unfermented juice of the grape. The ancients called it wine; the present inhabitants call it dibbs; and Dr. E. Smith calls it grape molasses. It is the same thing under these various designations. "A rose may smell as sweet by any other name."

The Rev. Henry Homes, American missionary to Constantinople, in the *Bibliothca Sacra* for May, 1848, gives the results of his observation. He wrote two years subsequently to Dr. Eli Smith, and has supplied what was lacking in Dr. E. Smith's statements which were "not full on every point." He did not rely on information from others, but personally examined for himself, and in every case obtained exact and authentic knowledge. He says: "Simple grape juice, without the addition of any earth to neutralize the acidity, is boiled from four to five hours, so as to reduce it *one-fourth* the quantity put in. After the boiling, for preserving it cool, and that it be *less liable to ferment*, it is put into earthen instead of wooden vessels, closely tied over with skin to exclude the air. It ordinarily has not a particle of intoxicating quality, being used freely by both Mohammedans and Christians. Some which I have had on hand for two years has undergone no change." "The manner of making and preserving this unfermented grape liquor seems to correspond with the receipts and descriptions of certain drinks included by some of the ancients under the appellation of wine."

"The fabricating of an intoxicating liquor *was never the chief* object for which the grape was cultivated among the Jews. Joined with bread, fruits, and the olive tree, the three might well be representatives of the productions most essential to them, at the same time that they were most abundantly provided for the support of life." He mentions sixteen uses of the grape, *wine making* being the *least important*. "I have asked Christians from Diabekir, Aintab, and other places in the interior of Asia Minor, and all concur in the same statement."

Dr. Eli Smith, as above, testifies that "wine is not the most important, but *the least*, of all the objects for which the vine was cultivated." These statements are fully confirmed by the Rev. Smylie Robson, a missionary to the Jews of Syria, who travelled extensively in the mountains in Lebanon, as may be seen by his letters from Damascus and published in the *Irish Presbyterian Missionary Herald* of April and May, 1845.

The Rev. Dr. Jacobus, commenting on the wine made by Christ, says: "This wine was not that fermented liquor which passes now under that name. All who know of the wines then used will understand rather the unfermented juice of the grape. The present wines of Jerusalem and Lebanon, as we tasted them, were commonly boiled and sweet, without intoxicating qualities, such as we here get in liquors called wines. The boiling prevents the fermentation. Those were esteemed the best wines which were least strong."

The ancients had a motive for boiling the unfermented juice. They knew from experience that the juice, by reason of the heat of the climate and the sweetness of the grapes, would speedily turn sour. To preserve it sweet, they naturally resorted to the simple and easy method of boiling. The art of distillation was then unknown; it was not discovered till the ninth century.

Wine with Water

There is abundance of evidence that the ancients mixed their wines with water; not because they were so strong with alcohol, as to require dilution, but because, being rich syrups, they needed water to prepare them for drinking. The quantity of water was regulated by the richness of the wine and the time of the year.

"Those ancient authors who treat upon domestic manners abound with allusions to this usage. Hot water, tepid water, or cold water was used for the dilution of wine according to the season." "Hesiod prescribed, during the summer months, three parts of water to one of wine." "Nicochares considers two parts wine to five of water as the proper proportion." "According to Homer, Pramnian, and Meronian, wines required twenty parts of water to one of wine. Hippocrates considered twenty parts of water to one of the Thracian wine to be the proper beverage." "Theophrastus says the wine at Thasos is wonderfully delicious." Athenæus states that the Tæniotic has such a degree of richness or fatness that when mixed with water it seemed gradually to be diluted, much in the same way as Attic honey well mixed.— *Bible Commentary* [sic], p. 17.

"Nor was it peculiar to pagans to mingle water with wine for beverage and at feasts; nor to profane writers to record the fact. It is written of Wisdom, she mingled her wine—Prov. ix. 2—and so written by an inspired penman."—*Nott*, London Ed. p. 84.

This mixed wine must be different from that named in Ps. lxxv, 8. [sic] "full of mixture," which we have seen is the symbol of the divine vengeance, the cup prepared for his enemies. But in Prov. ix. 2, it is a blessing to which friends are invited. If in this passage the mixture is of aromatic spices, in addition to the water necessary to dilute the syrup, it was not to fire the blood with alcohol, but to gratify the taste with delicate flavors.

The Passover was celebrated with wine mixed with water. According to Lightfoot, each person—man, woman, and child—drank four cups. Christ and His disciples having celebrated the Passover, He took of the bread and the wine that remained, and instituted the Lord's Supper. The wine was, as we believe, the rich syrup diluted with water. This kind of wine met all the requirements of the law concerning leaven—the true rendering of *Matsah*, according to Dr. F.R. Lees, being *unfermented things*.

"The Rev. R.M. Pattison, of Philadelphia, showed, from authorities of the highest repute as exegists or personal observation, some of them adverse to the main question, by their unanimous concurrence, that the sweet wine, or unfermented juice of the grape, was of old a popular beverage in Palestine."—*New York Evangelist*.

The conclusion to which these varied sources of proof bring us may thus be stated:

1. That unfermented beverages existed, and were a common drink, among the ancients.

2. That to preserve their very sweet juices, in their hot climate, they resorted to boiling and other methods which destroyed the power and activity of the gluten, or effectually separated it from the juice of the grape.

3. That these were called wines, were used, and were highly esteemed.

Prof. M. Stuart says, "Facts show that the ancients not only preserved their wine unfermented, but regarded it as of a higher flavor and finer quality than fermented wine."—*Letter to Dr. Nott*

That they also had drinks that would intoxicate cannot be denied. All that we have aimed to show is that intoxicating wines were *not the only wines in use.*[2]

Twenty Things God Wants You to Know about Wine and Strong Drink

There are four key passages of Scripture in Proverbs on the subject of wine and strong drink. These passages are: Proverbs 20:1, Proverbs 23:20–21, Proverbs 23:29–35, and Proverbs 31:4–7. Almighty God instructs us in these verses with just a few poignant words how we should view the subject of wine and strong drink. The teaching is clear and easy to understand for any and all who will receive it. These verses should be memorized by every member of the family. As family members memorize these scriptures and discuss them, they should be aware of the fact that by doing so, they are "receiving" wisdom training from the Lord Himself. We are the ones who do the memorizing, but it is the Lord who takes the Word and changes our worldly views. He drives out dark thinking from our minds and replaces it with light. (See chapter seven of this book.)

Proverbs 20:1

Wine is a mocker, and strong drink is raging, and whosoever is deceived thereby is not wise. (20:1)

1. It is a **mocker.** ⟶ "Wine is a **mocker.** ..."

"The history of the world since the days of Noah" (Gen. 9:21), said Charles Bridges, "proves that the love of *wine and strong drink* is a most insidious vice."[3] The "victims" are not convinced until "it's too late," he tells us, "that they have been *mocked* and grievously *deceived.*"[4] It overcomes them, Bridges states, before they are aware of what is happening and "promises pleasures which it can never give."[5] Bridges lectures "and yet so mighty is the spell, that the besotted slave consents to be *mocked* again and again, till 'at last it biteth like a serpent, and stingeth like an adder'" (chapter 22:29–32).[6]

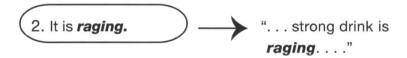

2. It is **raging.** ⟶ "... strong drink is **raging.** ..."

One of the "raging" problems associated with wine and strong drink is a problem sometimes referred to as "pathological intoxication." This condition is described as follows: "after downing a small amount of drink, a person suddenly breaks into a maniacal fury, smashing furniture, and attacking people. The seizure ends as suddenly as it began, and then the victim usually falls into a stuporous sleep, from which he awakens after some hours—usually without memory of the events."[7]

Another of the "raging" problems associated with wine and strong drink is a burning lust. Matthew Henry said, "Wine is oil to the fuel of lust."[8] Charles Bridges says, "Seldom does any sensual indulgence come alone. One lust prepares the way for others. The first step is sure to lead onwards. The poor, deluded victim cannot stop when he pleases. Drunkenness opens the door for impurity."[9]

3. It is a **deceiver.** ⟶ "... and whosoever is **deceived** thereby is not wise. ..."

A woman with a drinking problem wrote syndicated columnist Ann Landers a letter several years ago. Here is how it appeared in her column:

> DEAR ANN: You have said more than once in your column that alcoholism is the No. 1 health problem, not only in the United States, but also in many other countries in the world. Please print the enclosed message that came in the mail—anonymously. It was, I am sure, sent by someone who cared enough to let me know he (or she) was concerned about my drinking. I am taking the message to heart and hope others will too.
>
> POSITIVELY NEGATIVE
>> We drank for joy and became miserable.
>> We drank for sociability and became argumentative.
>> We drank for sophistication and became obnoxious.
>> We drank for friendship and became enemies.
>> We drank for sleep and awakened exhausted.
>> We drank for strength and became weak.
>> We drank for exhilaration and ended up depressed.
>> We drank for "medicinal purposes" and acquired health problems.
>> We drank to get calmed down and ended up with the shakes.
>> We drank for confidence and became afraid.
>> We drank to make conversation flow more easily, and the words came out slurred and incoherent.
>> We drank to diminish our problems and saw them multiply.
>> We drank to feel heavenly and ended up feeling like hell.
>> We drank to cope with life and invited death.[10]

Proverbs 23:20–21

Be not among winebibbers, among gluttonous eaters of flesh; for the drunkard and the glutton shall come to poverty, and drowsiness shall clothe a man with rags. (23:20–21)

4. It leads to **poverty.** ⟶ "For the drunkard . . . shall come to **poverty**. . . ." (v. 21)

Proverbs 23:29–35

Who hath woe? Who hath sorrow? Who hath contentions? Who hath babbling? Who hath wounds without cause? Who hath redness of eyes? They that tarry long at the wine; they that go to seek mixed wine. Look not thou upon the wine when it is red, when it giveth its color in the cup, when it moveth itself aright. At the last it biteth like a serpent, and stingeth like an adder. Thine eyes shall behold strange things, and thine heart shall utter perverse things. Yea, thou shalt be as he that lieth down in the midst of the sea, or as he that lieth upon the top of a mast. They have stricken me, shalt thou say, and I was not sick; they have beaten me, and I felt it not. When shall I awake? I will seek it yet again. (23:29–35)

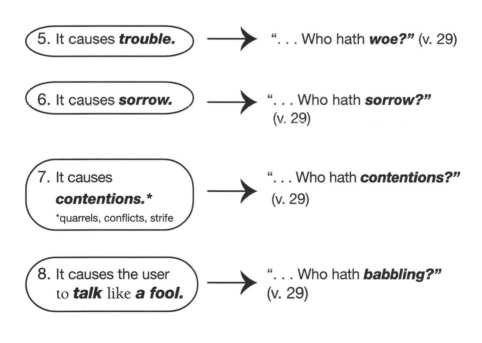

5. It causes **trouble.** ⟶ ". . . Who hath **woe?**" (v. 29)

6. It causes **sorrow.** ⟶ ". . . Who hath **sorrow?**" (v. 29)

7. It causes **contentions.*** ⟶ ". . . Who hath **contentions?**" (v. 29)
*quarrels, conflicts, strife

8. It causes the user to **talk** like **a fool.** ⟶ ". . . Who hath **babbling?**" (v. 29)

When wine comes in, mind goes out.[11]

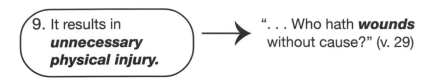

9. It results in **unnecessary physical injury.** → ". . . Who hath **wounds** without cause?" (v. 29)

Encyclopedia Britannica reports that alcoholics are:

- 7 times more likely to have fatal accidents as persons in the general population.
- 30 times more liable to fatal poisoning.
- 16 times more liable to death from a fall.
- 45 times more liable to death in a motor vehicle accident.

"These liabilities," reports *Britannica,* "obviously reflect not only the disablements of immediate intoxication but the whole life-style and state of the alcoholics."[12]

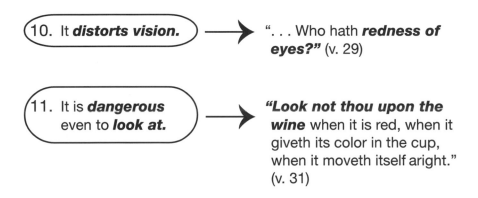

10. It **distorts vision.** → ". . . Who hath **redness of eyes?"** (v. 29)

11. It is **dangerous** even to **look at.** → *"Look not thou upon the wine* when it is red, when it giveth its color in the cup, when it moveth itself aright." (v. 31)

The dangers that come from this devil-brew pose such a great and horrible threat to us that the Lord commands us here not to even *look* at it. Satan has had thousands of years to perfect his "sales skills," and we need to be aware of how he operates. Here's how he got Eve to sin:

Satan's Seduction Process

1. He "told" her (Gen. 3:1–5).
2. He "showed" her (Gen. 3:6).
3. He "sold" her (Gen. 3:6)

Our children were not allowed to listen to or watch any advertisements for alcoholic beverages—and they knew the reason why. The psalmist said, "I will set no wicked thing before mine eyes . . ." (Ps. 101:3).

As much as possible, parents should prevent Satan's messages of seduction from reaching their children. We can also be seduced to drink by just being around those who do. We are told "be not among winebibbers" (Prov. 23:20), and are warned that "*evil company* corrupts good morals" (1 Cor. 15:33).

| 12. It **bites** like a snake. | → | "At the last it **biteth like a serpent.**" (v. 32) |

One cannot habitually play with rattlesnakes without getting bit. Satan is the most hateful, cunning, and despicable snake of all. He'll "play" with you for a while. He'll offer you "good times" and "the pleasures of sin for a season," but then suddenly comes his awful, awful bite. His bite is quick, unexpected, and hits us like a nightmare. His bite is often life-threatening and is nearly always life-changing. His goals are simple. His goals are vicious. His goals are: to steal, to kill, and to destroy (John 10:10). Millions of people who once said, "Alcohol won't get the best of me, I can handle it" eventually found out "*at the last* it biteth like a serpent."

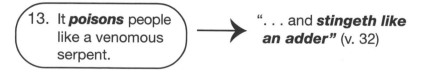

| 13. It **poisons** people like a venomous serpent. | → | ". . . and **stingeth like an adder**" (v. 32) |

Charles Bridges said:

> Whatever be its present jest, *at the last it biteth like a serpent, and stingeth like an adder*. (compare 20:17). Did it *bite* first, who would touch it? Did Satan present the cup in his own naked form, who would dare to take it? Yet it comes from his hand as truly, as if he were visible to the eyes. If poison was seen in the cup, who would venture upon it? Yet is the poison less dangerous, because it is unseen? The *adder's sting* is concealed, yet most fatal. . . .[14]

Health Problems

Encyclopedia Britannica reports that "in long-lasting alcoholism, one or more of the chronic nutritional deficiency diseases may develop."[13] *Encyclopedia Britannica* also reports that some of the deficiency diseases and health related problems caused by drinking are:

- Degeneration of the nervous system
- Beriberi heart disease
- Pellagra
- Scurvy
- Hypochromic microcytic anemia
- Severe open sores
- Zieve's Syndrome
- Severe pancreatitis
- Acute hepatitis
- Cirrhosis of the liver
- Marchiafava-Bignami's Disease
- Cortical laminar sclerosis
- Cerebellar degeneration
- Central pontine myelinolysis
- A generalized deterioration including the brain, muscles, endocrine system, and vital organs.

Encyclopedia Britannica also informs us that "alcoholics die more frequently in all types of accidents and from numerous diseases; their average life span is reduced by about ten or twelve years."[15]

14. It causes **delirium tremens.** → *"Thine eyes shall behold strange things."* (v. 33)

Alcoholic psychoses are psychiatric disorders caused from prolong and excessive drinking. The most common alcoholic psychosis is "delirium tremens." The person thinks he is seeing things like snakes and bugs on the wall, on the floor, or more commonly, on himself. It is often a terrifying experience. *Encyclopedia Britannica* describes this psychosis as follows: "Increasing tremulousness ('the shakes') is followed commonly by visual and auditory hallucinating. Most characteristic are visions of small animals, especially insects, crawling around the sufferer's body."[16]

Sometimes seizures accompany delirium tremens. The fatality for those suffering from delirium tremens ranges from one to twenty percent according to *Encyclopedia Britannica*. Delirium tremens have been known to last up to ten days.

Listed below are some other alcoholic psychoses:

- Alcoholic hallucinations
- Wernickle's encephalopathy
- Chronic alcoholic deterioration
- Korsakoff's psychosis
- Jolliffe's encephalopathy

These psychoses are characterized by such things as visual and auditory hallucinating, fear, confusion, excitement, stupor, loss of memory, crude and obscene behavior, vomiting, sweating, restlessness, and sleep disturbances.

15. It brings **perverse things** out of the heart. ➝ ". . . and thine heart shall utter **perverse things.**" (v. 33)

In the heart of every man, there are unclean and vile things, Jesus told us (Mark 7:21–23). A little alcohol consumed quickly deadens the moral conscience. Perverse thoughts, perverse words, and perverse deeds are the predicted results of men and women who use alcohol. Here are Dr. John Rice's comments on this subject:

> In the highest centers of control, I mean where conscience is, one is drunk first. The brain relaxes control in the area of moral inhibitions. I mean the part that inhibits and says, "Go easy. Remember you are your mother's boy. Remember your reputation." The part that says to a woman, "Remember you are a wife and a mother," or to a nice, sweet girl, "Remember you are a pure girl"—that part dies first. It takes but a few spoonfuls of alcohol to deaden that part.
>
> Now what do you have? Give a woman who is quiet and modest just one or two drinks and now she is loud-talking, laughing at her own jokes, patting everybody on the back. Now she is not careful to arrange her skirt, not concerned if her hair is ruffled and unkempt. . . . Alcohol goes first to the higher centers of the brain and then to certain areas that control sex functions so that a man's sex desires increase, but his control, the thing that makes him talk softly and like a gentleman, is gone. Now he will talk loud and coarse and vulgar, and swear, and insult women. . . .
>
> I warn you now: as certain as there is a God in heaven, when you take liquor in your mouth, you risk everything sacred, everything pure, everything holy, everything valuable! A curse of God is on the one who drinks. . . .
>
> Another curse of liquor is the curse of sex desire. It is many times mentioned in the Bible. Let me read it again here in Habakkuk 2:15, 16:

Wine and Strong Drink

Woe unto him that giveth his neighbour to drink, that puttest thy bottle to him, and makest him drunken also, that thou mayest look on their nakedness! Thou art filled with shame for glory: drink thou also, and let thy foreskin be uncovered: the cup of the Lord's right hand shall be turned unto thee, and shameful spewing shall be on thy glory.

Evidently it was known in Bible times that drunkenness made people take off their clothes and be immoral. There was Noah, a good man. God said that he, his wife, his three sons and their wives were the only ones of his entire generation worth saving. So God killed the whole race except them. Noah was a good man, one who walked with God. God spared him. But after he got out of the ark, he planted a vineyard, and then he made wine and got drunk. Do not say that he was intentionally bad, for he was not. But Noah got drunk. And the Bible tells in Genesis, chapter 9, how he lay naked in his tent. There, drunk and naked, his boy looked on him and laughed and laughed. Others, ashamed, came and covered their drunken dad, lying naked in the tent and not caring. That is what happens when people drink.

Turn to the nineteenth chapter of Genesis and we have the story of Lot. The wicked city of Sodom was destroyed, and Lot and his two daughters were taken out of the city and dwelt in a cave in the mountains. Lot had wine in the cave. And his two daughters talked among themselves and said, "It looks as if all the men in the world were killed, all the boys we knew, and we are going to turn out to be old maids, and not have a family. So let's make Dad drunk." And they got the old man to drink wine and then, under the influence of the wine, they each lay with their father and conceived through this wicked incest. And both of them became unmarried mothers.

That tragic story is an eternal indictment against liquor. Don't tell me that wine is better than whiskey, when wine is the kind of drink that will make a man like Lot so that he doesn't have any sensibility, so that his conscience is seared, so the sense of his own decency is gone. Now, drunken and committing incest with his own daughters. Liquor does that!

Now what part of a man gets drunk first? The pilot, that part that is the control; the part that holds the reigns, that guides the steering, that controls the passions and keeps a man or woman straight. I say, drunkenness leads to adultery, leads to nakedness, leads to lewdness.

In Exodus is the story of the Ten Commandments, given by God to Moses upon Mount Sinai. When Moses and Joshua came down off the mountain, they heard music and shouting. When they got down they found the people had said to Aaron, "Make us gods to worship," and gave him earrings and bracelets. So Aaron molded a golden calf and they worshipped it. Exodus 32:6 says:

> *And they rose up early on the morrow, and offered burnt-offerings, and brought peace-offerings: and the people sat down to eat and drink, and rose up to play.*

After they drank, what happened? God's Word tells us in Exodus 32:25:

> *And Moses saw that the people were naked: (for Aaron had made them naked unto their shame among the enemies. . . .)*

Now why is it when people drink that they do not mind pulling off their clothes? Do not mind cursing and blaspheming? Why is it when people drink they have no respect for God, no respect for womanhood, no care about little children? When a man drinks, why is it that he does not care whether his children have food or not? When a woman drinks, why is it that she does not mind leaving her babies shut up in a cold house while she goes to a tavern and spends the night drinking with soldiers and others? There is something horrible in the drink that steals away the brain, steals away the conscience, takes away modesty, takes away holy impulses in the mind and the heart!

Listen, I care not whether you are the best man or woman in the world, the most respected, how much you love God, how virtuous your mind, how true your conscience; you take a few drinks and that sense is gone. One cannot be trusted who drinks. You cannot be trusted to drive a car. You cannot be trusted with another man's wife. You cannot be trusted to pay your honest debts. You cannot be trusted to take care of your children.

It does not take eight glasses of beer to make you drunk. When you drink the first glass, you are one-eighth drunk. And that first glass goes to your head. The last glass may make you so your legs will wobble [sic]. The last glass may make you so you will go to sleep in a drunken stupor [sic]. But the first glass is the part that destroys the fine appreciation, the inhibition that keeps you from doing wrong, the sense of responsibility that makes you bring home your pay check, makes you take care of your children. That part that makes you respect virtue, that makes you tell the truth, makes you keep out of crime—that part is dead first, doped first, cursed first. God said, "Woe to the crown of pride, to the drunkards of Ephraim." Woe to the drunkard! What a curse on drink![17]

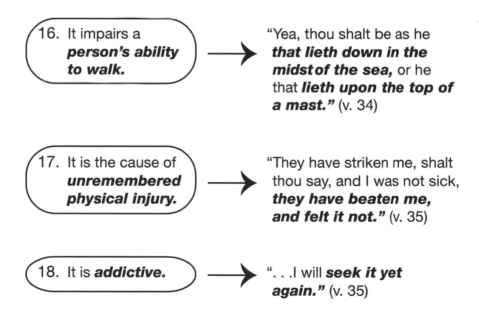

16. It impairs a **person's ability to walk.** ⟶ "Yea, thou shalt be as he *that lieth down in the midst of the sea,* or he that *lieth upon the top of a mast."* (v. 34)

17. It is the cause of **unremembered physical injury.** ⟶ "They have striken me, shalt thou say, and I was not sick, *they have beaten me, and felt it not."* (v. 35)

18. It is **addictive.** ⟶ ". . .I will **seek it yet again."** (v. 35)

These verses picture a man who is "hooked." Just look at all the trouble, and all the sorrow, and all the problems that this man has gone through. Furthermore, all of his troubles were avoidable.

If he had never taken that "first drink," none of these things would have happened to him. But, he reasoned, as millions of others have reasoned: "I can handle a little drink. A little drink never hurt anybody. I am just going to drink socially." Now this man is "hooked" by the mocker, "hooked" by the rager, "hooked" by the deceiver, and what will he do when he is able to get his sick, battered body up? Will he sober up, quit drinking, and change his ways? He will not! Some young, naive boy or girl says, "But why won't he stop? I would. I don't understand." Young person, you don't understand because you have not yet learned that sin is habit forming. Sin is easy to get into and hard to get out of. The man in these verses represents scores of people in our world today who are hooked on strong drink. When they were young, they never thought drink would enslave them. It was just "fun" to do. They were *sure* that they could handle it. Satan convinced them that "this is no big deal." Now here's the fact: Millions of these young people who thought that they could handle drink have become slaves to it. It has robbed them of their dignity, their self-respect, their hopes, their dreams, and their bank accounts; but tomorrow they will get their sick, hurting bodies up off the bed and they will say, as this sick man said: "I will seek it yet again."

Proverbs 31:4–7

It is not for kings, O Lemuel, it is not for kings to drink wine, nor for princes strong drink, lest they drink, and forget the law, and pervert the justice of any of the afflicted. Give strong drink to him that is ready to perish, and wine unto those that are of heavy hearts. Let him drink, and forget his poverty, and remember his misery no more.

19. It causes people to make **wrong decisions.** → "Lest they drink, and **forget the law, and pervert the justice** of any of the afflicted." (v. 5)

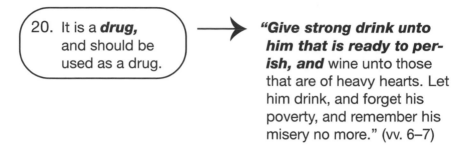

20. It is a **drug,** and should be used as a drug.

→ **"Give strong drink unto him that is ready to perish, and** wine unto those that are of heavy hearts. Let him drink, and forget his poverty, and remember his misery no more." (vv. 6–7)

For further comment on the use of wine and strong drink, see chapter 31 of this book.

Summary:

Almighty God gave us just four key passages in Proverbs on the wine and strong drink issue. He gave us just a few verses, but look at all He has told us in these verses. He has warned us in these verses in many ways that He is against intoxicating beverages, for they cause us much sorrow and trouble. He is a loving God. He loves us far too much to want to see us messed up with this drug called alcohol. Evangleline Booth, wife of William Booth who founded the Salvation Army, once said:

> Drink has drained more blood, hung more crepe, sold more homes, plunged more people into bankruptcy, armed more villains, slain more children, snapped more wedding rings, defiled more innocent, blinded more eyes, twisted more limbs, dethroned more reason, wrecked more manhood, dishonored more womanhood, broken more hearts, blasted more lives, driven more to suicide, and dug more graves than any other poisoned scourge that ever swept its death-dealing waves across the world.[18]

11 | The Finite Will of Man and the Sovereign Will of God

The Finite Will of Man

 Man is responsible for his decisions, his thoughts, and his actions; and he will one day give account for these before the Great God of heaven. All of the instructions in Proverbs from the earthly father to his son clearly show that the son has a free will. He can choose right or he can choose wrong. He can choose life or he can choose death. The earthly father encourages the son to exercise his will and choose for God (chapters 1–7).

Man Has the Ability to Respond But Many Times Refuses

Because I have called, and ye refused; I have stretched out my hand, and no man regarded, but ye have set at nought all my counsel, and would have none of my reproof, I also will laugh at your calamity; I will mock when your fear cometh; when your fear cometh as desolation, and your destruction cometh as a whirlwind; when distress and anguish come upon you. Then shall they call upon me, but I will not answer; they shall seek me early, but they shall not find me; because they hated knowledge, and did not choose the fear of the Lord. They would have none of my counsel; they despised all my reproof. Therefore shall they eat of the fruit of their own way, and be filled with their own devices. For the turning away of the simple shall slay them, and the prosperity of fools shall destroy them. But whoso hearkeneth unto me shall dwell safely, and shall be quiet from the fear of evil. (1:24–33)

Man Can Accept the Lord and Be Saved or Refuse the Lord, Thereby Condemning His Own Soul

Now, therefore, hearken unto me, O ye children; for blessed are they who keep my ways. Hear instruction, and be wise, and refuse it not. Blessed is the man who heareth me, watching at the posts of my doors. For whoso findeth me findeth life, and shall obtain favor of the Lord. But he that sinneth against me wrongeth his own soul; all they that hate me love death. (8:32–36)

The Sovereign Will of God

God has given man a limited free will. Man is free to exercise choice concerning attitudes of the heart. Included in man's available choices are things such as: "Shall I accept the Lord into my life? Shall I reject Him? Shall I search for His will? Shall I obey Him and serve Him with my life?" Man is allowed to plan his life's journey, but he is responsible for his choices. He will one day appear before the Lord, the righteous judge. His entire life will then be evaluated.

The Creator has given man freedom of choice, but man does not "control his own destiny." Man cannot determine the outcome of his choices, nor of his life. These things are in the hands of Almighty God. Mortal man journeys down the path of life thinking he's in control, "calling the shots," but it is the Lord who is directing his steps (16:9). Man chooses the path that he will travel, but Almighty God determines what is going to happen on that path.

God Directs a Man's Steps

A man's heart deviseth his way, but the Lord directeth his steps. (16:9)

A fine description of the sovereign government of God! Inscrutable indeed is the mystery, how He accomplishes His fixed purpose by free-willed agents. Man, without his free will, is a machine.

God, without His unchangeable purpose, ceases to be God (Mal. 3:6). As rational agents we think, consult, act freely. As dependent agents, the Lord exercises His own power in permitting, over-ruling, or furthering our acts. Thus man purposes, God disposes. *Man devises; the Lord directeth.* He orders our will, without infringing on our liberty, or disturbing our responsibility. For while we act as we please, we must be answerable.

We observe the supremacy in *directing*, not only an important end, but every step toward it; not only the great events, but every turn; not only in His own people, but in every child of man. . . .[1]

Man's goings are of the Lord; how can a man, then, understand his own way? (20:24)

Very few men and women really seek God's will in life; nevertheless, the events of our lives are directed by the invisible hand of the awesome God of heaven. We are directed along the path that we have selected (some on the King's highway, and some on the road of destruction), and most of the time we are not even aware of the part that He is having in our lives. Sometimes He is aiding us. Sometimes He is hindering us. Sometimes He is redirecting us ("this is the way, walk ye in it. . . ."). Sometimes He is leading us. Sometimes He is pushing us. Charles Bridges quotes Bishop Hall as saying: "Every creature walks blindfolded. Only he that dwells in light sees whither they go (2 Kings 5:2, 3)."[2]

God Has the Ability to Change Minds

When a man's ways please the Lord, he maketh even his enemies to be at peace with him. (16:7)

The king's heart is in the hand of the Lord, like the rivers of water; he turneth it withersoever he will. (21:1)

There are many, many examples in the Bible that show us that God changes minds. One example would be how God changed the minds of the Egyptians toward the Israelites, whom they had oppressed so badly. He told Moses:

And I will give this people favor in the sight of the Egyptians; and it shall come to pass, that, when ye go, ye shall not go empty; but every woman shall ask of her neighbor, and of her who sojourneth in her house, jewels of silver, and jewels of gold, and raiment, and ye shall put them upon your sons, and upon your daughters; and ye shall despoil the Egyptians. (3:21–22)

It happened just as God said it would. The Lord gave the Israelites "favor" by changing the minds of the Egyptians:

And the children of Israel did according to the word of Moses; and they asked of the Egyptians jewels of silver, and jewels of gold, and raiment. And the Lord gave the people favor in the sight of the Egyptians, so that they gave unto them such things as they required. And they despoiled the Egyptians. (Exod. 12:35–36)

Author Jerry Bridges comments:

How did God do this? We don't know. We only know what the text tells us. It is obvious that the Egyptians acted freely and voluntarily of their own wills. Yet they acted that way because as the text says, "The Lord had made (them) favorably disposed toward (the Israelites)." God, in some mysterious way, moved in their hearts so that they, of their own free choice, did exactly what He planned for them to do. God sovereignly intervened in the hearts—the desires and wills—of the Egyptians to accomplish His purpose for the Israelites.[3]

God Has Placed a Boundary on the Will of Men

There is no wisdom, nor understanding, nor counsel against the Lord. (21:30)

Man can only do what God *allows* him to do. The things that a man does falls into two categories: 1. Those things God *directs*, and 2. Those things that God *permits*.

God's Sovereign Will Always Prevails over Man's Finite Will

There are many devices in a man's heart; nevertheless, the counsel of the Lord, that shall stand. (19:21)

God Alone Knows a Man's Future

Boast not thyself of tomorrow; for thou knowest not what a day may bring forth. (27:1)

The plan of God cannot be thwarted, changed, or compromised. His purposes will always prevail, regardless of what schemes Satan may plant in the minds of wicked men. A man's plans can only succeed when the Lord permits them to. God determines the outcome of things (Prov. 16:9,33; 19:21, 20:24, 21:30–31).

12 | God and His People

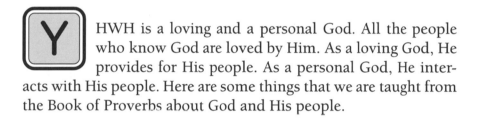HWH is a loving and a personal God. All the people who know God are loved by Him. As a loving God, He provides for His people. As a personal God, He interacts with His people. Here are some things that we are taught from the Book of Proverbs about God and His people.

He disciplines us so that we can do better.

My son, despise not the chastening of the Lord, neither be weary of His correction; for whom the Lord loveth He correcteth, even as a father the son in whom he delighteth. (3:11–12)

As a loving father corrects his son, the loving heavenly Father corrects us.

He favors us if we do right.

A good man obtaineth favor of the Lord, but a man of wicked devices will He condemn. (12:2)

The way of the wicked is an abomination unto the Lord, but He loveth him that followeth after righteousness. (15:9)

He that followeth after righteousness and mercy findeth life, righteousness, and honor. (21:21)

He feeds us.

The Lord will not suffer the soul of the righteous to famish, but He casteth away the substance of the wicked. (10:3)

The righteous eateth to the satisfying of his soul, but the belly of the wicked shall want. (13:25)

He hears all the prayers that we pray.

The Lord is far from the wicked, but He heareth the prayer of the righteous. (15:29)

He sees all the things that we do.

The eyes of the Lord are in every place, beholding the evil and the good. (15:3)

For the ways of man are before the eyes of the Lord, and He pondereth all his goings. (5:21)

He knows all the thoughts that we think.

All the ways of a man are clean in his own eyes, but the Lord weigheth the spirits. (16:2)

Every way of a man is right in his own eyes, but the Lord weigheth the hearts. (21:2)

If thou sayest, Behold, we knew it not; doth not he that weigheth the heart consider it? And He that keepeth the soul, doth not He know it? And shall not He render to every man according to his works? (24:12)

When You Trust Him:

• He will direct your paths.

Trust in the Lord with all thine heart, and lean not unto thine own understanding. In all thy ways, acknowledge Him and He shall direct thy paths. (3:5–6)

• He will make you happy.

He that handleth a matter wisely shall find good; and whoso trusteth in the Lord, happy is he. (16:20)

• He will prosper you.

He that is of a proud heart stirreth up strife, but he that putteth his trust in the Lord shall be made fat. (28:25)

• He will keep you safe.

The fear of man bringeth a snare; but whoso putteth his trust in the Lord shall be safe. (29:25)

When You Commit Your Life to Him:

• He will redirect your thoughts and you'll discover His purpose for your life.

Commit thy works unto the Lord, and thy thoughts shall be established. (16:3)

13

Things That Delight the Lord, Things That Disgust the Lord

Things That Delight the Lord

R *âcôn* is a Hebrew word that is translated (in Proverbs) as "delight," or "favor." It is also translated one time as "what is acceptable." Râcôn comes from the Hebrew word *râcâh,* which means "to be pleased with" or "to satisfy a debt." God tells us in the following verses of things that "please" Him. These are things in which He delights:

1. Those who find God (8:35)
2. A man who takes a wife (18:22)
3. Honest people (11:1, 12:22)
4. The "good people" of this world (11:27, 12:2)
5. The "upright" and "righteous" (11:20, 14:9)
6. The prayer of the upright (15:8)

Things That Disgust the Lord

The Hebrew word for abomination in Proverbs is *tôw'êlâh* and describes something that is "disgusting" to the Lord. These abominations or disgusting things are:

1. Pride (6:17, 16:5)

2. A lying tongue (6:17, 12:22)

3. Hands that shed innocent blood (6:17)

4. The thoughts of the wicked (6:18, 15:26)

5. Feet that run to do evil (6:18)

6. A slanderer (6:19)

7. A person who sows discord among brethren (6:19)

8. A sacrifice offered by a wicked person (15:8, 21:27)

9. The life-style of the wicked (15:9)

10. Rulers who commit wickedness (16:12)

11. One who acquits a wicked person (17:15)

12. One who condemns an innocent person (17:15)

13. Dishonest people (20:10, 23)

14. He who will not hear the Word of the Lord (28:9)

14 | Marriage

Marriage is the first institution that God set up for the human race, dating back to our first ancestors, Adam and Eve (Gen. 2:18, 20–24). Marriage is of God and is therefore good, right, and profitable for men and women. Marriage was designed by Almighty God for the happiness and procreation of the human race. Marriage works beautifully for people who follow the rules and guidelines that the Lord gave us for its protection.

There are, in the final analysis, only two reasons why a marriage ends: The first reason is death. This is God's way of ending a marriage. In the plan of Almighty God, marriage is to be "until death do us part." The second reason why a marriage ends is sin. We are all sinners, so God did not design marriage for perfect people. When He designed marriage, He knew full well that the human race would reject His absolute Lordship. The good news is that we do not have to be sinless to make marriage work. The bad news is sin so often results in divorce. Divorce is always the result of somebody's sin. There are no exceptions. This is not God's way of ending a marriage. Divorce is man "putting asunder" what "God hath joined together" (Matt. 19:6). It is Satan's way of destroying that which God designed: marriage. Divorce brings sorrow, loneliness, discouragement, depression, heartbreak, and almost always an increased tendency to sin further. Divorce has left us with a nation full of confused, hurting, and unstable children and teenagers. These are the "innocent victims" of divorce. Matthew Henry said:

> Let him that is married take delight in his wife, and let him be very fond of her, not only because she is the wife that he himself has chosen and he ought to be pleased with his own choice, but because she is the wife that God, in His providence, appointed for him and he ought much more be pleased with the divine appointment, pleased with her because she is his own.[1]

The Rejoicing and Ravished Husband

Proverbs 5:15–20

This passage deals with the intimate relationship in marriage. It is covered in more detail in chapter five of this book. Notice the important points God gives us here.

- A man should have sexual relations **with his wife only** (vv. 15, 19, 20).
- A woman should have sexual relations **with her husband only** (v. 17).
- Husband and wives are told to *rejoice* together (v. 18).
- A man is to be all taken up with his wife and her love *(ravished* v. 19).

Trouble in the Home

A. Caused by the husband:

He that troubleth his own house shall inherit the wind; and the fool shall be servant to the wise of heart. (11:29)

And why wilt thou, my son, be ravished with a strange woman, and embrace the bosom of a foreigner. (5:20)

B. Caused by the wife:

1. The unfaithful wife.

*A virtuous woman is a crown to her husband, but **she that maketh ashamed** is rottenness in his bones.* (12:4)

2. The foolish wife.

*Every wise woman buildeth her house: but the foolish **plucketh it down** with her hands.* (14:1)

3. The angry wife.

*It is better to dwell in a corner of the housetop, than with a **brawling woman** in a wide house.* (21:9)

Other scriptures on the angry wife include: Proverbs 19:13, 21:19, 25:24, 27:15–16.

A Good Wife

***Whoso findeth a wife findeth a good thing,** and obtaineth favor from the Lord.* (18:22)

*House and riches are the inheritance of fathers, and a **prudent wife is from the Lord.*** (19:14)

*Who can find a virtuous woman? For **her price is far above rubies.*** (31:10)

The qualities of the virtuous woman are covered in this book in chapter 31. When you read that chapter, you will discover why her value is so high. Here are some points from the above verses about a (good) wife.

- A good wife is very important (18:22).
- A good wife is a gift from God (18:22, 19:14).
- A good wife is priceless (31:10).

15 | Children

- **Children need to be trained:**

  Train up a child in the way he should go and, when he is old, he will not depart from it. (22:6)

- **Children need to be taught the Word of God:**

  Hear, O my son, and receive my sayings, and the years of thy life shall be many. I have taught thee in the way of wisdom; I have led thee in the right paths. When thou goest, thy steps shall not be hindered; and when thou runnest, thou shalt not stumble. (4:10–12)

- **Children have "reputations" just like grown-ups do:**

  Even a child is known by his doings, whether his work be pure, and whether it be right. (20:11)

- **Children, when grown, should still listen and respect their parents:**

  Hearken unto thy father that begot thee, and despise not thy mother when she is old. (23:22)

- **Children who are rebellious make parents sad:**

  A foolish son is a grief to his father, and bitterness to her that bore him. (17:25 [See also 10:1, 17:21, 19:13])

- **Children who do the right thing cause parents to rejoice:**

  The father of the righteous shall greatly rejoice, and he that begotteth a wise child shall have joy of him. Thy father and thy mother shall be glad, and she that bore thee shall rejoice. (23:24–25)

A ll children need some discipline. Some children need very little corporal punishment. These children respond very quickly to correction. Other children disobey more, break the rules more, and just seem to have a real struggle in the area of obedience. These children need more corporal punishment. Parents should never spank a child when they are angry. The only biblical reason that a child is to be spanked is for correction of bad behavior. Discipline should be administered firmly, but with a heart of love and concern for the child. The child should always understand before being disciplined what unacceptable behavior has caused this action to be taken. The parent should not withhold forgiveness. If the child, having been spanked, is repentant, he or she should be forgiven by the parent immediately.

The "Dirty Dozen"

Twelve Reasons Why Parents Don't Discipline Their Children

1. They have embraced the philosophy of the culture on "child-rearing" instead of the Bible. → Many influential voices in our culture are saying: "Spanking children is wrong."

2. They feel guilty because they aren't home much. → "We both work, and so we are hardly ever home, hardly ever see him—how can we spank him?"

3. They are preoccupied with their own problems. They don't want "the hassle." It's too much trouble to raise the kids right.

→ "I know I should be teaching my children to behave better, but I've got too much on my mind."

4. There is a dislike of the child—either openly or secretly (13:24).

→ *He that spareth the rod hateth his son; but he that loveth him chasteneth him early. (13:24)*

5. They do not know that foolishness is bound up in a child's mind.

→ *Foolishness is bound in the heart of a child, but the rod of correction shall drive it far from him. (22:15)*

6. They do not realize that discipline, lovingly administered when needed, causes a child to increase in wisdom.

→ *The rod and reproof give wisdom, but a child left to himself bringeth his mother to shame. (29:15)*

7. They do not realize that without it, the child is headed for trouble.

→ *The rod and reproof give wisdom, but a child left to himself bringeth his mother to shame. (29:15)*

8. They are often afraid of hurting the child.

→ *Withhold not correction from the child; for if thou beatest him with the rod, he shall not die. (23:13 [See also 20:30])*

9. They don't understand that great issues are at stake. How will an undisciplined child live as an adult? Where will he/she spend eternity?

→ *Thou shalt beat him with the rod, and shalt deliver his soul from sheol.* (23:14)

10. They do not realize that a day may come when "hope" to correct the child's unacceptable behavior will be gone.

→ *Chasten thy son while there is hope, and let not thy soul spare for his crying.* (19:18)

11. They do not realize that it is the thing that will end the confusion in the home and bring joy.

→ *Correct thy son, and he shall give thee rest; yea, he shall give delight unto thy soul.* (29:17)

12. They have not carefully considered the lifelong benefits of raising obedient children.

→ *The father of the righteous shall greatly rejoice, and he that begotteth a wise child shall have joy of him. Thy father and thy mother shall be glad, and she that bore thee shall rejoice.* (23:24–25)

16 | Taking Care of Business

Sometimes we make the mistake of looking enviously at the "success" of the ungodly people of this world. All of us know of men and women who have sinned their way to "success." "Evil men" (Prov. 24:1) often have a "whatever-it-takes-to-get-to-the-top" attitude. They will break the law, they will lie, they will steal, and they will cheat. Although they are often found in respectable occupations, if they are "evil men," they are not to be respected. Other people have profited from businesses that pander to man's sinful nature. They make their fortunes at the expense of the health, morals, and well-being of their customers and their families. Great fortunes have been made in marketing sex (Hollywood is just one example), alcohol, and drugs.

People who are attempting to live right and obey God reject these money-making techniques and this philosophy of business for two reasons: the first reason is conscience. The second reason is the knowledge that after man's "brief day in the sun," there is an eternal God to face. The Book of Proverbs gives us some guidelines that, when followed, will bring the right kind of success. Follow these, and you will know that your Maker is pleased, for the Holy Spirit Himself will stamp upon your heart God's seal of approval. He will also vocalize His approval to you when you appear before Him with these words: "Well done, thou good and faithful servant . . ." (Matt. 25:21).

Twelve Laws for Success in Business
from the Ancient Near East

The Book of Proverbs has much to say about being a good manager of time and assets. I have selected twelve important things that YHWH told the ancient people of Israel that, when followed, would bring them earthly rewards. These twelve laws are just as important today as they were in Solomon's day. They will work for men and women today just as they worked for men and women in Solomon's day. As you consider these twelve laws from the ancient Near East, remember their original source is God, *not* man. These are, therefore, twelve laws of good business from God to you.

Law #1
Do not envy evil men: Do not desire to be with them. Do not take counsel from them.

*Be not **envious** of evil men, **neither desire** to be with them.* (24:1)

Cease, my son, to hear the instruction that causeth thee to err from the words of knowledge. (19:27)

Law #2
Acquire wisdom and knowledge.

*Through **wisdom** is an house builded, and by understanding is it established; and by **knowledge** shall the chambers be filled with all precious and pleasant riches. A wise man is strong; yea, **a man of knowledge increaseth strength**.* (24:3–5)

To achieve success in man's eyes, you may only need human knowledge. To attain real success (definition: doing the best at whatever God gives you to do), you will need both human wisdom and divine wisdom. See chapter four of this book. Get as much education in the field that God has placed you in as you can. It was Lord Bacon of England who said: "Knowledge is power." Proverbs 19:2 tells us that "It is not good for a person to be without knowledge . . ." (NAS). You should be growing continually in both schools of wisdom.

Law #3
Develop your business or profession first.
And then build your home.

Prepare thy work outside, and *make it fit for thyself in the field; and afterwards build thine house.* (24:27)

Law #4
Commit your business or profession to the Lord.

Commit thy works unto the Lord, and *thy thoughts shall be established*. (16:3)

Most people's work goal is "to get rich." Is that your goal? That is the wrong goal. That is a goal that comes from man's mind, not God's. It is a goal based on man's wisdom and not divine wisdom. The Lord instructs us in Proverbs 23:4: "Labor not to be rich; cease from thine own wisdom." If your goal is simply "to get rich," you have a goal that is in conflict with God's purpose for your life. God wants you to commit your business, your life, and all that you are to Him, to bring glory to Him. There is no higher calling for your life than this. The ultimate goal for you and me is to glorify our Lord. "Whether, therefore, ye eat, or drink, or whatever ye do, do all to the glory of God," we are told (1 Cor. 10:31). The unsaved mind, in many cases, will not be able to comprehend this concept. A pagan cannot commit to a Lord that he does not know. If you are a believer, and you *commit your all* to the Lord, even your "thoughts shall be established" (16:3).

Law #5	*He that covereth his sins shall not*
Confess your sins and forsake them.	***prosper***, *but whoso **confesseth** and **forsaketh them** shall have mercy.* (28:13)

We cannot hear from, nor fellowship with, a Holy God when there is unconfessed sin in our lives. Christian business men and women who want to hear from God must deal with the issue of sin regularly (1 John 1:8–10).

Law #6	***Honor*** *the Lord with **thy substance**, and with the **first fruits of thine increase**. **So shall thine barns be filled with plenty**, and*
Honor the Lord with your tithes and offerings . . . and He will honor you.	*thy presses shall burst out with new wine.* (3:9–10)

Law #7	*The simple believeth every word, but*
Spend sufficient time in research.	*the **prudent man looketh well** to his going.* (14:15)

Law #8	***Be thou diligent to know the state of thy flocks, and look well to thy herds***; *for riches are not forever. And doth the crown endure to every generation? The hay appeareth,*
Watch your business interests carefully.	*and the tender grass showeth itself, and herbs of the mountains are gathered. The lambs are for thy clothing, and the goats are the price of the field. And thou shalt have goats' milk enough for thy food, for the food of thy household, and for the maintenance for thy maidens.* (27:23–27)

Stay current with and know the state of your business or profession. This includes such things as customers, accounts, the competition, market trends, your investments and assets (see also 22:29).

Law #9
Work hard, and you'll be rewarded.

*The **hand of the diligent shall bear rule**, but the slothful shall be put to forced labor. (12:24)*

Law #10
Be honest.

*A **false balance** is an **abomination to the Lord**, but a **just weight** is **His delight**. (11:1 [see also Proverbs 16:11, 20:10, 23])*

Law #11
Help the poor.

*He that **hath pity upon the poor** lendeth unto the Lord, and that which he hath given will He pay him again. (19:17)*

Law #12
When your business becomes successful—do not trust in your riches.

*He that **trusteth in his riches shall fall**, but the righteous shall flourish like a branch. (11:28)*

As we become successful, we have a tendency to become more independent from God. We begin to trust in the power of our money, rather than in the power of the Living God. We are warned about this in both the Old and New Testaments. Do not neglect to walk with God and to trust in Him when you become successful. Agur prayed that God would give him "neither poverty not riches; feed me with food convenient for me, lest I be full, and deny thee, and say, Who is the Lord? Or lest I be poor, and steal, and take the name of my God in vain" (30:8–9).

17 | Money

here is an abundance of information in Proverbs on the subject of money, poverty, and wealth. Many, many verses in Proverbs deal with these subjects. I have assembled a list of twelve wealth-building strategies from the Book of Proverbs. These are obviously similar in nature to the laws of success discussed in chapter sixteen. Although there is some overlap in these two chapters, chapter sixteen deals primarily with making money whereas chapter seventeen deals with the proper handling of the money.

Twelve Wealth Building Strategies from the Mind of God

Strategy #1   **Commit the fruit of your hands to the Lord.**

Commit thy works unto the Lord, and thy thoughts shall be established. (16:3)

Strategy #2   **Do not invest in ventures that conflict with who you are (a child of God).**

*Better is the poor that walketh in his uprightness, than he that is **perverse in his ways***, *though he be rich.* (28:6)

He that by interest and **unjust gain** increaseth his substance, he shall gather it for him that pity the poor. (28:8)

Whoso is **partner with a thief** hateth his own soul; he heareth cursing, and revealeth it not. (29:24)

Whoso robbeth his father or his mother, and saith, It is not transgression; the same is a **companion of a destroyer.** (28:24)

Strategy #3   Expect God to bless your investments as you serve Him.

The blessing of the Lord, it **maketh rich**, and He addeth no sorrow with it. (10:22)

A **good man leaveth an inheritance** to his children's children; and the wealth of the sinner is laid up for the just. (13:22)

In the **house of the righteous** is **much treasure**, but in the revenues of the wicked is trouble. (15:6)

There is **treasure** to be desired, and **oil, in the dwelling of the wise**, but a foolish man spendeth it up. (21:20)

By humility and the fear of the Lord there are **riches, and honor, and life**. (22:4)

Strategy #4   Determine to honor the Lord with the "first fruits" of all your profits.

Honor the Lord with thy substance, and with the **first fruits** of **all thine increase**; so **shall thy barns be filled with plenty**, and thy presses shall burst forth with new wine. (3:9–10)

There is he that scattereth, and yet **increaseth**; and there is he that withholdeth more than is fitting, but it tendeth to poverty. **The liberal soul shall be made fat**, and he that watereth shall be watered also himself. (11:24–25)

Strategy #5 **Learn to be "harvest minded" like the ant.**

*Go to the **ant**, thou sluggard; and **consider her ways**, and **be wise**, which, having no guide, overseer, or ruler, provideth her food in the summer, and **gathereth** her food **in the harvest**.* (6:6–8)

Chapter six of this book deals with the subject of the harvest. Please review that chapter for further help on this subject.

*The **thoughts** of the **diligent** tend only to **plenteousness**; but of every one that is hasty, only to want.* (21:5)

***There is treasure** to be desired, **and oil, in the dwelling of the wise**, but a foolish man spendeth it up.* (21:20)

Strategy #6 **Seek God's direction before investing in anything.**

*In **all** thy ways **acknowledge Him**, and **He shall direct** thy paths.* (3:6)

***Commit thy works unto the Lord**, and **thy thoughts** shall be **established**.* (16:3)

Strategy #7 **Do not be taken in by "hot tips" or hearsay, and do careful research before investing.**

*The **simple believeth every word**, but the **prudent** man **looketh well** to his going.* (14:15)

Strategy #8 **Be diligent in monitoring your investments.**

***Be thou diligent to know the state of thy flocks, and look well to thy herds**; for riches are not forever. And doth the crown endure to* *every generation? The hay appeareth, and the tender grass showeth itself, and herbs of the mountains are gathered. The lambs are for thy clothing, and the goats are the price of the field. And thou shalt have goats' milk enough for thy food, for the food of thy household, and for the maintenance for thy maidens.* (27:23–27)

Strategy #9   **Do not borrow money unless it is absolutely necessary.**

*The rich ruleth over the poor, and the **borrower is servant** to the lender.* (22:7)

Borrowing money makes you a servant to someone else. Borrowing money puts you in bondage to men. God promised to supply all of our needs (Phil. 4:19). It is better to trust God to supply the need than to borrow money and go in debt. Many times we go in debt for "wants," not "needs." Going into debt for "wants" is not a good strategy. Major purchases like a home or an automobile are necessary exceptions. As a rule of thumb for most other expenses, it is better to "pay as you go."

Strategy #10   **Do not co-sign a note.**

*My son, **if thou be surety** for thy neighbor, if thou hast struck thy hand with a stranger, **thou art snared** with the words of thy mouth, thou art taken with the words of thy mouth. Do this now, my son, and deliver thyself, when thou art come into the hand of thy neighbor: go, humble thyself, and importune thy neighbor. Give not sleep to thine eyes, nor slumber to thine eyelids. **Deliver thyself** like a roe from the hand of the hunter, and like a bird from the hand of the fowler.* (6:1–5)

These verses are dealt with in chapter six of this book. Other verses that deal with co-signing are: Proverbs 11:15, 17:18, 20:16, 22:26, and 27:13.

Strategy #11 **Always be aware that wealth and increase come from the Lord.**

Riches and honor **are with me**; *yea, durable riches and righteous-ness. My fruit is better than gold, yea than fine gold; and my revenue than choice silver. I lead in the way of righteousness, in the midst of the paths of justice, that I may cause those who love me to inherit substance; and **I will fill their treasuries**. (8:18–21)*

Strategy #12 **Never put your trust in your bank account or in your investments.**

He that trusteth in his riches shall fall, *but the righteous shall flourish like a branch. (11:28)*

Trust in the Lord with all thine heart, *and lean not unto thine own understanding. (3:5)*

*Wilt thou set forth thine eyes upon that which is not? For **riches** certainly **make themselves wings**; **they fly away** like an eagle to-ward heaven. (23:5)*

18 | Reward in Labor, Mind Your Own Business, Punishment for Murder, Judgment Day, Gray Hair

Reward in Labor

He that tilleth his land shall be satisfied with bread, but he that followeth vain persons is void of understanding. The wicked desireth the net of evil men, but the root of the righteous yieldeth fruit. The wicked is snared by the transgression of his lips, but the just shall come out of trouble. A man shall be satisfied with good by the fruit of his mouth; and the recompense of a man's hands shall be rendered unto him. (12:11–14)

He becometh poor that dealeth with a slack hand, but the hand of the diligent maketh rich. He that gathereth in the summer is a wise son, but he that sleepeth in harvest is a son that causeth shame. (10:4–5)

The labor of the righteous tendeth to life; the fruit of the wicked, to sin. (10:16)

In all labor there is profit; but the talk of the lips tendeth only to penury. (14:23)

He that keepeth his mouth keepeth his life, but he that openeth wide his lips shall have destruction. The soul of the sluggard desireth, and hath nothing; but the soul of the diligent shall be made fat. (13:3–4)

Wealth gotten by vanity shall be diminished, but he that gathereth by labor shall increase. (13:11)

The slothful man roasteth not that which he took in hunting, but the substance of a diligent man is precious. (12:27)

The hand of the diligent shall bear rule, but the slothful shall be put to forced labor. (12:24)

For more on the subject of labor, see chapter six of this book.

Mind Your Own Business

He that passeth by, and meddleth with strife belonging not to him, is like one that taketh a dog by the ears. (26:17)

We are cautioned not to be hasty to strive even for our own cause (25:8). How much more caution, then, is needed before entering somebody else's quarrel? When you take this "dog by the ears," suddenly somebody else's problems become yours. If you have an angry, snarling dog by the ears, you've got your hands full, indeed! He's angry, and defensive, and trying to bite you! How are you going to get out of this mess? You can't hang on to his ears and fight him off forever, but as soon as you let go, you quickly become "dog-meat!"

Solution: mind your own business!

Punishment for Murder

A man that doeth violence to the blood of any person shall flee to the pit; let no man sustain him. (28:17)

God established the death penalty for murder way back in the days of Noah. It is an offense to Almighty God when people rally behind a known murderer and attempt to save his life. *Let no man sustain him*, declares the Word of God. Genesis 9:6 tells us why God requires the death penalty for murder: "Whoso sheddeth man's blood, by man shall his blood be shed; *for in the image of God made He man.*"

It is a horrible outrage against the God of heaven to destroy one who was created in His image. The Bible clearly teaches that the murderer's life is not to be spared. The murderer is to be put to death.

Judgment Day

Be not afraid of sudden fear, neither of the desolation of the wicked, when it cometh; for the Lord shall be thy confidence, and shall keep thy foot from being taken. (3:25–26)

The wise shall inherit glory, but shame shall be the promotion of fools. (3:35)

If thou sayest, Behold, we knew it not; doth not He that weigheth the heart consider it? And He that keepeth thy soul, doth He not know it? And shall not He render to every man according to his works? (24:12)

Riches profit not in the day of wrath, but righteousness delivereth from death. (11:4)

Gray Hair

The hoary head is a crown of glory, if it be found in the way of righteousness. (16:31)

The glory of young men is their strength, and the beauty of old men is the gray head. (20:29)

19 | The Nation, The Poor

The Nation

Kings

- **Who really selects the rulers?**

  By me kings reign, and princes decree justice. By me princes rule, and nobles, even all of the judges of the earth. (8:15–16)

- **Our loyalty is encouraged.**

  My son, fear thou the Lord and the king, and meddle not with them that are given to change; for their calamity shall rise suddenly, and who knoweth the ruin of them both? (24:21–22)

- **Ungodly leaders v. Godly leaders.**

  When righteous men do rejoice, there is great glory; but when the wicked rise, a man is hidden. (28:12)

  As a roaring lion, and a ranging bear, so is a wicked ruler over a poor people. The prince that lacketh understanding is also a great oppressor; but he that hateth covetousness shall prolong his days. (28:15–16)

  When the righteous are in authority, the people rejoice; but when the wicked beareth rule, the people mourn. (29:2)

  The king by justice established the land, but he that exacteth gifts overthroweth it. (29:4)

- **The importance of the types of people who surround the king:**

  Take away the wicked from before the king, and his throne shall be established in righteousness. (25:5)

  If a ruler hearken to lies, all his servants are wicked. (29:12)

Things That May Affect a King's Decisions:

Lack of counsel

Where no counsel is, the people fall; but in the multitude of counselors there is safety. (11:14)

Wrong counsel

If a ruler hearken to lies, all his servants are wicked. (29:12)

Wrong beverage

It is not for kings, O Lemuel, it is not for kings to drink wine, nor princes strong drink. Lest they drink, and forget the law, and pervert the justice of any of the afflicted. (31:4–5)

Wrong gifts (bribes)

The king by justice establisheth the land, but he that exacteth gifts overthrow it. (29:4)

The Lord

The king's heart is in the hand of the Lord, like the rivers of water; he turneth it at withersoever He will. (21:1)

What Righteousness Does:

- **Righteousness benefits communities.**

  When it goeth well with the righteous, the city rejoiceth; and when the wicked perish, there is shouting. (11:10)

- **Righteousness exalts communities.**

  By the blessing of the upright is the city exalted, but it is overthrown by the mouth of the wicked. (11:11)

- **Righteousness exalts a nation.**

  Righteousness exalteth a nation, but sin is reproach to any people. (14:34)

What Sin Does:

- **Sin brings disgrace.**

  Righteousness exalteth a nation, but sin is reproach to any people. (14:34)

- **Sin causes governments to be overthrown.**

  By the blessing of the upright the city is exalted, but it is overthrown by the mouth of the wicked. (11:11)

The Poor

A man there was
Though some called him mad,
The more he cast away, the more he had.
He that bestows his goods upon the poor
Should have as much again
and ten times more.[1]

The Relationship between the Lord and the Poor

We please our Maker:	We reproach our Maker:
• By having mercy on the poor (14:31)	• By mocking the poor (17:5)
• By having pity on the poor (19:17)	• By oppressing the poor (14:31)
• By giving food to the poor (22:9)	

The Lord's Promises and Warnings Concerning the Poor

⟶ **Give to the poor, and God Himself will repay you.**

He that hath pity on the poor lendeth unto the Lord, and that which he hath given will He pay him again. (19:17)

⟶ **Feed the poor, and God will bless you.**

He that hath a bountiful eye shall be blessed; for he giveth of his bread to the poor. (22:9)

⟶ **Give to the poor, and you won't lack.**

He that giveth to the poor shall not lack. . . . (28:27a)

⟶ **God blesses the king who watches out for the poor.**

The king that faithfully judgeth the poor, his throne shall be established forever. (29:14)

⟶ **Be generous to the poor, and the Lord shall prosper you.**

There is he that scattereth, and yet increaseth; and there is he that withholdeth more than is fitting, but it tendeth to poverty. The liberal soul shall be made fat, and he that watereth shall be watered also himself. (11:24–25)

➤ **He that oppresses the poor often comes to a time of need.**

He that oppresseth the poor to increase his riches, and he that giveth to the rich, shall surely come to want. (22:16)

➤ **He that covers his ears to the cry of the poor may one day cry himself.**

Whoso stoppeth his ears at the cry of the poor, he also shall cry himself, and not be heard. (21:13)

➤ **He that covers his eyes to the poor shall suffer many curses.**

He that giveth unto the poor shall not lack, but he that hideth his eyes shall have many a curse. (28:27)

Instructions and Facts from Proverbs Concerning the Poor

■ **The poor are not to be mocked.**

Whoso mocketh the poor reproacheth his Maker; and he that is glad at calamities shall not be unpunished. (17:5)

■ **The poor are not to be oppressed.**

He that oppresseth the poor reproacheth his Maker, but he that honoreth him hath mercy on the poor. (14:31)

■ **The poor are often shunned by friends, families, and neighbors.**

Wealth maketh many friends, but the poor is separated from his neighbor. All the brethren of the poor do hate him. How much more do his friends go far from him! He pursueth them with words, yet they are lacking to him. (19:4, 7)

■ **When the poor come to us for help, we are to help them.**

Whoso stoppeth his ears to the cry of the poor, he also shall cry himself, and not be heard. (21:13)

■ **God sometimes takes money from those who are unscrupulous and gives it to someone who will pity the poor.**

He that by interest and unjust gain increaseth his substance, he shall gather it for him that will pity the poor. (28:8)

■ **Righteous people are concerned for the poor.**

The righteous considereth the cause of the poor, but the wicked regardeth not to know it. (29:7)

■ **Kings are to plead the cause of the poor.**

The words of King Lemuel, the prophecy that his mother taught him. . . . Open thy mouth, judge righteously, and plead the cause of the poor and needy. (31:1, 9)

■ **The virtuous woman in Proverbs 31 helped the poor.**

She stretcheth out her hand to the poor; yea, she reacheth forth her hands to the needy. (31:20)

We have just studied the Word of God on the subject of the poor. If we are to be a godly people, we must align our thinking with the mind of God. Most of us (myself included) have not done much, and surely not enough, for the poor. Now that we know what the Word of God says on this subject, if we are really serious about obeying the Lord, we must adjust our thinking, and we must take action.

Here are some suggestions:

1. Give something on a regular basis to the poor. Save a set amount out of each paycheck or a small percentage of your income.

2. As these funds begin to accumulate, ask God to show you who He would have you to help.

3. Before a gift of cash or food, verify carefully that the party is in need.

4. Give the appropriate gift of money or food in the name of the Lord and in obedience to His Word.

20 | Sin, Repentance

What Sin Does

❏ Sin makes life hard.

Good understanding giveth favor, but the way of the transgressors is hard. (13:15)

❏ Sin brings trouble and problems.

Behold, the righteous shall be recompensed in the earth; much more, the wicked and the sinner. Proverbs 11:31

Evil pursueth sinners; but, to the righteous, good shall be repaid. (13:21)

❏ Sinful thoughts are an abomination to the Lord.

The thoughts of the wicked are an abomination to the Lord, but the words of the pure are pleasant words. (15:26)

❏ Sin shortens life.

The fear of the Lord prolongeth days, but the years of the wicked shall be shortened. (10:27)

❏ Sin results in destruction.

Whoso despiseth the word shall be destroyed, but he that feareth the commandment shall be rewarded. (13:13)

❏ **Sin robs a person of all hope when life on earth is over.**

The hope of the righteous shall be gladness, but the expectation of the wicked shall perish. (10:28)

When a wicked man dieth, his expectation shall perish; and the hope of unjust men perisheth. (11:7)

Man's Universal Problem of Sin

*Who can say, I have made my heart clean, **I am pure from my sin**? (20:9)*

God's Universal Answer to the Sin Problem

For the Unbeliever:

GOD'S ANSWER IS JESUS CHRIST.

I love those who love me, and those who seek me early shall find me. (8:17)

*For whoso **findeth me findeth life**, and shall obtain favor of the Lord. But he that sinneth against me wrongeth his own soul; all they that hate me love death.* (8:35–36)

For the Believer:

GOD'S ANSWER IS REPENTANCE.

*He that covereth his sins shall not prosper, **but whoso confesseth and forsaketh them shall have mercy**.* (28:13)

21 | **Flattery, Pride, Humility**

Proverbs on Flattery

▌ Flattering words can destroy lives:

*With her much fair speech she caused him to yield; with the **flattering of her lips** she forced him. He goeth after her straightway, as an **ox to the slaughter**, or as a fool to the correction of the stocks, till an arrow strike through his liver-as a bird hasteneth to the snare, and knoweth not that **it is for his life**.* (7:21–23)

One of the things for young men to learn from this story is to beware of the flatterer. We can be led into all kinds of sin through flattery. The words of the flatterer, if believed, can cause great trouble and even ruin one's life.

▌ Flattering words do not reveal what is in the heart:

*When he speaketh pleasantly, believe him not; for there are **seven abominations in his heart**. A lying tongue hateth those who are afflicted by it, and a **flattering mouth worketh ruin**.* (26:25, 28)

There is a great difference between a genuine compliment and words of flattery. The compliment comes from one whose heart is sincere. His heart matches his words. The flatterer's heart does not match his words. He is insincere. He is a liar.

▌ Flattery is never designed for the good of the person:

He that rebuketh a man afterwards *shall find more favor than he that flattereth* with his tongue. (28:23)

What an interesting thought. There are three people in verse 23. There is the "rebuker," there is the "flatterer," and there is the man to whom they addressed their remarks. The rebuker makes the man feel *uneasy*. It's not pleasant to be rebuked. The flatterer's words are *appealing* and *pleasant* to the ears. As time passes, however, the man realizes through his experiences that the sincere rebuker told him what he *needed* to hear, while the flatterer told him what he *wanted* to hear.

▌ Flatterers often lay traps:

A man that flattereth his neighbor *spreadeth a net* for his feet. (29:5)

Their words often sound like music and flow like "honey from the comb." Accept sincere compliments when they are given by well meaning people but beware of the flatterer's "net." If you know the person is not a truthful person, you need to ask, "What's behind the smile? What's behind the smooth words? What is really in this person's heart?" Listen to their words carefully and prayerfully, and if you are dealing with a flatterer, the Holy Spirit will surely show you that "it's a setup." Graciously reject the flattering words from the one whose heart does not match his statement. The flatterer may seem like an "angel of light," but beware—he is not your friend but your enemy (2 Cor. 11:13–15).

Summary:

The dangers that we are exposed to by the tongue of the flatterer are many and would include: a loss of fellowship with the Lord (flattery can cause a person to take his eyes off the Lord and focus on himself), pride, destroyed morals, ruined lives, and other satanic traps (Prov. 29:5 with 2 Tim. 2:26).

Proverbs on Pride

The subject of pride is covered in chapter six of this book. Pride is a serious topic because it is a mindset that Almighty God is against. Following are eight important truths from Proverbs on the subject of pride that come to us from the mind of God.

◆ 1. God hates pride.

*These six things doth the Lord **hate**; yea, seven are an abomination unto Him: **A proud look**, a lying tongue, and hands that shed innocent blood.* (6:16–17)

*The fear of the Lord is to hate evil; **pride**, and arrogance, and the evil way, and the perverse mouth, **do I hate**.* (8:13)

◆ 2. God sometimes causes financial ruin to the proud.

***The Lord will destroy the house of the proud**, but He will establish the border of the widow.* (15:25)

◆ 3. Pride is sin.

*An high look, and a **proud heart**, and the plowing of the wicked are **sin**.* (21:4)

◆ 4. Pride in the heart causes strife in the church.

*Only by **pride** cometh **contention**, but with the well-advised is wisdom.* (13:10)

*He that is of a **proud heart stirreth up strife**, but he that putteth his trust in the Lord shall be made fat.* (28:25)

◆ 5. Pride leads to destruction.

***Pride** goeth before **destruction**, and an haughty spirit before a fall.* (16:18)

◆ 6. Pride leads to shame.

*When **pride** cometh, then cometh **shame**; but with the lowly is wisdom.* (11:2)

◆ **7. Pride brings a man low.**

*A man's **pride** shall bring him **low**, but honor shall uphold the humble in spirit.* (29:23)

◆ **8. Pride causes someone who is filthy in the sight of God to think that he (or she) is clean and pure.**

*All the ways of a man are **clean in his own eyes**, **but the Lord** weigheth the spirits.* (16:2)

***Every way of a man** is **right in his own eyes**, **but the Lord** weigheth the hearts.* (21:2)

*There is a generation that are pure in their own eyes, and yet are **not washed from their filthiness**. There is a generation, oh, how lofty are their eyes! And their eyelids are lifted up.* (30:12–13)

> For more on the subject of pride, see chapter six of this book.

Proverbs on Humility

▲ **Humility is not a characteristic of those who promote themselves.**

Put not thyself in the presence of the king, and stand not in the place of great men; for better it be said unto thee, come up hither, than that thou shouldest be put lower in the presence of the prince whom thine eyes have not seen. (25:6–7)

▲ **Humility is not a characteristic of those who praise themselves.**

Let another man praise thee, and not thine own mouth; a stranger, and not thine own lips. (27:2)

▲ **Humility is a characteristic of those who are growing in divine wisdom.**

When pride cometh, then cometh shame; but with the lowly is wisdom. (11:2)

▲ **Humility is the road to honor.**

The fear of the Lord is the beginning of wisdom; and before honor is humility. (15:33)

Before destruction the heart of man is haughty, and before honor is humility. (18:12)

▲ **Humility brings good things.**

By humility and the fear of the Lord are riches, and honor, and life. Proverbs 22:4

22 | Emotions

motional illness has often been called "the nation's number one health problem." Medical doctor S.I. McMillen states that "one out of every twenty Americans will have a psychotic disturbance severe enough to confine him in a hospital for the insane."[1]

Emotional turmoil is also the cause of many kinds of physical and often fatal illness. Nerve fibers go out from the emotional center of the brain to every organ of the body. Doctor McMillen reports that over fifty diseases can be triggered by our emotions. A "self-centered" attitude often causes strong emotional responses. These emotions, out of control, often cause health problems, disease, and death. Some of these "disease-producing" emotions are: fear, desire for love or approval, sorrow, jealousy, envy, ambition, frustration, rage, hatred, resentment. "Observe that these disease-producing emotions," said Dr. McMillen, "are concerned with protecting and coddling the self, and they could be summarized under one title—*self-centeredness*."[2] Carnal emotions are definitely related to the works of the flesh that are listed in Galatians 5:19–21.

The human nervous system, with respect to behavior and feeling, basically has two sides, according to Dr. Jay Adams. He states that:

> One side is emotional and involuntary. The other side, associated with problem-solving and voluntary action has to do with

behavior. The importance of this fact is that it is in the client's behavior that changes can be made directly, because behavior, in contrast to emotion is controlled by the voluntary, not the involuntary side of men. . . . While there is no direct voluntary access to the emotions, the emotions can be reached indirectly through the voluntary system, because extensive fiber overlapping in the cortex allow unified correlation of the two systems. Thus, actions affect emotions. Voluntary behavioral alterations will lead to involuntary emotional changes. It is important to understand, therefore, that feelings flow from actions.[3]

Envy/Jealousy

Envy is an emotion, like several others, that only gives us trouble when we don't fear God as we should. ⟶

*Let not thine heart **envy** sinners, **but be thou in the fear of the Lord** all the day long.* (23:17)

Envy causes believers to desire the things of the ungodly. ⟶

*Let not thine heart **envy sinners**, but be thou in the fear of the Lord all the day long.* (23:17)

*Be not thou **envious of evil men**, neither desire to be with them.* (24:1)

*Fret not thyself because of evil men, **neither be thou envious of the wicked**.* (24:19)

Jealousy can fill you with uncontrollable rage. ⟶

*For **jealousy is the rage of a man**; therefore he will not spare in the day of vengeance.* (6:34)

Envy is one of the emotions that can destroy your health. ⟶

*A sound heart is the life of the flesh; but **envy, the rottenness of the bones**.* (14:30)

Fear

Fear causes people all kinds of problems and often results in sinful behavior. Being fearful can cause a person to lie, steal, and even kill. When a person puts his trust in the Lord, the Lord can help him to overcome all of his fears. Proverbs 29:25 teaches that fear brings a snare (or a noose). The Lord has removed many necks from the noose named "fear."

> *The fear of man bringeth a **snare**; but **whoso putteth his trust in the Lord shall be safe**. (29:25)*

Greed

A **greedy** person is never satisfied but always wants more. →	*Sheol and destruction are never full; so the **eyes of man are never satisfied**. (27:20)*
Greed practiced in the market place causes trouble at home. →	*He that is greedy for gain troubleth his own house, but he that hateth bribes shall live. (15:27)*
Greed often leads to dishonest business practices and criminal activity. →	*Better is the poor that walketh in his uprightness, than he that is **perverse in his ways**, though he be rich. (28:6 [See also 1:10–19.])*
Greed can bring a person to poverty. →	*He that hasteneth to be rich hath an evil eye, and considereth not that **poverty shall come upon him**. (28:22 [See also 11:24; 22:16.])*

Anger

Being **slow to anger** is a valuable trait. →

*He who is **slow to anger** is **better than the mighty***; *and he who ruleth his spirit, than he that taketh a city.* (16:32)

Clear thinking can keep a man from ***losing his temper.*** →

*The **discretion** of a man **deferreth his anger**, and it is his glory to pass over a transgression.* (19:11)

An **uncontrolled temper** can literally **ruin your life.** →

*He that hath no rule over his own spirit is **like a city that is broken down,** and without walls.* (25:28)

A quick temper is a sure sign of **foolishness.** →

*He that is **soon angry dealeth foolishly**, and a man of wicked devices is hated.* (14:17 [See also 14:29])

A **hot temper** stirs up others and causes **strife.** →

*A **wrathful man stirreth up strife**, but he who is slow to anger appeaseth strife.* (15:18 [See also 29:22])

A **bad temper** will cause you to **suffer the consequences.** →

*A man of **great wrath shall suffer punishment***; *for if thou deliver him, yet thou must do it again.* (19:19)

Hang out with the angry man and you'll become angry and **suffer the consequences.** →

Make no friendship with an angry man; *and with a furious man thou shalt not go, lest thou learn his ways, and get a **snare to thy soul**.* (22:24–25)

An angry man has a lot of **sin.** →

*An **angry man** stirreth up strife, and a **furious man aboundeth in transgression**.* (29:22)

300

Vengeance

When someone does evil to us, the natural thing for us to do is to devise a plan to retaliate. "I'll get even" is a phrase that expresses that the heart is set on revenge. The natural thing to do is to repay evil with evil. Evil thoughts, after all, are already present in the natural mind (Mark 7:21). God has some instructions for us on this important subject from Proverbs.

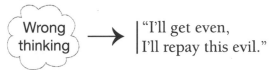

Say not thou, I will recompense evil. . . . (20:22a)

Say not, I will do so to him as he hath done to thee; I will render to the man according to his work. (24:29)

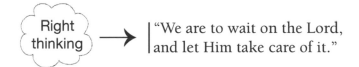

*Say not thou, I will recompense evil; but **wait on the Lord**, and He shall save thee.* (20:22)

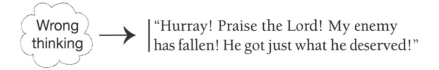

Rejoice not thou when thine enemy falleth, and let not thine heart be glad when he stumbleth, lest the Lord see it, and it displease Him, and He turn away his wrath from him. (24:17–18)

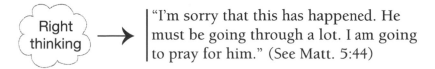

Hate

The more you study human emotions, the more you will realize that the underlying cause for many emotional problems is not mental or physical but spiritual. Emotional problems develop when we are not in a right relationship with our Creator. Hatred is just one example of a powerful, wrong emotion that can surface in a person's mind who is not in a right relationship with the Lord. Following are four important facts from Proverbs that God wants us to know about hate.

Hate causes **strife.** → *Hatred stirreth up strifes, but love covereth all sins.* (10:12)

Hate is sometimes **concealed.** (You may not be aware of the fact that someone hates you.) → *He that **hideth hatred** has lying lips, and he that uttereth slander is a fool.* (10:18)
*He whose **hatred is covered** by deceit, his wickedness shall be revealed before the whole congregation.* (26:26)

Wicked people often **hate God's people.** → *The bloodthirsty **hate the upright,** but the just seek his soul.* (29:10)
*An unjust man is an abomination to the just; and **he that is upright** in the way is an **abomination to the wicked**.* (29:27)

People who hate Christ love the things that will **bring them to death.** → *But he that sinneth against me wrongeth his own soul; **all they that hate me love death**.* (8:36 [This is Christ speaking—see chapter eight of this book.])

The Broken Spirit

"In Scripture," states Jay Adams, "physical illness is compared and contrasted with a spirit broken under the burden of a guilty heart."[4] Adams goes on to say: "Painful emotions are more serious than the pain of a serious disease. The right spirit within enables one to bear physical pain, but what is there to sustain one with a broken spirit crushed in pain?"[5]

The following diagram based on statements from the Book of Proverbs may help to understand how emotional problems, if not resolved, tend to become more complex and harmful.

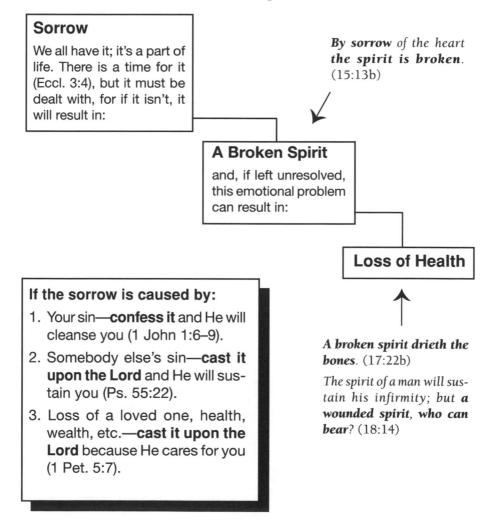

Sorrow

We all have it; it's a part of life. There is a time for it (Eccl. 3:4), but it must be dealt with, for if it isn't, it will result in:

By sorrow of the heart the spirit is broken. (15:13b)

A Broken Spirit

and, if left unresolved, this emotional problem can result in:

Loss of Health

If the sorrow is caused by:

1. Your sin—**confess it** and He will cleanse you (1 John 1:6–9).

2. Somebody else's sin—**cast it upon the Lord** and He will sustain you (Ps. 55:22).

3. Loss of a loved one, health, wealth, etc.—**cast it upon the Lord** because He cares for you (1 Pet. 5:7).

A broken spirit drieth the bones. (17:22b)

*The spirit of a man will sustain his infirmity; but **a wounded spirit, who can bear**?* (18:14)

The Merry Heart

We are not dealing with the "merry heart" as a personality type here. The "merry heart" that is described in Proverbs is a condition that exists in a person's life when all is well between him and the Lord. The "merry heart" of the believer will manifest itself in different ways in different people depending on personality type. Regardless of your personality type, however, when all is right between you and the Lord, you will normally have a "merry heart."

It **shows on the face** of the believer.   →   *A merry heart maketh a **cheerful countenance**. (15:13a)*

> When your heart is filled with the joy of the Lord, it will show on your face.

Life is like **a "continual banquet"** to the merry heart.   →   *All the days of the afflicted are evil, but he that is of a **merry heart hath a continual feast**. (15:15)*

In spite of all the many trials and problems that we face in life, the Lord fills us with His joy when our hearts are right with Him. Why settle for an occasional hamburger at the table of life when you can have a continual feast at the Lord's banquet table that He has *reserved* for "merry hearts only"?

A **merry heart** is one of the secrets of long-term **good health**.   →   *A **merry heart doeth good like a medicine**, but a broken spirit drieth the bones. (17:22)*

*A **sound heart is the life of the flesh**; but envy, the rottenness of the bones. (14:30)*

Dr. William Sadler stated that:

No one can appreciate so fully as a doctor the amazingly large percentage of human disease and suffering which is directly traceable to worry, fear, conflict, immorality, dissipation, and ignorance—to unwholesome thinking and unclean living. The sincere acceptance of the principles and teachings of Christ with respect to the life of mental peace and joy, the life of unselfish thought and clean living, would at once wipe out more than half the difficulties, diseases, and sorrows of the human race.[6]

Love

Love is slow to condemn and **quick to overlook** the faults of others. ——→ *Hatred* stirreth up strifes, but **love covereth all sins**. (10:12)

> The opposites in this verse are obviously hate and love. They are opposite emotions, and they produce opposite actions. Hate, like the school yard bully, is always looking to stir up trouble. Love, on the other hand, is patient (1 Cor. 13:4), kind, and has no desire to stir up trouble. It would rather excuse the one who has sinned against us whenever possible.

Love is an emotion that **can bring great joy** to people even when **there is very little else**. ——→ *Better is a dinner of herbs where love is*, than a stalled ox and hatred therewith. (15:17)

Summary: Emotions

People do not accept the Lord into their lives because of the health benefits. They normally accept the Lord because of a present need (the here and now), and a future need (heaven v. hell). Millions of people, however, having accepted the Lord into their lives, have found that there are many other "bonuses" for being a follower of

Christ. Two of these bonuses are improved emotional health and improved physical health. Dr. William Saddler stated that:

> The teachings of Jesus applied to our modern civilization—understandingly applied, not merely nominally accepted—would so purify, uplift, and vitalize us that the race would immediately stand out as a new order of beings, possessing superior mental power and increased moral force. Irrespective of the future rewards of living, laying aside all discussion of future life, *it would pay any man or woman to live the Christ-life just for the mental and moral rewards it affords here in this present world.*[7]

23 Sexual Sin, Gifts, A Good Name

Sexual Sin: The High Price of Immorality

Sex education in the home is the subject in chapter five of this book. Below are some important facts that Almighty God wants us all to know. Wise parents will instill these truths from God into the hearts of their children, and will impress upon them the moral, physical, spiritual, and emotional problems that people encounter when they break God's laws. The dangers are many and very real.

1. Sexual sin can lead to an *early death.* → *For her house inclineth unto death, and her paths unto the dead.* (2:18 [See also 7:27; 9:18])

2. Sexual sin can lead to frightening *diseases.* → *And thou mourn at the last, when thy flesh and thy body are consumed.* (5:11)

3. Sexual sin results in great *remorse.* → *And say, How have I hated instruction, and my heart despised reproof; and have not obeyed the voice of my teachers, nor inclined mine ear to them that instructed me!* (5:12–13)

4. Sexual sin **cannot be hidden** from the eyes of the Lord. He sees all that we do.

→ *For the **ways of man are before the eyes of the Lord**, and **He pondereth all his goings**. His own iniquities shall take the wicked himself, and he shall be held with the cords of his sin.* (5:21–22)

5. Sexual sin brings people to **poverty.**

→ *For **by** means of **an unchaste woman a man is brought to a piece of bread**; and the adulteress will hunt for the precious life.* (6:26)

6. Sexual sin will **"burn" you.**

→ ***Can a man take fire** in his bosom, and his clothes be not burned? Can one go upon hot coals, and his feet **not be burned**? So he that goeth in to his neighbor's wife; whosoever toucheth her shall not be innocent.* (6:27–29)

7. Sexual sin is **deceiving.**

→ *With her much fair speech she caused him to yield; with the flattering of her lips she forced him. **He goeth after her** straightway, as an ox goeth to the slaughter, or as a fool to the correction of the stocks, till an arrow strike through his liver—as a bird hasteneth to the snare, **and knoweth not that it is for his life**.* (7:21–23)

Gifts

Have you ever thought of the "power of a gift?" The right gift given at the right time can be a powerful tool for good. In fact, even a small and seemingly insignificant gift given in love can be a great blessing to someone. God teaches us about the "power of a gift" in three separate verses in Proverbs. Study these and use the "power of a gift" to bring glory to God and to encourage people for Him.

Gifts can **open doors and hearts.** →
*A **man's gift maketh room for him**, and bringeth him before great men.* (18:16)

Those who give gifts will **receive friendships.** →
*Many will entreat the favor of the prince, and **every man is a friend to him that giveth gifts**.* (19:6)

Gifts can **soften an angry heart.** →
*A **gift** in secret **pacifieth anger**; and a reward in the bosom, strong wrath.* (21:14)

Every time we give a gift, let us mention on the accompanying card God's unspeakable gift (Jesus Christ)! *Thanks be unto God for His unspeakable gift.* (2 Cor. 9:15)

A Good Name

Your good name **will remain** after you are gone. →
*The **memory of the just is blessed**, but the name of the wicked shall rot.* (10:7)

A good name is a far **greater inheritance** to leave your children **than great riches.** →
*A **good name** is **rather to be chosen than great riches**, and loving favor rather than silver and gold.* (22:1)

24 | The Tongues of Proverbs

How important are the words we speak! Our words can encourage people, give people hope for the future, help shape lives, and bring about positive change. Our words can also discourage people, rob them of their hope, and even cause some to have "broken spirits." The tongue has great power, the Lord tells us, and we need to be reminded of that again and again. Proverbs 18:21 states that *"Death and life are in the power of the tongue. . . ."* In this chapter we will look at six different tongues from the Book of Proverbs.

The Godly Tongue

The words from a person's mouth normally reveal what is in that person's heart. Jesus said "out of the abundance of the heart the mouth speaketh" (Matt. 12:34). A person whose heart is in a right relationship with God is one who is obeying the command in Proverbs 4:23, which says: "Keep thy heart with all diligence; for out of it are the issues of life." God is indeed pleased with those who walk "upright" (11:20) before Him, for these are the people that He uses to communicate to others. A person whose heart is fully set on obeying God will have a godly tongue. I think that you will be surprised and challenged to see the high value that God places upon the tongue of the righteous. "Born as we are for eternity," said Charles Bridges, "no utterance of our tongue can be called trifling."[1]

1. The godly tongue **brings forth wisdom.** →

> In the **lips of him** that **hath understanding, wisdom is found.** (10:13a)
>
> The **mouth** of the **just bringeth forth wisdom.** (10:31a)
>
> The **lips** of the **wise disperse knowledge.** (15:7a)

2. The godly tongue **"feeds" others** the nourishing words of the Lord. →

> The **lips** of the **righteous feed many.** (10:21a)

3. From the godly tongue flows the words which **give everlasting life.**

   (But whosoever drinketh of the water that I shall give him shall never thirst, but the water that I give shall be in him a well of water springing up into **everlasting life.** John 4:14) →

> The **mouth** of a **righteous man** is a **well of life.** (10:11a)
>
> The words of a man's mouth are like deep waters, and the **wellspring of wisdom** like **a flowing brook.** (18:4)
>
> **He** that **winneth souls** is **wise.** (11:30b)

4. The godly tongue speaks **words of encouragement** that bring hope and gladness to the discouraged heart. →

> **Heaviness in the heart** of man maketh it stoop, but a **good word maketh it glad.** Proverbs 12:25

5. The godly tongue speaks words that **cause believers to grow.** ⟶ (Their words are "sweet," not bitter.)

*The wise in heart shall be called prudent, and the **sweetness** of the **lips increaseth learning**. (16:21)*

6. The godly tongue is comparable to **choice** ⟶ **silver.**

*The tongue of the **just** is like **choice silver**. (10:20a)*

7. The godly tongue actually **promotes health** in ⟶ other people.

***Pleasant words** are like an honeycomb, **sweet** to the **soul**, and **health to the bones**. (16:24)*

8. The godly tongue **brings healing.** ⟶

*The **tongue** of the **wise brings healing**. (12:18b NAS)*

9. The godly tongue not only **blesses others,** it **blesses its owner** as well. ⟶

*A **man** shall be **satisfied** with good by the **fruit of his mouth.** (12:14a)*

*A **man shall eat good** by the **fruit of his mouth.** (13:2a)*

*A **man hath joy** by the **answer of his mouth.** (15:23a)*

10. The godly tongue that faithfully teaches you the Word of God is ⟶ **worth more to you than great riches.**

*There is gold, and an abundance of jewels; but **the lips of knowledge** are a **more precious thing**. (20:15a NAS)*

The Ungodly Tongue

When our hearts are not given over totally to the Lord, we will have problems with our tongue. No man can tame the tongue, we are told in James 3:8, for "it is an unruly evil full of deadly poison." It takes strict self-discipline and constant monitoring to keep the tongue in check. We should be careful to commit ourselves afresh to God each day. David C. Egner, writing for *Our Daily Bread* devotional, once said, "The tongue's unruly nature lurks dangerously below the surface. You can tame a tiger, but only by prayer and watchfulness can you control your tongue."

> Lord, set a watch upon my lips,
> My tongue control today;
> Help me evaluate each thought
> And guard each word I say.
> — Hess

1. The tongue of the ungodly can **burn like fire.** → *An **ungodly** man diggeth up evil, and in **his lips** there is as **a burning fire**. (16:27)*

2. The tongue of the ungodly can **cut like a sword.** → *There is **he that speaketh like the piercings of a sword**, but the tongue of the wise is health. (12:18)*

3. The tongue of the ungodly **causes strife.** → *A **perverse man soweth strife.** . . . (16:28a)*

4. The tongue of the ungodly **breaks up friendships.** → *A **whisperer separateth chief friends**. (16:28b)*

5. The tongue of the un-godly **causes him trouble.** → *He that hath a perverse heart findeth no good; and* **he that hath a perverse tongue falleth into mischief.** (17:20)

6. The tongue of the un-godly can **destroy people.** → **Death and life are in the power of the tongue.** (18:21a)

The Talebearer's Tongue

1. A talebearer hurts people by **"sharing" things that shouldn't be shared.** → *A* **talebearer revealeth secrets,** *but he that is of a faithful spirit concealeth a matter.* (11:13)

2. A talebearer's words are often **readily received.**

   People "swallow" the words of the talebearer like they would **"dainty morsels."** → *The* **words** *of a* **whisperer are like dainty morsels,** *and they go down into the innermost parts of the belly.* (18:8 NAS [See also 26:22.])

3. A talebearer **breaks up friendships.** → *A perverse man soweth strife, and a* **whisperer separateth** *chief* **friends.** (16:28)

   He that covereth a transgression seeketh love, but **he that repeateth a matter separateth friends.** (17:9)

4. When the talebearer **is removed,** the contention and fiery **strife ceases.** → *Where no wood is, there the fire goeth out; so **where there is no talebearer, the strife ceaseth**. As coals are to **burning coals**, and wood to fire, so is a **contentious man** to kindle strife.* (26:20–21)

5. We are told **not to associate** with a talebearer. → *He who goes about as a slanderer reveals secrets, therefore **do not associate with a gossip.*** (20:19 NAS)

The Yacker's Tongue

1. The yacker has **a sin problem** that is at least partially caused by the fact that he **talks too much!** → *In the **multitude of words** there **lacketh not sin**, but he that refraineth his lips is wise.* (10:19)

2. The yacker's **endless talking** causes him much trouble. → *He that keepeth his mouth keepeth his life, but he that **openeth wide his lips shall have destruction**.* (13:3)

*Whoso **keepeth his mouth and his tongue, keepeth** his soul **from troubles**.* (21:23)

3. The yacker has **never learned to speak sparingly.** → *He that hath knowledge spareth his words; and a man of understanding is of an excellent spirit. **Even a fool, when he holdeth his peace**, is counted wise; and he that shutteth his lips is esteemed a man of understanding.* (17:27–28)

The Flatterer's Tongue

The tongue of the flatterer is discussed in chapter twenty-one of this book. The flatterer is a hypocrite. The words of his mouth do not match the thoughts of his mind. He deceives people by speaking words that they like to hear, but oh, if they only knew what is really in his heart! Remember these important points about the flatterer:

- **The flattering tongue can destroy lives.** (7:21–23)

- **The flatterer's tongue does not reveal what is in his heart.** (26:25, 28)

- The flatterer's words are **never designed for the good of the person.** (28:23)

- **The flatterer often lays traps.** (29:5)

The Lying Tongue

Lying is so common in our culture that we have come to accept it as "not too bad," because after all, "everybody does it." We even "excuse" our lies by pointing out that "they were just little white lies." Search the Scripture from cover to cover, and you will not find a single example where God defines an untruth as a "little white lie." I asked myself the question: "Who tells little white lies?" The answer came back to me swiftly: "Little white **liars.**" Because of our fallen nature, we do not view our own lies as significant sins. In fact, we tend to view other people's lies much more critically than we do our own. (Didn't Jesus say something in Luke 6:41–42 about dealing with the beam in our own eye before dealing with the mote in our brother's eye?)

317

Lying is a big deal to God, for He is Truth. He groups "all liars" with a wicked assortment of people in Revelation 21, and tells us that "these shall have their part in the lake which burneth with fire and brimstone, which is the second death" (v. 8). In Revelation 22, He describes for us those who shall be outside of the holy city. Included in this infamous list are: dogs, sorcerers, fornicators, murderers, idolators, and *whosoever loveth and maketh a lie* (v. 15). As you will see, the God of ancient Israel had much to say about lies and liars. This same God is our God today. "Jesus Christ, the same yesterday, and today, and forever" (Heb. 13:8). All of us have lied. All liars are unrighteous and cannot inherit the kingdom of God without first coming to the Lord and being cleansed from their sins. "And such were some of you; but ye are washed, but you are sanctified, but ye are justified in the name of the Lord Jesus, and by the Spirit of our God" (1 Cor. 6:11). Aren't you glad that Jesus paid for all our sins, including our lies, by His death on the cross?

⟫ **1. God hates a lying tongue.**

*These six things doth the Lord hate; yea, seven are an abomination unto Him: . . . **a lying tongue**.* (6:16–17)

⟫ **2. Liars are an abomination to the Lord.**

***Lying lips** are an **abomination to the Lord**, but they that deal truly are his delight.* (12:22 [See also 6:16–17])

⟫ **3. A righteous man hates lying.**

*A **righteous** man hateth **lying**.* (13:15a)

⟫ **4. Wicked people lie constantly.**

*A righteous man hateth lying, but a **wicked** man is **loathesome**, and cometh to shame.* (13:5)

▥➡ **5. A liar is a deceiver.**

*He that speaketh truth showeth forth righteousness, but **a false witness, deceit**.* (12:17)

▥➡ **6. Liars enjoy the wrong company.**

*A wicked doer giveth heed to false lips, and **a liar giveth ear to a mischievous tongue**.* (17:4)

▥➡ **7. Liars are soon exposed.**

*The lip of truth shall be established forever, but **a lying tongue** is but **for a moment**.* (12:19 [See also 19:9])

▥➡ **8. Liars do not go unpunished.**

*A false witness shall not be unpunished, and **he that speaketh lies shall not escape**.* (19:5)

▥➡ **9. All liars shall perish.**

*A false witness shall not be unpunished, and **he** that speaketh lies **shall perish**.* (19:9)

25 | Counsel and Reproof

Counsel

1. **The wise man listens to counsel.**

The way of a fool is right in his own eyes, but **he that hearkeneth unto counsel is wise**. (12:15)

2. **The way to add safety to any organization is to add many counselors.**

Where no counsel is, the people fall; but **in the multitude of counselors there is safety**. (11:14)

3. **It takes many counselors to make plans succeed.**

Without counsel *purposes are* **disappointed**, *but in the* **multitude of counselors they are established**. (15:22)

4. **The Word of God commands all of us to "hear counsel and receive instruction."**

Hear counsel, and receive instruction, *that thou mayest be wise in thy latter end*. (19:20)

5. **The counsel of a friend is sweet and causes rejoicing.**

Ointment and perfume **rejoice** *the heart; so doth the* **sweetness** *of a* **man's friend**, *by hearty* **counsel**. (27:9)

6. **Wise counsel is necessary for victory.**

*Every purpose is established by counsel; and with **good advice make war**. (20:18)*

*For **by wise counsel** thou shalt **make thy war**, and in the multitude of counselors there is safety. (24:6)*

Reproof

1. **All of us need to be reproved from time to time.**

*For the commandment is a lamp, and the law is the light, and **reproofs of instruction are the way of life**. (6:23)*

*My son, despise not the chastening of the Lord, neither be weary of His correction; **for whom the Lord loveth** He **correcteth**, even as a father the son in whom he delights. (3:11–12)*

2. **It is not profitable to reprove scoffers and wicked people.**

*He that **reproveth a scoffer** getteth to himself **shame**, and he that rebuketh a **wicked man getteth himself a blot**. (9:7)*

3. **A man who refuses reproof will go astray.**

*He is in the way of life that keepeth instruction, but **he that refuseth reproof erreth**. (10:17)*

4. **A man who hates reproof is stupid.**

*Whoso loveth instruction loveth knowledge, but **he that hateth reproof is stupid**. (12:1)*

5. **There are times when a person must listen to reproof or die.**

*Correction is grievous unto him that forsaketh the way, and **he that hateth reproof shall die**. (15:10)*

6. **Listening to reproof will bring a man to honor.**

*Poverty and shame shall be to him that refuseth instruction, but **he that regardeth reproof shall be honored**.* (13:18)

7. **Reproof and the reprover are valuable to one growing in wisdom.**

***As an earring of gold**, and an **ornament of fine gold**, so is a **wise reprover** upon an obedient ear.* (25:12)

8. **A wise man welcomes and appreciates a proper reproof.**

*Reprove not a scoffer, lest he hate thee; **rebuke a wise man**, and **he will love thee**.* (9:8)

*A **reproof entereth** more **into a wise man** than an hundred stripes into a fool.* (17:10)

9. **A man who consistently rejects reproof will suddenly be destroyed.**

*He that, being **often reproved, hardeneth his neck**, shall **suddenly be destroyed**, and that without remedy.* (29:1 [Study also 1:23–30])

What to Do When You Are Reproved *

A. Receive reproof with an open mind.

- Listen carefully to the reprover's words.

B. Ask yourself these questions:

- Is this reproof valid?
- Is God attempting to correct me through this person?

*or "corrected"

C. Approach God humbly, with an open mind and seek His mind on this reproof.

- By prayer.
- By searching Scripture for information on the subject of the reproof (take notes, gather data).
- Arrange and review your data.

D. Make a final evaluation.

- "I'm okay"—no adjustment necessary.
- "I need this reproof"—
  1. Confess your sin and thank the Lord for the reproof.
  2. Make the adjustment.
  3. Thank the person for giving you the needed reproof.

E. Recognize with joy and anticipation that you are now "one step closer to the gold."

*But He knoweth the way that I take, when he hath tested me, **I shall come forth as gold!*** (Job 23:10)

26 | Self-Discipline, Overstaying One's Welcome

Self-Discipline

We live in a society where multitudes of people do not have control over some area of their lives. Being "out of control" is often frightening, unhealthy, and can be extremely dangerous. If we were to make a list of all the ways that we could become "out of control," the list would be, for all practical purposes, endless. We have all known people who were "out of control" in such areas as sex, drugs, or alcohol. There are eating disorders, emotional disorders, and multitudes of behavior disorders. Here is what the book of wisdom says about being "out of control":

✳ **1. It is better to have control of your life than to have rule over many.**

He who is slow to anger is better than the mighty; and he who ruleth his spirit, than he that taketh a city. (16:32)

✳ **2. Out-of-control people get into situations that bring them to shame.**

Go not forth hastily to strive, lest thou know not what to do in the end thereof, when thy neighbor hath put thee to shame. (25:8)

325

✳ **3. Your defense is your self-control.**
Lose your self-control and you have lost your defense.

He that **hath no rule over his own spirit is like a city** that is **broken down**, *and without walls*. (25:28)

Being "out of control" is not an issue for the person whose mind and will are yielded to the Lord. He is the one who has brought self-control to millions of weak and sinful people. "Self-control" is a fruit of the Spirit of God (Gal. 5:23–24). A person who selfishly refuses to give God control of his life is in danger of *losing control to Satan and the flesh*. The way to experience victorious self-control is to give oneself to the Lord. It is He who gives us the power over lusts, passions, "hang-ups," disorders, and idiosyncrasies. In other words, *we gain control by giving control, or we lose control by keeping control.*

Overstaying One's Welcome

*Let your feet **rarely** be in your neighbor's house, **lest he become weary of you** and hate you.* (25:17 NAS)

27 | Friends and Enemies

Wrong Friends

⭐ **Wrong friends will influence you to do wrong.**

*Cease, my son, to **hear** the **instruction that causeth thee to err** from the words of knowledge.* (19:27)

⭐ **Wrong friends can lead to your destruction.**

*He that walketh with wise men shall be wise, but a **companion of fools** shall be **destroyed**.* (13:20 [See also 1:10–19])

"Friends"

⭐ **Some friends are "fair weather" friends only.**

*There are **friends who pretend to be friends**, but there is a friend who sticks closer than a brother.* (18:24 RSV)

⭐ **God instructs us to be loyal to our friends.**

Thine own friend, *and thy father's friend, **forsake not**; neither go into thy brother's house in the day of calamity; for better is a neighbor that is near than a brother far off.* (27:10)

☆ **Choose wise friends and you'll become wise.**

He that walketh with wise men shall be wise, but a companion of fools shall be destroyed. (13:20)

Close Friends

☆ **A close friend will love you regardless of your circumstances.**

A close friend is an "all weather" friend. He is a friend in fair weather, and he is a friend in foul weather.

A friend loveth at all times, and a brother is born for adversity. (17:17)

☆ **A godly friend can give you good advice.**

Ointment and perfume rejoice the heart; so doth the sweetness of a man's friend, by hearty counsel. (27:9)

☆ **Two more benefits of having a friend:**

1. God can use *you* to sharpen your friend.

2. God can use *your friend* to sharpen you.

Iron sharpens iron, so one man sharpens another. (27:17 NAS)

The Best Friend of All

☆ **The best friend of all is a friend who will stick closer to you than a brother.**

There are friends who pretend to be friends, but there is a friend who sticks closer than a brother. (18:24 RSV)

Do you have a friend that meets that description? You are very fortunate if you do and you should thank God daily for such a friend. What a comfort that friend can be to you in times of sorrow or trial in your life.

Those of us who know the Lord have a friend that sticks closer than a brother. For He Himself has said, "I will **never** leave you nor forsake you" (Heb. 13:5). Millions of believers have found Him to be a **"very present help"** when they were going through trouble (Ps. 46:1). Jesus said, "I am with you always" (Matt. 28:20), and if you **know Him** you have the **very best friend** in the whole world. "There are friends who pretends to be friends, but **there is a friend who sticks closer than a brother"** (18:24 RSV).

Enemies

➔ 1. **The Lord says that you are not to seek revenge on your enemy.**

> **Say not** thou, **I will recompense evil**; but wait on the Lord, and He shall save thee. (20:22)

> **Say not**, **I will do so to him** as he hath done to me; I will render to the man according to his work. (24:29)

➔ 2. **The Lord tells you to do good to your enemy.**

> If thine enemy be hungry, **give him bread to eat**; and if he be thirsty **give him water** to drink; for thou shalt heap coals of fire upon his head, and **the Lord shall reward thee**. (25:21–22)

➔ 3. **The Lord tells you not to rejoice if your enemy falls.**

> **Rejoice not when thine enemy falleth**, and let not thine heart be glad when he stumbleth, lest the Lord see it, and it displease Him, and He turn away His wrath from him. (24:17–18)

➔ 4. **Evil people will sometimes become your enemies simply because you are living for the Lord.**

*The **bloodthirsty hate the upright**, but the just seek his soul.* (29:10)

*An unjust man is an abomination to the just; and he that is **upright** in the way is an **abomination** to the **wicked**.* (29:27)

➔ 5. **The Lord has power over the minds of your enemies.**

*When **a man's ways please the Lord**, he maketh **even his enemies to be at peace with him**.* (16:7)

Summary

The Spirit of God wrote the Holy Scriptures, which reveal to us the mind of God and the nature of God. The instruction that the Lord has given us in these verses is just the opposite of what many of us have practiced in times past. It goes "against our nature" to be good to our enemies, not to seek revenge, and not to rejoice if they fall. "But these are enemies," we argue. What we need to remember is that prior to our salvation, we too were God's enemies (Rom. 5:10), and He loved us, didn't he (Rom. 5:8)? We were "children of wrath" (Eph. 2:3), "alienated" from Him (Col. 1:21), but "while we were yet sinners, Christ died for us" (Rom. 5:8).

28 | Man Without God, Evangelism

Man Without God

1. The **universal problem** of sin.

> **Who can say, I have made my heart clean, I am pure** *from my sin?* (20:9)

2. Many people are **lost and don't know it.**

> *There is a* **way which seemeth right** *unto a man, but* **the end** *thereof are the ways of* **death.** *(14:12 [Note: This verse is repeated in 16:25, emphasizing its importance.])*

3. The **man of darkness** contrasted with the **man of light.**

> *The way of man is froward and strange: but as for the pure, his work is right.* (21:8)

4. Humanism (the deification of man) **is foolish.**

> **He that trusteth in his own heart is a fool,** *but whoso walketh wisely, he shall be delivered.* (28:26)

5. The "self-righteous" man is **spiritually blind.** He is filthy and doesn't know it.

> *There is a generation that are pure in their own eyes, and* **yet** *are* **not washed from their filthiness**. (30:12)

6. Where the gospel is not proclaimed, *people perish.*

> **Where there is no vision**, *the* **people perish**; *but he that keepeth the law, happy is he.* (29:18)

Evangelism

1. The Lord said you are wise if you win people to Him.

The fruit of the righteous is a tree of life; and **he that winneth souls is wise**. (11:30)

2. The description of a true witness for God:

A true witness delivereth souls, *but a deceitful witness speaketh lies.* (14:25)

3. From the godly tongue flows the words that give everlasting life.

The **mouth** *of a* **righteous man** *is a* **well of life**, *but violence covereth the heart of the wicked.* (10:11)

The **lips** *of the* **righteous feed many**, *but fools die for lack of wisdom.* (10:21)

4. What this lost, thirsty world needs is the good news of salvation that is sent from that far off country named heaven.

As cold water to a **thirsty soul**, *so is* **good news** *from a* **far off country**. (25:25)

29 The Joy of the Righteous, The Misery of the Unrighteous

Those who are living for Christ tend to be happy and blessed. Have you noticed? Those who do not know the Lord often do not have this happiness. In fact, the contrasts, in real life as well as in Scripture, are sometimes like night and day! There are many verses on this subject in the Bible. Here are some selected scriptures from the Book of Proverbs on this subject. If you know the Lord, rejoice and praise Him as you review His blessings.

Thirteen Statements from God on the Joy of the Righteous and the Misery of the Unrighteous — from Proverbs —

1. The Blessings of God (10:6 TLB)

The Righteous	The Unrighteous
*The good man is covered with **blessings** from **head to foot**. . . .* (a)	*. . . but an evil man inwardly **curses his luck**.* (b)

2. Desires and Fears (10:24)

The Righteous	The Unrighteous
. . . but the desire of the righteous shall be granted. (b)	The **fear** of the **wicked**, it shall **shall come upon him** . . . (a)

3. Hope (10:28)

The Righteous	The Unrighteous
The hope of the righteous shall be **gladness** . . . (a)	. . . but the **expectation** of the wicked **shall perish**. (b)

4. Man's Thought Life (11:20)

The Righteous	The Unrighteous
. . . but such as are upright in their way are His delight. (b)	They that are of a perverse heart are an abomination to the Lord . . . (a)

5. Life-styles (15:9)

The Righteous	The Unrighteous
. . . but He loveth him that followeth after righteousness. (b)	The way of the wicked is an abomination to the Lord . . . (a)

6. The Word of God (13:13)

The Righteous	The Unrighteous
. . . but he that feareth the commandment **shall be rewarded**. (b)	**Whoso despiseth** the word shall be **destroyed** . . . (a)

The Word of God cont. (13:13–15)

The Righteous	The Unrighteous
Whoso despiseth the word shall be destroyed, but he that feareth the commandment shall be rewarded. The law of the wise is a foundation of life, to depart from the snares of death. **Good** *understanding giveth* **favor** *. . .* (13–15a)	*. . . but the* **way** *of* **transgressors is hard**. (15b)

7. Length of Life (10:27)

The Righteous	The Unrighteous
The fear of the Lord **prolongeth days** *. . .* (a)	*. . . but the* **years** *of the* **wicked** *shall be* **shortened**. (b)

8. The Way of the Lord (10:29)

The Righteous	The Unrighteous
The way of the Lord is **strength** *to the* **upright** *. . .* (a)	*. . . but* **destruction** *shall be to the* **workers of iniquity**. (b)

9. Foundations (13:13)

The Righteous	The Unrighteous
. . . but the righteous is an **everlasting foundation**. (b)	*As the whirlwind passeth, so the* **wicked** *is* **no more** *. . .* (a)

10. Inheritance (10:30)

The Righteous	The Unrighteous
The righteous shall **never be removed** . . . (a)	. . . but the wicked **shall not inhabit** the **earth**. (b)

11. Riches

The Righteous	The Unrighteous
(16:8)	
Better is a little with righteousness . . . (a)	. . . than great revenues without right. (b)
(16:19)	
Better it is to be of an humble spirit with the lowly . . . (a)	. . . than to divide the spoil with the proud. (b)
(28:6)	
Better is the pure that walketh in his uprightness . . . (a)	. . . than he that is perverse in his ways, though he be rich. (b)

12. The Lord as Judge (12:2)

The Righteous	The Unrighteous
A good man **obtaineth favor** of the Lord . . . (a)	. . . but a man of wicked devices **will he condemn**. (b)

13. Judgment Day (11:4)

The Righteous	The Unrighteous
. . . but **righteousness delivereth** from death. (b)	**Riches profit not** in the day of wrath . . . (a)

30 | The Personalities of Proverbs

Many different personalities are mentioned in Proverbs. Almighty God focuses our attention on a whole variety of people found throughout the "book of wisdom." He speaks to us of the evil man and the just. He tells us of the teacher as well as the fool. He tells us of the false witness, and He tells us of the witness who is faithful. He speaks of the drunkard, the bloodthirsty, the furious man, and the lazy man. He also tells us of the prudent man, the diligent man, and the man of understanding.

No one understands the minds of men like the Creator. He knows all there is to know about the human race that He created. He alone is worthy to tell us what is right and what is wrong. Studying the different personalities found in Proverbs helps us to understand more clearly the issues of sin and righteousness. A list of the various types of people found in Proverbs follows.

Type	Scripture	Type	Scripture
Women:		**Men** (continued):	
Angry Woman	21:19	Faithful Ambassador	13:17
Brawling Woman	21:9; 25:24	Faithful Witness	14:5, 25
Contentious Woman	21:19; 27:15	False Witness (includes the deceitful witness and the liar.)	6:19; 12:17; 14:5, 25; 17:4; 19:5, 9, 22; 21:28; 25:18; 30:6
Gracious Woman	11:16		
Prudent Wife	19:14	Fool, Foolish	7:22; 9:6; 10:8, 10, 14, 18, 23; 11:29; 12:15; 13:16; 14:3, 7, 16; 15:5, 7, 20; 17:7, 10, 12, 16, 21, 24, 28; 18:2; 19:1, 10; 20:3; 21:20; 23:9; 24:7; 26:1, 4–6, 8, 10–12; 27:22; 28:26; 29:9, 11, 20; 30:22
Virtuous Woman	12:4; 31:10		
Wicked Woman (includes evil, harlot, foolish, strange, and foreign.)	5:3, 5:8–11, 20; 6:24; 7:5, 8–27; 9:13–18; 12:4; 14:1; 22:14; 23:27–28; 26:12; 29:23, 30:20		
Widow	15:25	Foolish Son	10:1; 17:25; 19:13
Wise Woman	14:1	Furious Man	22:24; 29:22
Men:		Glutton	23:2, 21; 28:7
Angry Man	14:17; 22:24; 29:22	Good Man	2:20; 12:2; 13:22; 14:14, 19
Bloodthirsty Man	29:10	Hypocrite	11:9
Borrower	22:7	Just	3:33; 4:18; 9:9; 10:6, 7, 20, 31; 11:9, 12:13, 21; 13:22; 17:15, 26; 18:17; 20:7; 21:15, 16; 29:10, 27
Contentious Man	26:21		
Diligent Man	10:4; 12:24, 27; 13:4; 21:5; 22:29; 27:23		
Drunkard	23:21; 26:9	Liberal Soul	11:25
Evil Man	2:12; 4:14–17; 17:11; 24:1; 19:20; 29:6	Lowly	3:34; 11:2; 16:19

The Personalities of Proverbs

Type	Scripture	Type	Scripture
Men (continued):		**Men** (continued):	
Man of Understanding	1:5; 3:13; 10:13, 23; 11:12; 14:29, 33; 15:14, 21; 17:27; 20:5; 28:2	Righteous Man, Men (cont.)	14:9, 19, 32; 15:6, 19, 28, 29; 16:13; 18:5, 10; 21:12, 18, 26; 23:24; 24:15, 24; 25:26; 28:1, 10, 12, 28; 29:2, 7, 16
Merciful Man	11:17		
Oppressor	3:31; 14:31; 28:16	Scorners (scoffers)	3:34; 9:7–8; 13:1; 14:6; 15:12; 19:25, 28; 21:11, 24; 22:10; 24:9
Perfect Man	2:21; 11:5		
Perverse Man	2:12, 15; 3:32; 4:24; 6:12; 8:8, 13; 10:31; 11:20; 12:8; 14:2; 16:28, 30; 17:20; 19:1; 21:8; 22:5; 28:6, 18	Simple	1:4, 22–32; 7:7; 8:5; 9:4, 13, 16; 14:15, 18; 19:25; 21:11; 22:3; 27:12
Poor	10:4, 15; 13:7, 8, 23; 14:20, 21, 31; 17:5; 18:23; 19:1, 4, 7, 17, 22; 21:13, 17; 22:2, 7, 9, 16, 22; 28:3, 6, 8, 11, 15, 27; 29:7, 13, 14; 30:9, 14; 31:9	Sinners	1:10–19; 8:36; 11:31; 13:6, 21; 14:21; 19:2; 20:2; 23:17
		Sluggard (includes slothful)	6:6, 9; 10:26; 12:24, 27; 13:4; 15:19; 18:9; 19:24; 20:4; 21:25; 22:13; 24:30; 26:13–16
Proud	15:25; 16:5, 19; 21:4, 24; 28:25		
		Stupid Man	12:1; 30:2
Prudent Man	12:16, 23; 13:16; 14:8, 15, 18; 15:5; 16:21; 18:15; 22:3; 27:12	Talebearers	11:13; 18:8; 20:19; 26:20, 22
		Teachers	5:13
Rich Man	10:15; 11:28; 13:7; 14:20, 24; 18:11, 23; 22:2, 7; 28:6, 11	Transgressors	2:22; 11:3, 6; 13:2, 15; 21:18; 22:12; 23:28; 26:10
Righteous Man, Men	2:7, 20; 3:32; 10:3, 11, 16, 21, 24, 25, 28, 30, 32; 11:8, 10, 21, 23, 28, 30–31; 12:3, 5, 7, 10, 12, 26; 13:5, 9, 21, 25;	Unfaithful Man	25:19
		Ungodly Man	16:27; 19:28

Type	Scripture	Type	Scripture
Men (continued):		**Men** (continued):	
Unjust Men	11:7; 29:27	Workers of Iniquity	10:29; 21:15
Upright Men	2:21; 10:29; 11:3, 6, 11, 20; 12:6; 13:6; 14:11; 15:8; 16:17; 21:18, 29; 28:10; 29:10, 27	Worthless Person	6:12
		Wrathful Man	15:18
Violent Man	16:29		
Wicked Man	2:14, 22; 3:25, 33; 4:14, 19; 5:22; 6:12; 9:7; 10:3, 6–7, 11, 16, 20, 24–25, 27–28, 30, 32; 11:5, 7–8, 10–11, 18, 21, 23, 31; 12:5–7, 10, 12–13, 21, 26; 13:5, 9, 17, 25; 14:11, 17, 19, 32; 15:6, 8, 9, 26, 28, 29; 16:4; 17:4, 15, 23; 18:3; 18:5, 28; 20:26; 21:4, 7, 10, 12, 18, 27, 29; 24:15, 16, 19–20, 24; 25:5, 26; 26:23; 28:1, 4, 12, 15, 28; 29:2, 7, 12, 16, 27		
Wise	1:5; 3:35; 9:8–9; 10:8, 14, 19; 11:29, 30; 12:15, 18; 13:20; 14:16, 24; 15:2, 7, 31; 16:21; 17:10; 18:15; 21:11, 20, 22; 22:17; 24:5; 29:8, 9, 11		
Wise King	20:26		
Wise Reprover	25:12		
Wise Servant	17:2; 14:35		
Wise Son	10:1, 5; 13:1; 15:20; 28:7		

Wisdom –
The Principal Thing
Section Three

This section deals with the final chapter in Proverbs,
chapter thirty-one.

31 | The Ideal Woman

King Lemuel is the human author of this chapter. The words, however, are not his words. They are the words that "his mother taught him" (v. 1). Just as we cannot identify Agur, the author of Proverbs 30, we cannot identify King Lemuel. Many believe that Lemuel was another name for Solomon. The name Lemuel means "devoted to God."

When Solomon was born, God named him Jedidiah, which means: "Beloved of the Lord" (2 Sam. 12:25). If Lemuel is Solomon, then we are reading the words of Bathsheba, for she was Solomon's mother. Some have reasoned that since Solomon tells us what his *father* taught him (4:1–4), then it would seem clear that here he is telling us what his *mother* taught him. They reason that his mother probably referred to him affectionately and proudly as "my son Lemuel: devoted to the Lord." Since they reason he is writing of her, he would be inclined to use the name that she called him. Even the rabbinical commentators identify Lemuel as Solomon. These are interesting thoughts, but since we cannot *prove* who Lemuel is, let's just say: "There is a good chance that Lemuel is Solomon."

A Mother Instructs Her Son, the Future King
(vv. 1–9)

As we begin this chapter, we will notice from the very first verse a significant change. The words that we are about to read are not from Solomon in his role as father, nor in his role as earth's wisest man. The words King Lemuel tells us are the "words . . . that his mother taught him." We are about to go back into an ancient Near East home where a wisdom training session is in progress. This time, however, as we enter the home (through the text), we quickly discover that it is not the father teaching the son. It is a loving, tender, and wise mother teaching the son that she had birthed a few short years before. She knows that he will one day be the king, so she approaches this training session from that perspective. How wonderful it would be if parents today would convey to their children during wisdom training sessions that "You are special. You are God's child. God has something special for you to do in life, something special for you to accomplish for Him. We are training you in His Word, and are praying that you will become all that God wants you to be, for His glory."

> Arise, O child of God,
> The Father calleth thee.
> Arise and do His will,
> And find thy destiny.
>
> Arise, O child of God,
> The Father's work to do.
> Arise, O child of God
> For He has need of you.
>
> Arise, O child of God,
> Above a life of sin.
> Arise, O Child of God,
> By faith and follow Him.
> — Don Manley

She Instructs Her Son About Wrong Women

The words of King Lemuel, the prophecy that his mother taught him. What, my son? And what, the son of my womb? And what, the son of my vows? Give not thy strength unto women, nor thy ways to that which destroyeth kings. (31:1–3)

The mother speaks with concern and compassion. She senses that her son's future rests on what he will do with her words, and oh, how she wants to communicate to him effectively these important truths. She struggles at first, trying to find the right words. "What, my son? And what, the son of my womb? And what the son of my vows?" She seems to be thinking: "What shall I tell you? What, my son, shall I teach you? How can I properly express how deeply I feel about your future, my son?" Parents, we need the same intense compassion concerning our children's future as we see displayed here by the words of a very concerned mother.

345

Sexual sin is a sin "which destroyeth kings" (v. 3). This is a sin that messed up David's life and his kingdom (2 Sam. 12:7–12). Scripture tells us that "King Solomon loved many foreign women," and that when he was old, "his wives turned away his heart after other gods, and his heart was not perfect with the Lord . . ." (1 Kings 11:1, 4). Here are some thoughts from England's great Bible scholar Matthew Henry (1710): "It (sexual sin) lessens the honor of kings and makes them mean. Are these fit to govern others that are themselves slaves to their own lusts? It makes them unfit for business and fills their court with the basest and worst of animals. . . . If they would preserve their people from the unclean spirit, they must themselves be patterns of purity."[1]

She Instructs Her Son About Wrong Use of Strong Drink

It is not for kings, O Lemuel, it is not for kings to drink wine, nor for princes strong drink, lest they drink, and forget the law, and pervert the justice of any of the afflicted. (31:4–5)

Intoxicating beverages have been one of Satan's favorite tools for thousands of years. The long, tragic history of "strong drink" has its beginning in Scripture in Genesis 9. Satan has captured legions of victims throughout history with this scourge called "strong drink," and continues to add scores of names daily to his endless, filthy list of prey. He has strewn the highways of the ages with a multitude of victims so vast that no man can count them. It was Shakespeare who had one of his characters say:

O thou invisible spirit of wine,
if thou hast no name to be known by,
let us call thee devil.

Wise words, indeed, young Lemuel, your mother gives you here. Do not drink, young man, lest your mind become perverted (v. 5). We have covered the other scriptures in Proverbs that deal with the subject of strong drink elsewhere.

She Instructs Her Son About the Right Use of Strong Drink

Give strong drink unto him that is ready to perish, and wine unto those that are of heavy hearts. Let him drink, and forget his poverty, and remember his misery no more. (31:6–7)

Alcohol is a drug that was often used for health purposes in ancient times. It was used as a disinfectant (Luke 10:34), as a medicine (1 Tim. 5:23), as a pain reliever, and a memory suppressant to those who were about to die (31:6–7). Medicines were limited in ancient days. Even in early America, alcoholic beverages were often the best medicine available and were widely used as a relief from pain. Whiskey was popular for treating snakebites and colds. It was also used to numb the pain before removing a bullet from a wound or before pulling a tooth. *Encyclopedia Britannica* states that "alcohol is administered by physicians in hospitals, usually by vein, sometimes for anesthesia before minor surgery; more often it is given for sedation after surgery. . . ."[2] The biblically approved uses of intoxicating beverages were strictly medicinal. God never intended that they be consumed as beverages.

Sinful minded men and women have used this mind-altering drug for thousands of years to "get high" or to have a "mind-bending" experience." Those who are schooled in divine wisdom realize the foolishness of ingesting a drug that alters a person's ability to reason and to think clearly (v. 5).

She Instructs Her Son About Those Who Cannot Help Themselves

Open thy mouth for the dumb in the cause of all such as are appointed to destruction. Open thy mouth, judge righteously, and plead the cause of the poor and needy. (31:8–9)

The mother of the future king urges her son to defend the weak, the poor, the defenseless. The Hebrew word for destruction in verse 8 is used nowhere else in the Bible. The literal meaning is "the sons of leaving behind."[3] These are children that have either been abandoned or whose parents have died. She instructs her son to "open thy mouth" for those who cannot defend themselves. A good king, or a good ruler of any kind, will have compassion on the poor, the orphans, and all of the "little people" of this world who cannot help themselves. "Pure religion," James tells us, is to "visit the fatherless and widows in their affliction . . ." (1:27). Rulers have a grave responsibility to "judge righteously and plead the cause of the poor and needy" (v. 9). The Old Testament contains passage after passage concerning the care of the widow and the fatherless. Rulers need to be aware that God has ordained that they should be His ministers to the people for good (Rom. 13:4), and that one day they will give an account directly to Him for their rule (2 Cor. 5:10, Rev. 20:12).

A Mother Instructs Her Son, the Future Husband and Father (vv. 10–31)

We have noticed Lemuel's mother in the early portion of this chapter (vv. 1–9) instructing him on three subjects: women, wine, and justice. She covers the negative side of the strong drink issue ("it is not for kings . . . to drink wine, nor for princes strong drink" [v. 4]), and then she covers the positive side of the strong drink issue ("give strong drink unto him that is ready to perish . . ." [v. 6]). She covers the positive side of the justice issue first ("open thy mouth . . ." [vv. 8–9]), and then she covers the negative side of the justice issue ("in the cause of all such as are appointed to destruction" [v. 8], "the poor and the needy" [v. 9]). She covers the negative side of the woman issue ("give not thy strength unto woman . . ." [v. 3]), but notice no positive womanhood statement is to be found in these verses. We have positive and negative sides addressed on the strong drink issue and on the justice issue. On the woman issue, however, we only have the negative side. The positive side of the woman issue is totally nonexistent in these verses. I refer to this as "the missing positive" in the following illustration.

The Mother's Instruction
(31:1–9)

She instructs her son about:

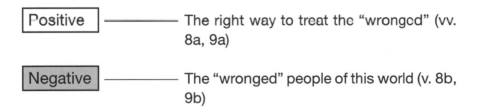

| ? ? ? | ⟶ | *The Missing Positive* |

| Negative | ——————— Wrong Women (v. 3) |

She instructs her son about:

| Negative | ——————— The wrong use of strong drink (vv. 4–5) |

| Positive | ——————— The right use of strong drink (vv. 6–7) |

She instructs her son about:

| Positive | ——————— The right way to treat the "wronged" (vv. 8a, 9a) |

| Negative | ——————— The "wronged" people of this world (v. 8b, 9b) |

The "missing positive" is the subject of the right woman. Although this subject is not covered in the above verses, it is covered in great detail in the remaining verses of the chapter. It is not by accident that the positive teaching of womanhood is the *last* subject in this *last* chapter of the Book of Proverbs. The Holy Spirit, the author of the Word, designed it this way. Here is an overview of the entire chapter:

The Mother's Instruction
(Proverbs 31)

Introduction: Vv. 1–2

SUBJECT #1 Woman

| ? ? ? | *The Missing Positive* |

| Negative | v. 3 |

SUBJECT #2 Strong Drink

| Negative | vv. 4–5 |

| Positive | vv. 6–7 |

SUBJECT #3 "Wronged People"

| Positive | vv. 8a, 9a |

| Negative | vv. 8b, 9b |

SUBJECT #1 Woman (continued from above)

Positive
(The Right Woman) ◄ vv. 10–31

The Ideal Woman

The order of this last chapter in Proverbs, along with the overall design of the entire book, suggests a distinct emphasis by the Holy Spirit on the subject of womanhood. The unwritten message of this arrangement of the sacred text comes through to us loud and clear. The unspoken message from God could be stated as follows: "I have saved the best for last." God focuses our attention in the last portion of this last chapter on the subject of the godly woman. We believe that the speaker is Lemuel's mother. She speaks to her son now not of "women" as in verse three, but of "a woman." We see her giving extremely valuable teaching to her son. She not only speaks to him, but she also paints pictures for him. Skillfully, she takes her carefully chosen words, goes to the canvas of her young son's mind, and there she paints beautiful pictures of a "virtuous woman." His mind becomes a gallery for the magnificent pictures that she creates with her paint of words.

In the early verses of this chapter (vv. 3–9), we see the godly mother instructing her son: *the future king.* In this final portion of the chapter (vv. 10–31), we see the godly mother teaching her son: *the future husband and father.* Seven verses of Scripture are used for mother's instruction to her son, *the future king* (vv. 3–9). Twenty-two verses of Scripture are used, however, by the mother in training her son, *the future husband and father* (vv. 10–31). This godly mother takes a mere seven verses to speak to her son about his future role as king, but she takes twenty–two verses to talk to him about the "right woman" to marry and to raise his children. Do you see what God is teaching us through Lemuel's mother? She knows how important it will be for him to have the *right* kind of wife, and so she describes for him the qualities to look for in a woman.

What is a godly woman suppose to be like? What does God tell us about her role? What qualities does God desire in a Christian woman? The answers to these questions are found in this chapter. This is that special section of Scripture where God shows us what a truly godly woman looks like.

What's an Acrostic?

The verses that follow (10–31) are unique in all of literature. The beauty of these verses is unsurpassed by the pen of man. They are colorful, practical, and are magnificently arranged. These verses are in the form of an acrostic. So what's an acrostic? There are actually several types of acrostics. The one found here is a poem in which each verse begins with a consecutive letter of the Hebrew alphabet. To give you an idea what an acrostic looks like, I devised one as a sample in English.

Truth
An Acrostic for Children

A lways tell the truth
B ecause the truth is always right
C overing up the truth will only get you into more trouble
D ecide, therefore, that you will always tell the truth
E ven if you are afraid of the consequences, you should always tell the truth
F athers are always pleased when their children tell the truth
G od is also pleased when children tell the truth

The Hebrew alphabet has twenty-two letters, thus there are twenty-two verses in the Proverbs 31 acrostic. Memorization is made easier if the acrostic form is used. This was, no doubt, the biggest reason for the use of the acrostic here and in several other places in the Old Testament. Ted A. Hildebrandt suggests two other reasons why the acrostic was used here, as follows:

> In Proverbs 31, the acrostic is significant on several levels. As an artistic device, the poet adorned the virtuous woman with a poem aesthetically fitted to her character. In addition, the idea of completeness was emphasized as the acrostic listed everything from A to Z and gave the sense that the topic under discussion had been thoroughly and completely discussed.[4]

The "virtuous" woman is a woman of many virtues. I have gleaned 22 of these virtues from our text. Mothers should model the virtues of the Proverbs 31 woman in their lives, and should teach those virtues to their sons and daughters. No boy or girl should grow up and not be well acquainted with the virtues that make a woman's worth "far above rubies."

Twenty-two Virtues of the Virtuous Woman

Virtue 1

She possesses rare qualities.
Verse 10: *Who can find a virtuous woman? . . .*

Virtue 2

She is worth more than valuable treasures.
Verse 10b: *. . . for her price is far above rubies.*

Virtue 3

She is faithful to her husband.
Verse 11a: *The heart of her husband doth safely trust in her . . .*

Virtue 4

She doesn't spend money foolishly.
Verse 11b: *. . . so that he shall have no need of spoil.*

Virtue 5

She will do good things for him all the days of her life.
Verse 12: *She will do him good, and not evil, all the days of her life.*

Virtue 6

She is "family focused," not "career focused."
Verse 12: *She will do him good. . . .*

(See also vv. 15, 21, 27.)

Virtue 7

She enjoys working with her hands for her family.

Verse 13: *She seeketh wool, and flax, and worketh willingly with her hands.*

Virtue 8

She is a good shopper.

Verse 14: *She is like the merchants' ships; she bringeth forth her food from afar.*

Virtue 9

She is a good businesswoman.

Verse 16: *She considereth a field and buyeth it; with the fruit of her hands she planteth a vineyard.*

See also vv. 18–19, 24.

Virtue 10

She is physically strong.

Verse 17: *She girdeth her loins with strength, and strengtheneth her arms.*

Virtue 11

She is confident in herself, knowing that the quality of her work is good.

Verse 18: *She perceiveth that her merchandise is good.*

Virtue 12

She is ambitious and pursues worthy goals with great energy.

Verse 15: *She riseth also while it is yet night, and giveth food to her household, and a portion to her maidens.*

Verse 18b: *. . . her lamp goeth not out by night.*

(See also vv. 13, 14, 16, 19, 24, 27.)

Virtue 13

She has a compassionate heart—she helps the poor and those in need.

Verse 20: *She stretcheth out her hand to the poor; yea, she reacheth forth her hands to the needy.*

Virtue 14

She takes pride in her personal appearance—she dresses elegantly.

Verse 22: *She maketh herself coverings of tapestry; her clothing is silk and purple.*

Virtue 15

She was careful in selecting a husband.

Verse 23: *Her husband is known in the gates, when he sitteth among the elders of the land.*

(See also verse 28b.)

Virtue 16

She is a woman of strong character and dignity.

Verse 25: *Strength and honor are her clothing, and she shall rejoice in time to come.*

Virtue 17

She is a woman that others can learn from, for she speaks words of wisdom.

Verse 26a: *She openeth her mouth with wisdom . . .*

Virtue 18

She has a tongue that is governed by "the law of kindness."

Verse 26b: *. . . and in her tongue is the law of kindness.*

Virtue 19

She is self-disciplined—she keeps herself busy with her God-given role as a homemaker and has no time for frivolous things.

Verse 27: *She looketh well to the ways of her household, and eateth not the bread of idleness.*

Virtue 20

She has earned the love and admiration of her children and husband—they praise her as the "best mom" and "best wife" of all.

Verses 28–29: *Her children rise up and call her blessed; her husband also, and he praiseth her. Many daughters have done virtuously, but thou excellest them all.*

Virtue 21

She is a godly woman.

Verse 30: *Favor is deceitful, and beauty is vain, but a woman who feareth the Lord, she shall be praised.*

Virtue 22

She will be praised in the community because she has performed so many good deeds, and the quality of her work is so high.

Verse 31: *Give her of the fruit of her hands, and let her own works praise her in the gates.*

Matthew Henry said these verses are a "looking glass for ladies, which they are desired to open and dress themselves by, and, if they do so, their adorning will be found to be praise, and honor, and glory at the appearance of Jesus Christ."[5] Parents who have daughters should dedicate themselves to bring them up to honor God by training them to develop these virtues. They should instill within their daughters' young teachable hearts the fact that God desires that they will one day become *women of honor* and women whose value is *far above rubies*. These are the pictures that should be painted on the canvas of their young minds. Parent, paint these pictures *quickly*, while your girls are young and teachable. Paint these pictures *vividly*, to make a lasting impression. Paint these pictures *repeatedly* to stress their continued significance. Paint these pictures *enthusiastically* to show them that being a "virtuous" woman pleases God, and that the benefits for doing so are many!

Parents should teach their sons that these are the qualities that a young woman should be *developing* if she is to become a good wife and mother. The key word here is *developing*. These qualities are not expected to be fully developed in a very young woman. She should, however, be developing these qualities as she gets to know God through His Word and through prayer. Every young woman should set out on a sacred quest, with firm determination to become a woman who truly pleases God.

Parents should teach these scriptures to their young sons and daughters with great passion. They should have their children memorize this entire section of Scripture (vv. 10–31). This should be done a verse at a time until the children have committed the entire passage to memory. "Why should this scripture be memorized?" someone asks. It should be memorized because it is here that Almighty God tells a young man what to look for in a wife and shows young women what they should strive to become. When young men and women memorize these scriptures, they are **learning the mind of God** on these important issues. The Word of God properly explained and then memorized by our sons and daughters has power, with the aid of the Holy Spirit, to mold and shape their views to the glory of God and to make them wise. Wisdom is the principal thing. Therefore, I encourage you to "get wisdom" (4:7) and to also become a teacher of wisdom.

Proverbs: The Beginning and the End

✱ **Proverbs:**	Begins with a man (Solomon). Ends with a woman (Lemuel's mother).

✱ **Proverbs:**	Begins with a father. Ends with a mother.

✱ **Proverbs:**	Begins with a warning to avoid wrong companions (1:10–19). Ends with a glorious description of the proper companion (31:10–31).

✱ **Proverbs:**	Begins with a father giving advice to his son. Ends with a mother giving advice to her son.

✱ **Proverbs:**	Begins with a family: father, mother, son (1:8). Ends with a family: father, mother, children (31:28).

✱ **Proverbs:**	Beginning was written by a king (1:8). Ending was written by a king (31:1).

✱ **Proverbs:**	Begins with the fear of the Lord (1:7). Ends with the fear of the Lord (31:30).

Notes

Introduction

1. J. Sidlow Baxter, *Explore the Book* (Grand Rapids: Zondervan Publishing House, 1972), 131.

2. D. Brent Sandy and Ronald L. Giese, Jr., *Cracking Old Testament Codes* (Nashville: Broadman and Holman Publishers, 1995), 246.

3. Ibid., 248.

4. Baxter, 133.

5. Herbert Lockyer, *All of the Books and Chapters of the Bible* (Grand Rapids: Zondervan Publishing House, 1996), 149.

Chapter One

1. C.I. Scofield, *The New Scofield Study Bible* (New York: Oxford University Press, 1967), 609.

2. Merrill F. Unger, *The New Unger's Bible Dictionary* (Chicago: Moody Press, 1988), 404.

3. Charles Bridges, *Proverbs* (Carlisle: Banner of Truth Trust Company, 1994), 3–4.

4. A.R. Fausset, *A Commentary on the Old and New Testaments* (Grand Rapids: Eerdmans Publishing Co., 1967), 415.

5. Ibid.

6. Ibid.

7. Bridges, 12.

8. Ibid., 11.

Chapter Two

1. Matthew Henry, *Matthew Henry's Commentary on the Whole Bible* (McLean: MacDonald Publishing Company, 1710), 799.

2. Ibid.

3. Ibid.

4. Jay E. Adams, *The Christian Counselor's Commentary, Proverbs* (Woodruff: Time-less Texts, 1997), 18–19.

5. Bridges, 14–15.

6. Adams, 19.

7. Fausset, 417.

Chapter Three

1. John Wesley, *John Wesley's Commentary on the Bible*, ed. G. Roger Schoenhals (Grand Rapids: Zondervan, 1990), 78.

2. Bridges, 23.

3. Oswald Chambers, *My Utmost for His Highest* (Westwood: Barbour and Company, 1984), 64.

4. Henry, 803.

5. Charles Stanley, *Clear Guidance in Major and Minor Matters*, (Audio Tape) (Atlanta: In Touch Ministries, 1995).

6. J. Vernon McGee, *Proverbs* (Pasadena: Thru the Bible Books, 1981), 40.

7. Chambers, 121.

8. McGee, 41.

9. Fausset, 421.

Notes

Chapter Four

1. Fausset, 423–424.

2. Bridges, 45.

3. John H. Walton, *Ancient Israelite Literature in its Cultural Context* (Grand Rapids: Zondervan, 1989), 178.

4. Fred John Meldau, *Why We Believe in Creation Not Evolution* (Denver: Christian Victory Publishing Company, 1968), 238.

5. Ibid., 54.

6. R.C. Sproul, *The Mystery of the Holy Spirit* (Wheaton: Tyndale House Publishers, Inc., 1990), 14.

7. Christopher B. Adsit, *Personal Disciplemaking* (Nashville: Thomas Nelson, Inc., 1993), 165.

8. Billy Graham, *The Home* (A pamphlet of a radio message from "The Hour of Decision," 1956), 10.

9. Bridges, 47.

Chapter Five

1. Bridges, 56–57.

2. Henry, 816.

3. Wesley, 306.

Chapter Six

1. Sandy and Giese, Jr., 237–238.

2. John Phillips, *Exploring the Scriptures* (Chicago: Moody Press, 1965), 115.

3. Fausset, 428.

4. Scofield, 725.

5. John W. Peterson, *Living Praise Hymnal* (Grand Rapids: Singspiration, Division of the Zondervan Corporation, 1974), 64.

6. McGee, 71.

7. C.H. Spurgeon, *The Treasury of David* (McLean: MacDonald Publishing Company), 168.

8. Ibid., 168.

9. W. E. Vine, *An Expository Dictionary of New Testament Words* (Old Tappan: Fleming H. Revell Company, 1966), 264.

10. Joseph H. Thayer, *Greek-English Lexicon of the New Testament* (Grand Rapids: Baker Book House, 1977), 3816.

11. McGee, 71.

12. Spurgeon, 342.

13. Bridges, 64.

14. Henry, 824.

15. Adams, 55.

16. Ibid.

Chapter Seven

1. Fausset, 433.

2. Ibid.

3. Henry, 829.

4. Fausset, 434.

5. Bridges, 69.

6. Henry, 830.

Chapter Eight

1. Adams, 62.

2. Henry, 833.

3. Ibid.

4. Bridges, 75.

5. Ibid., 76.

6. Henry, 834.

7. Bridges, 84.

Chapter Nine

1. Walton, 246.

2. Emory H. Bancroft, *Elemental Theology Doctrinal and Conservative* (Hayward: J.F. May Press, 1945), 178.

3. R.A. Torrey, *What the Bible Teaches* (New York: Fleming H. Revell Company, 1898), 84.

4. Mark G. Cambron, *Bible Doctrines, Beliefs that Matter* (Grand Rapid: Zondervan, 1954), 95–96.

5. Ibid., 255.

6. H.G. Moule, *The Fundamentals, Volume 3* (Grand Rapids: Baker Book House Company, 1993), 141.

7. Ibid., 79–80.

8. Bridges, 72–73.

9. John Pollack, *George Whitefield and the Great Awakening* (Garden City: Doubleday and Company, Inc., 1972), 82–83.

10. Henry, 840.

11. Fausset, 442.

12. McGee, 89–90.

13. Bridges, 87.

14. G. Campell Morgan, *The Analyzed Bible* (Westwood: Fleming H. Revell Company, 1964), 183.

15. Bridges, 89–90.

Chapter Ten

1. William Patton, *Bible Wines or Laws of Fermentation and Wines of the Ancients* (Oklahoma City: Sane Press, 1975), 16–17.

2. Ibid., 26–53.

3. Bridges, 334.

4. Ibid.

5. Ibid.

6. Ibid., 334–335.

7. Encyclopedia Britannica, (1974), Macropaedia, Volume 1, 440.

8. Henry, 928.

9. Bridges, 443.

10. Ann Landers, *St. Petersburg Times*, November 30, 1982.

11. Fausset, 479.

12. Encyclopedia Britannica, Volume 1, 440.

13. Bridges, 442–443.

14. Encyclopedia Britannica, 441.

15. Ibid., Volume 15, 178.

16. Ibid.

17. John R. Rice, *The Double Curse of Booze* (Murfreesboro: Sword of the Lord Foundation, 1960), 10–12.

18. Byram H. Glaze, *Devil's Juice* (Columbus: Calvary Crusade), 19.

Chapter Eleven

1. Bridges, 232–233.

2. Ibid., 233.

3. Jerry Bridges, *Trusting God even when Life Hurts* (Colorado Springs: Navpress, 1988), 57.

Chapter Fourteen

1. Henry, 819.

Chapter Nineteen

1. Lockyer, 150.

Chapter Twenty-Two

1. S.I. McMillen, M.D., *None of these Diseases* (Old Tappan: Spirebooks, 1970), 114.

2. Ibid., 64.

3. Adams, 96–97.

4. Ibid., 143.

5. Ibid.

6. McMillen, 64–65.

7. Ibid., 65.

Chapter Twenty-Four

1. Bridges, 229.

Chapter Thirty-One

1. Henry, 972.

2. Encyclopedia Britannica, Volume 1, 440.

3. George V. Wigram, *The New Englishman's Hebrew Concordance* (Hendrickson Publishers, 1984), 431.

4. Sandy Giese, Jr., 245.

5. Henry, 977.

Index

Index

To order additional copies of

Have your credit card ready and call

toll free **(877) 421-READ (7323)**

or send $29.95* each plus
Shipping & Handling**

$5.95 - USPS 1st Class

to

**WinePress Publishing
PO Box 428
Enumclaw, WA 98022**

www.winepresspub.com

*WA residents, add 8.6% sales tax

** Add $1.00 S&H for each additional book ordered.